1929

THE GOLDSTEIN-GOREN SERIES IN AMERICAN JEWISH HISTORY

GENERAL EDITOR: HASIA R. DINER

We Remember with
Reverence and Love
*American Jews and the Myth
of Silence after the Holocaust,
1945–1962*
HASIA R. DINER

Is Diss a System?
A Milt Gross Comic Reader
EDITED BY ARI Y. KELMAN

All Together Different
*Yiddish Socialists, Garment
Workers, and the Labor Roots
of Multiculturalism*
DANIEL KATZ

Jews and Booze
*Becoming American in the
Age of Prohibition*
MARNI DAVIS

Jewish Radicals
A Documentary History
TONY MICHELS

1929
Mapping the Jewish World
EDITED BY HASIA R. DINER
AND GENNADY ESTRAIKH

1929

Mapping the Jewish World

Edited by

HASIA R. DINER AND GENNADY ESTRAIKH

NEW YORK UNIVERSITY PRESS

New York and London

NEW YORK UNIVERSITY PRESS
New York and London
www.nyupress.org

References to Internet Websites (URLs) were accurate at the time of writing.
Neither the author nor New York University Press is responsible for URLs
that may have expired or changed since the manuscript was prepared.

LIBRARY OF CONGRESS CATALOGING-IN-PUBLICATION DATA
1929 : mapping the Jewish world / edited by Hasia R. Diner and Gennady Estraikh.
pages ; cm— (The Goldstein-Goren series in American Jewish history)
Includes bibliographical references and index.
ISBN 978-0-8147-2020-2 (cloth : alk. paper)—ISBN 978-0-8147-2021-9 (pbk. : alk. paper)
1. Jew—United States—History—20th century. 2. Jew—History—20th century.
3. Jews—United States—Politics and government—20th century. 4. Jews—Politics
and government—20th century. 5. Jews—United States—Intellectual life—20th
century. 6. Jews—Intellectual life—20th century. 7. Jews—United States—Social life and
customs—20th century. 8. Jews—Social life and customs—20th century. 9. Jews—United
States—Charities.—History—20th century. 10. Jews—Migrations—History—20th
century. I. Diner, Hasia R., editor. II. Estraikh, G. (Gennady), editor. III. Title: Nineteen
twenty nine.
E184.354.A14   2013
973'.04924—dc23   2013006920

New York University Press books are printed on acid-free paper,
and their binding materials are chosen for strength and durability.
We strive to use environmentally responsible suppliers and materials
to the greatest extent possible in publishing our books.

Manufactured in the United States of America

c 10 9 8 7 6 5 4 3 2 1
p 10 9 8 7 6 5 4 3 2 1

Contents

Introduction

HASIA R. DINER AND GENNADY ESTRAIKH

Conventional thinking about Jewish history has pivoted around a number of key dates, going from 70 CE with the destruction of the Temple in Jerusalem by the Romans to 1492 and the expulsion from Spain. Most commentators would agree that 1881 with the outbreak of the pogroms in the Czarist empire, 1933 and the rise of Adolf Hitler to power, and finally 1948 and the declaration of the State of Israel as a sovereign Jewish state constitute the key years from which to imagine the flow of Jewish historical time. Many also regard 1967 as a dividing line, as the June War changed tangibly the international image and situation of Israel, stimulated new interpretations of history, and triggered the Jewish emigration from the Soviet Union.

But since Jewish history cannot, and ought not, be divorced from the larger history of the world, other dates also suggest themselves as possible moments which can provide a framework for understanding the Jewish past. 1096 and the launch of the First Crusade, 1516 when Martin Luther ripped apart the unity of Christendom, and the French Revolution of 1789, which offered citizenship to all men, divorcing the benefits offered by the state from religious affiliation, offer a few other dates drawn from world history which could be considered as transformative of Jewish life and worthy of exploration.

1929, the subject of this volume, proved to be a watershed in modern Jewish history. The reaction of Jewish communities, organizations, and individuals to the dramatic events of that year was determined by, particularly, although not limited to, the great crisis of the world economy ushered in by the crash of the stock market. The developments of 1929 as they played out in the Jewish world reflected the reality that changes, for better or worse, in the larger society impacted upon the Jews. Jews in the modern world, or the premodern world for that matter, never lived in splendid isolation from others. Their internal communal practices, their relationships with each other, and the bonds they forged with non-Jews took their shape as much from the issues and events of the larger society as they reflected Jewish concerns and consciousness. Additionally, 1929 offers a clear example of the transnational connections which linked Jews to each other, regardless of where they lived.

While Jews functioned as American Jews, Russian—or, better, Soviet—Jews, German Jews, Palestinian Jews, Polish Jews, and the like, they behaved politically in a global context. They understood their fates to be tied up with each other despite the fact that each Jewish community had a particular bundle of political, social, and economic rights, based on place of residence. Each had to react to and interact with the particularities of their specific societies. Yet each Jewry took the worldwide condition of the Jewish people to be a matter of grave concern. 1929 proved to a year when Jews, regardless of where they lived, saw themselves as affected by developments that took place far away. No matter how far away, the crises endured by other Jews became part of a transnational Jewish consciousness.

As the historians and literary scholars whose essays make up this book engage with so many other watershed dates, they have taken 1929 as more that just a singular year. But they contemplate it as a key moment in time from which to assess the trends set in motion in the decade that preceded it and in the immediate period of time which followed. As such, they have not limited themselves to the events of only that one year. Rather, 1929 provides this book with a vantage point from which to survey and analyze the revolutions in Jewish life, set in place by developments in the post–World War I world, as they shaped Jewish intellectual, political, and communal conditions. 1929 likewise provides a lens from which to contemplate the changes which that year brought about, some of which left indelible marks on the history of the Jewish people.

In 1929, the world Jewish population hovered at just a bit over 17 million, a striking figure retrospectively, given that in less than ten years, political forces would be unleashed in Germany which would annihilate one-third of them, and in fewer than twenty years, the image of the six million Jewish victims of the Holocaust would dominate Jewish thinking and political action. That, however, lay in the future. In 1929, over 7 million of the Jewish people lived in central and eastern Europe, including Poland, Russia, Austria, Czechoslovakia, Hungary, Latvia, and Lithuania, where they constituted about 6 percent of the total population. 300,000, on the other hand, made their home in the Jews' ancestral homeland, Palestine. Almost 5 million Jews lived in the Americas, north and south, with the lion's share of over 4 million in the United States. While eastern Europe, across national boundaries, represented the single largest concentration of Jews anywhere, the United States had the largest single Jewish community in any one country.

To a considerable degree, this book takes a decidedly American focus, reflecting not only the flowering of scholarship in the field of American Jewish history and literature but also the size of the Jewish community and the fact that the United States experienced World War I so differently than did the nations of Europe, which had fought so much longer and lost so many more men and on whose soil the battles had raged. Reflecting that postbellum reality as well as the migration trends which had brought nearly one-third of European Jewry across the Atlantic to the United States, in the 1920s, the Jews of the United States had become the dominant constituent of world Jewry. Fundraising campaigns all over the United States helped continue Zionist projects in Palestine. In Europe, many individuals, organizations, or even whole communities depended on American Jewish charities such as the American Jewish Joint Distribution Committee (JDC), which played a central role in assisting Jews in World War I–torn Europe and after the war, helping secure their economic position by providing direct relief and by establishing hundreds of cooperative credit unions to assist Jewish-owned businesses in eastern Europe, among other projects.

American Jews experienced steady and solid economic mobility in the 1920s, making it comfortable for them to provide assistance to their coreligionists abroad. And despite the rising levels of anti-Semitism, both in rhetoric and in action, which characterized the 1920s, they by and large evinced a positive outlook on their place in American life, an optimistic view toward the future, and an eagerness to fulfill their self-imposed obligations to Jews around the world in distress. In 1929, however, the stock-market crash brought profound economic, social, and ideological changes to the American Jewish community and limited its ability to support humanitarian and Jewish nationalist projects in other countries.

The particularities of the United States shaped the relationships between its Jews and those elsewhere. This played itself out most importantly in terms of the ways in which American Jews connected to those in the Soviet Union, a political entity forged in the crucible of World War I. Given the absence of official relations between the United States and Soviet Russia until 1933, Jewish channels of economic assistance sometimes served diplomatic ends. Charitable activities directed at foreign causes by the JDC, *landsmanshaftn* (hometown societies), and various other organizations helped reinforce their members' and sponsors' positions on the Jewish and general political landscape. It also strengthened and particularized the American Jewish identity.

The post–World War I remapping created, inter alia, new Jewish identities, for instance, that of the "Finnish Jewish" and the "Latvian Jewish." At the same time, the "Ukrainian Jewish" self-identification began to replace previous regional identifications, such as "Volhynian" and "Podolyan." One of the most significant identity changes took place in the Soviet Union. Lazar Fagelman, a heavyweight among the New York Jewish journalists, wrote on 12 July 1943, in the *Forverts* (which he would edit in the 1960s) about the abyss that had divided the Soviet Jewish and the western Jewish worlds. An American Jew and a Soviet Jew, especially of the younger generations, began to speak essentially different languages, even if both remained fluent Yiddish speakers. According to Fagelman, Soviet Jews developed different habits, values, and manners; their vision of life differed; they had a different attitude to people, to the world, and to all political, economic, and moral problems.

While many Jewish intellectuals mourned the decline of the relatively homogeneous Jewish cultural terrain in eastern Europe, they anticipated the emergence of distinctive centers of strong cultural gravitation, most notably in New York, Warsaw, and Moscow, with Berlin as the main crossroads. Latin America, South Africa, and Australia each supported a lively Jewish cultural and communal life. At the same time, international Jewish organizations countered these centrifugal tendencies.

In August 1929, a constituent assembly met in Zurich, establishing the Jewish Agency for Palestine, or *sokhnut*, responsible for emigration, *aliyah*, to the future Jewish state. The Fourth Aliyah (1924–1926) brought to Palestine about 70,000 Jews, most notably middle-class migrants from Poland. This bourgeois population included many fewer supporters of the socialist ideals than earlier waves of immigration had, and more advocates of the Revisionist Zionism of Vladimir Jabotinsky. The newcomers reinforced the urban population of Palestine, especially Tel Aviv, which increased in size from 16,000 in 1924 to 46,000 in 1929. This period saw the opening of the Hebrew University in Jerusalem and the Technion in Haifa.

The Jewish organizations for vocational training, ORT, and for health protection, OZE, which initially appeared in imperial Russia, morphed into international bodies with fundraising and relief operations in scores of countries. The establishment of the Yiddish section at the PEN Club and the international popularity of its honorary chairman, the novelist and playwright Sholem Asch, underscored the Diasporic character of Jewish cultural life. The Jewish Scientific Institute (YIVO), a 1925 brainchild of a few Berlin-based intellectuals, by 1929 had sunk strong roots in Vilna, the capital of Lithuania, and established affiliates in Warsaw and Berlin. It also enlisted to its ranks a worldwide constituency of scholars and supporters.

Cosmopolitans populated the headquarters of international and national Jewish organizations. Born and educated between East and West, these Jews devoted themselves not to a homeland but to ideas, be they Zionism, Bundism (the socialist Jewish workers' movement), Communism, Jewish nation-building in the Diaspora, Westernization and other forms of acculturation. These globally focused Jewish activists built their worlds on Yiddish, Hebrew, Russian, Polish, English, and German, as the spoken and written mediums of their polyglot institutions. Some among these activists not only spoke all of these—and other—languages fluently but also used them in their creative work. Linguistic, cultural, and ideological affinity of activists living in various countries contributed to the success of Jewish international projects.

Some uprooted disillusioned intellectuals became recruits of the international Communist movement. In the Soviet Union, the consolidation of power in the hands of Josef Stalin created by 1929 a much more dogmatic policy and reality intolerant of dissent, whether in the USSR itself or around the world in the international network of the Communist movement. This included the Jewish branches. In the 1920s and 1930s, legal and illegal outlets of the Communist International, or Comintern, had more than a fair share of Jewish activists. The international character of the Communist movement appealed to some literati, turning them into fellow travelers. Jewish, notably Yiddish-speaking, Communist substructures mushroomed in the United States and other countries with a significant Jewish population. 1929 proved pivotal in the history of American Communists. In March 1929, the Workers Party of America, during its sixth convention, stopped hiding its real identity and became the Communist Party of the USA (CPUSA), merging into one organization. The new ideological and organizational path of the Communist movement sparked vast and volatile conflicts in Jewish trade unions in the United States and elsewhere. It split Jewish fraternal organizations such as the Arbeiter Ring (the Workmen's Circle) and inspired disputes that would persist for decades, well into the period following World War II.

The new departure of the international Communist movement played itself out in other very specific Jewish settings and forced some Jewish Communists to have to decide if their Jewish loyalties trumped their Communist ones, or the other way around. In the fall of 1929, a group of Jewish believers in the Soviet experiment abandoned the movement following the Kremlin's siding with the Arabs and hailing the Jewish bloodshed in Palestine as an anticolonial uprising.

The outbreak of violence in Palestine ought not be thought of as a localized event of limited geographic reach. On 11 October 1929, the highbrow Warsaw Yiddish weekly *Literarishe Bleter* (Literary Pages), which favored promoting unity in the ranks of Yiddish literati, indicated that the events in Palestine had created a schism in the Jewish world and had driven virtually everyone to participate in a bitter debate. The riots in Hebron and other towns of Palestine underscored the vulnerability of the Zionist enterprise and ignited hot discussions among various Jewish political groupings about the matters of establishing a Jewish state on its historical site. Jacob Lestschinsky, one of the foremost Jewish social scientists, published an article in the Warsaw-based Bundist daily *Naye Folkstsaytung* (New People's Newspaper, 11 and 18 April 1930), arguing that after the riots, Palestine became simply another dangerous place in the Jewish world. He compared Zionists with followers of the seventeenth-century "false messiah" Shabbatai

Zvi. Being ready to accept the Zionists' commitment to building Jewish life in Israel, Lestschinsky condemned those radicals who undermined Jewish life by "ruining the Jewish soul" and depriving "the Jewish masses of their feelings of citizenship, of having birthrights to the country of their residence, and of equality with the surrounding population. . . . Instead, it [Zionism] exhilarates them with illusions and promises, which can intoxicate but cannot produce results."[1] Meanwhile, American and other Western donors provided funds for such projects as the building a Jewish republic in the Crimea and, later, in Birobidzhan. While both projects never achieved their goals, the enthusiastic support of non-Soviet sponsors, representing a range of ideologies, revealed widespread skepticism toward Zionism and assimilation and demonstrated global Jewish connections.

Wherever Jews lived, wherever they maintained organized communities which both participated in global Jewish philanthropy—as either receivers or donors—and wherever they maintained a Jewish press and supported Jewish movements, they followed these and other developments. They understood that their fate and their status, while surely determined by the policies of their home countries and national governments, could not be extricated from the fate and status of Jews elsewhere. Their definition of the "Jewish community" or the "Jewish world" did not stop at the lines of their cities, states, or countries. Rather, looking outward, they defined themselves as bound together with other Jews, no matter how far away they lived.

Because of the global interconnection of Jews and Jewish politics, an international team of leading experts have contributed to *1929: Mapping the Jewish World*. This book takes as its conceptual framework the idea of the various "(tree-)rings" of this year in Jewish history. The local may have very well served as the lived center, but each ring represented meaningful places in the world Jewish imagination and in the political reality which shaped Jewish community life.

NOTES
1. Jacob Lestschinsky, "Men kon zikh filn fray in goles, un golesdik in erets-yisroel," *Naye Folkstsaytung*, 11 and 18 April 1930.

PART I

Global Ties

.

1

Living Locally, Organizing Nationally, and Thinking Globally

The View from the United States

HASIA R. DINER

The 1929 volume of the *American Jewish Yearbook* included a lengthy obituary for Louis Marshall, a constitutional lawyer and American Jewish communal activist who died that year while attending a Zionist conference in Lausanne, Switzerland. Marshall, decidedly not a Zionist, had come in the 1920s to recognize the fact that except for Palestine, no place in the world existed to which mass Jewish migration might go and that the problems of east European Jewry had deteriorated to such a point that any solution trumped the unacceptable status quo.[1] That *AJY* obituary lauded Marshall as someone who had devoted his life at one and the same time to the betterment of the status of Jews in the United States and to those around the world. The domestic concerns which preoccupied Marshall, according to the writer of this article, Cyrus Adler, himself a notable American Jewish community figure and also a non-Zionist, existed in perfect harmony with his global Jewish vision. Marshall, commented Adler, had been "a dominant figure in the Jewish affairs of America and of the world." The obituary and the actual contents of the *AJY* demonstrated the emergence of American Jewry to a dominant place in world Jewish affairs at the same time that it sought to make itself "at home in America."[2]

1929, the year of Marshall's death and the year that ushered in the great worldwide depression, an event which would profoundly mark America and nearly all of the world, a year which would unleash forces that arguably catalyzed some of the most profound events of the modern age, at first blush does not stand out in and of itself as a milestone moment in the history of the Jews of the United States. The year in that decade which might arguably occupy that premier place of importance, 1924, spelled the end of mass Jewish migration west across the Atlantic, a phenomenon which both froze the American Jewish population and rendered it increasingly American born and English speaking.

But retrospectively, 1929 emerges as pivotal. During that year, the world, as American Jewry knew it, began to unravel, setting in motion a chain of events that transformed it and profoundly altered its place in America and in the global Jewish world. That process stretched out from the collapse of the world economy to the devastation of the Great Depression to the rise of Nazism in Germany, ultimately leading to the destruction of European Jewry.

With that liquidation of Jewish life in Europe and the extirpation of one-third of the Jewish people, the United States emerged as the largest and most significant Jewish community, in its own time and perhaps in modern history. At no time prior to this had one center of Jewish political and cultural life been able to set the tone and terms for Jewries around the globe.[3]

Ironically, in the decades, indeed centuries, before the end of World War II and the Holocaust, both of which can be seen as deeply related to the economic devastation of the Depression ushered in by the 1929 crash, American Jewry had been an outpost of European Jewry, a receiver of texts, leaders, and ideas from abroad. The intellectual and political elite of European Jewries had primarily viewed the American Jewish community as a local, insignificant, shallow, derivative entity, notable for its materialism and lack of cultural authenticity. After the debacle of the 1930s and 1940s, no one could for decades to come challenge American Jewry's hegemony in Jewish politics, broadly defined.

That centrality in world Jewish politics began to emerge only slowly in the early twentieth century when a handful of notable individual American Jewish powerbrokers, men associated with the American Jewish Committee, such as Jacob Schiff, Felix Warburg, Oscar Straus, and Louis Marshall, began to make their influence felt both at home and abroad in their quest to protect and secure Jewish rights.[4] The 1914 founding of the Joint Distribution Committee in New York made American Jewish philanthropy a formative force in the making and remaking of Jewish communities around the world, including but not limited to the Soviet Union, the former Ottoman Empire, Palestine, eastern Europe, central Europe, and Latin America.[5]

Until that point, America figured into the realm of world Jewry as basically a place to which impoverished Jews and those in distress could migrate. Until the middle of the 1920s, it had been the place of destination for European Jews. In the century which had culminated in the 1920s, nearly one-third of Europe's Jews had left the continent, and of these somewhere between 85 to 90 percent had opted for the United States.

Who and what constituted the American Jewish "community," a term which implies a unity and integration which did not in fact exist? Of the approximately 123 million people who made up the population of the United States, estimates put the number of Jews at 4 million, who constituted about 3.58 percent of the population of their country and functioned as a communally, politically, and culturally active yet divided people.[6] In global terms, these 4 million represented something below one-quarter of the 17 million people around the world who defined (or were defined by others) as Jews.

Like the Jews in most places in the world, those in America divided along the lines of where in Europe they had come from and also according to a variety of ideologies, political and religious. While most of America's Jews hailed from someplace in eastern Europe, they maintained, to some degree, a set of loyalties to the lands, regions, and towns from which they or their parents had hailed. Although by 1930 a majority of Jews in America would have been born in their destination home, they, particularly the older ones among them, continued to evince a sense that those who traced their roots to eastern Europe differed in some meaningful way from those American Jews who looked to family origins in Germany. That latter group constituted a distinctive cadre within the communal body, and that group, although small in number, functioned as the communal elite.

Equally important, American Jews splintered denominationally between Reform, Orthodoxy, Conservativism, and religious nonaffiliation, as well as between socialists, Communists, and supporters of America's conventional two parties. Zionists of various persuasions hoped, with little success, to convince the masses of American Jews that they needed to do more than express their vague commitment to the Jews in Palestine by becoming a member of a Zionist body. Proponents of Yiddish furthermore constituted a distinctive segment of the community, and their schools, summer camps, mutual-aid associations, and social institutions served their particular sensibilities. In addition, a wide class spectrum existed; and while some Jews belonged to the nation's economic elite and others constituted a substantial body of merchants, with smaller or larger enterprises to their credit, a significant Jewish working class, which concentrated in the garment trades, still existed, and it complicated the profile of American Jewry.

By 1929, the number of Jews who had been born in the United States just about equaled the number who had been born abroad. American Jewish historians have consistently cited 1930 as the year when the percentage of the native born first surpassed that of the foreign born. The great age of Jewish immigration had come to an end several years earlier as a result of congressional legislation, and immigration by and large ceased to be a factor in changing the nature of American Jewry. In 1929, about 18,000 new Jewish immigrants had been admitted to the United States, with about 360 leaving, some as a result of deportation. Jewish women outnumbered men among the newcomers to the United States, and the relatively high number of children and older people demonstrated the family character of the migration. In fact, of the arrivals, 96 percent came to join relatives already in the country.[7]

Where American Jews lived, their places of residence and the size of the country in which they made their homes, demonstrated the degree to which they resembled each other. Although the women and men who constituted American Jewry in the year 1929 not only lived in every one of the forty-eight states and had dispersed themselves among no fewer than 8,500 nodes of residence, most dwelled in the nation's largest cities. New York remained the single largest center. Of the city's almost 6,000,000 residents, Jews numbered 1,765,000, making up well over one-quarter of the Jews of the United States. Another 300,000 lived in Chicago, 200,000 in Philadelphia, 90,000 in Boston. A very urban people, Jews in America lived in a nation which only in the previous census, that of 1920, registered that a majority, a bare one at that, lived in "cities," defined as communities of at least 2,500 people. This residential profile made them distinctive within the American population.[8]

The clustering of Jews in America's cities had a profound impact on their lives. Much of what constituted Jewish communal patterns played itself out through the informal mechanisms of family and neighborhood. Nearly every place they lived they formed some kind of enclave, living in physical proximity to each other and making the streets of their neighborhoods places for the maintenance of Jewish life, through the convergence of shared space and retail activity.

While the organic flow of Jewish life took much of its shape from informal relationships, forged by the ties of family and neighborhood life, American Jews in the 1920s, as before, participated in an array of community institutions. They did not all participate in the same way, but by and large they affiliated themselves in one way or another with some organized activity that constituted Jewish communal life. Regardless of where they or their parents had emigrated from, or if they considered themselves middle or working class, they built and sustained, through voluntary contributions and membership, a wide array of Jewish institutions. For most, in fact, being Jewish meant belonging to something. Most American Jews of 1929 primarily structured their lives around local Jewish institutions, particularly the synagogues (Reform, Orthodox, and Conservative), community centers, schools (those sponsored by religious institutions as well as those that espoused some form of Zionism, socialism, or the Yiddish language), clubs, charitable endeavors, and mutual-aid and self-help societies.[9]

Despite the presence of American Jews in all sorts of scattered places and their nearly even split between those of American and of foreign nativity, they had banded together to "live in" 128 national organizations, which dedicated themselves to performing functions of every kind including religious, political, educational, social, cultural, and charitable. Of these national Jewish organizations, seven came into being in 1929, and just a quick listing of some of the innovations of this year in Jewish history gives us some sense of the multiplicity of concerns which impelled some of them into action. In 1929, the first group of graduates of the Jewish Institute of Religion, which had been founded in 1922, banded together into an alumni association to sustain the New York Reform-oriented rabbinical school. So, too, in 1929 the American Society for Jewish Farm Settlements in Russia, the Federation of American Jews of Lithuanian Descent, and the Union of Sephardic Congregations formed to serve their particular constituents. The League for Safeguarding the Fixity of the Sabbath Against Possible

Encroachment by Calendar Reform attracted a small group of Jews in 1929 from across the Orthodox to Reform spectrum to serve as the Jewish voice in opposition to a campaign by the National Committee on Calendar Simplification, which had proposed that Congress pass a bill which would have pledged the United States to participate in an international conference on changing the calendar to a thirteen-month year, with twenty-eight calendar days. According to Jewish opponents of this plan, while it might have "simplified" the calendar, it would however have wreaked havoc on the Jewish Sabbath. Finally, a group of Jews, representing a number of younger intellectuals, created the Menorah Association in 1929 with the goal of advancing the study of Jewish culture and propagating Jewish ideals among colleges and universities in the United States. This group over time became a breeding ground for a new generation of American Jewish intellectuals such as Elliott Cohen who would particularly in the postwar period shape the discourse about America, the place of Jews in it, and the nature of American democracy and pluralism.[10]

These 1929 American Jews contributed much money, collecting over $15 million, to sustain Jewish community life through fifty-two local Jewish philanthropic federations, which encompassed 465 constituent societies. This figure does not include money contributed to synagogues and other religious institutions, nor does it include for the most part funds contributed to small, local projects, to charitable institutions in communities that had not yet federated, or to more informally constituted family funds and free loan societies.[11] To this hefty sum, impressive in itself, particularly in a year which included the several months which followed the crash of the New York Stock Exchange, must be added the $6 million shipped from American Jewry to the Jewries of eastern Europe and Palestine, collected in America by various worldwide Jewish bodies.

The profile of American Jewry and its inner complexities can be demonstrated also by the kinds of institutions which they built and sustained on a community-by-community level. The helping and social-welfare institutions encompassed some fifty-seven Jewish hospitals, forty-seven Jewish homes for the care of dependent children, and forty-five homes for the aged.[12] In the matter of diffusing information among these American Jews, they sustained a Jewish press, which consisted of 113 periodical, exclusive of the newsletters, bulletins, and magazines produced for members of organizations, which circulated either nationally or, more often, locally. These publications included dailies, weeklies, bimonthlies, and monthlies, most of which served readers of English, although thirty-two Yiddish publications, six Hebrew ones, and one in Ladino appealed to Jews who preferred, or needed, their news to come to them in some language other than English. These publications, like American Jews themselves, reflected their diversity in ideology and intent. While some of the newspapers disseminated general Jewish information, others articulated the particularistic religious, political, and cultural sensibilities of their subscribers and their producers.[13]

American Jews consumed and produced a vast reservoir of words and texts which made up their public culture, and in their words and deeds, they demonstrated their understanding of themselves as Jewish women and men who lived in particular places: New York, Chicago, Pittsburgh, Minneapolis, Cleveland, and the like. Their print culture also reflected the degree to which they considered themselves to be Americans, concerned with the life of the nation as a whole and their place in it. Indeed, a few years earlier, a major study came out under the authorship of Mordecai Soltes on the Yiddish press. That volume, based on content analysis of several Yiddish dailies, the records of the newspapers themselves, and studies of the readers, asserted emphatically that this foreign-language press functioned as an "Americanizing agency."[14]

They sustained an elaborate array of communal institutions, all of which depended on their own voluntary efforts, sustained by a system of self-taxation. Jewish institutions, including those which provided direct services to the poor, to the infirm, and to others of their group who faced severe distress, could not, nor did they want to, accept outside funding, be it from government agencies or general community philanthropic funds. They devoted much of their action in the public sphere to fretting over the status of Jews in other lands, worrying about their fate, and advocating activism on their behalf. American Jews manifested a profound sense of internationalism as they contemplated themselves as part of a transnational people. American Jews in 1929 both resembled their non-Jewish American neighbors and behaved in distinctive ways.

Given the bewildering range of identities, institutions, and texts of the Jewish people in America, how can we then explore the ways in which American Jews experienced and made sense of the events of 1929? How can we uncover the patterns of meaning that the year played in their lives as Americans, as Jews, and as American Jews? One text, the *American Jewish Yearbook*—the 1929 volume of which provided the tribute to Louis Marshall as a "dominant figure in the Jewish affairs of America and of the world"—offers at least a partial window into their world, broadly defined. Although this annual reference book, sponsored by the American Jewish Committee and published by the Jewish Publication Society, represented the worldview of a particular elite, it still provides an accessible guide to evaluating the year 1929 in the consciousness of American Jews, allowing for an exploration of a set of questions about that year and the Jews of the United States.[15] What did they see as new and transformative about that year? What factors which had once dominated their list of concerns had now faded in significance? How did they see the future? To what degree did that volume of the *AJY* which covered 1929 define the fate of American Jews as within their own control or as dependent on the actions of other Americans? And finally, in what ways did they discern connections between themselves and the Jewish people around the world?

Published since 5660, corresponding to the year 1899–1900, the *AJY*, which marked its volumes by the dates of the Hebrew calendar rather than the Gregorian, had since its inception sought to avoid ideology and to concentrate on data collection. Conceived of initially as a project of the Jewish Publication Society, due to financial problems, the American Jewish Committee adopted it in 1907 as one of its notable undertakings. Even before the shift in sponsorship, the *AJY*, under the meticulous care of Henrietta Szold, strove to offer a full picture of American and world Jewry and to place it in the context of the world in which it functioned. Both before and after its takeover by the AJC, the *AJY*, with its annual lists, directories, and extensive articles, served as both an insider document, telling American Jews about themselves and their coreligionists around the world, and provided a profile of American Jewry for the benefit of outsiders. It showed up on the shelves of public and university libraries, and after the AJC took it over, it was distributed free of charge to members of Congress, governors, and mayors of places that housed substantial Jewish communities.[16]

Since volumes straddled years corresponding to the Hebrew calendar, volume 32, chronicling the events of the year 5691, covered most of what transpired in 1929 and serves as the key text for analysis here. As in all previous years and as befits an almanac-type volume, its first regular section was a calendar arranged according to both "general" time and the Hebrew months, including the Jewish holy days, candlelight time for each Sabbath, and the weekly Torah portions. As an initial comment about the *AJY* as a text, by opening this way, it not only provided a useful, albeit mundane, guide to time in the most literal sense, but it made a statement about the universality of Jewish culture.[17]

As in previous years, the *AJY* editor, Harry Schneiderman, then moved to the "Review of the Year" sections, which subdivided into "United States," "Latin America," "Australia," and so on, covering Europe, the "Eastern Countries" (under which he listed Austria, Hungary, Romania, Czechoslovakia, Yugoslavia, Poland, Russia, Turkey, and Palestine). As to what the volume did not consider as newsworthy or noteworthy, it had no information on the Jews of North Africa or the Near East. With the exception of Turkey, it included information only about the Jews of Europe or the "new world." How much this reflected a lack of interest, a lack of knowledge, or a lack of access to information cannot be ascertained from the book itself.

For sure, the activities and issues involving American Jews took center stage here, and the *AJY* offered facts about their activities and problems in a more specific and detailed manner than it did about other Jews. The names of their publications, the listing of their organizations, and long enumerations of their major philanthropic and charitable efforts represented the core of the volume. It did not publish in such detail and at such a length analogous information about other Jewish communities.

But regardless of the *AJY*'s essential American orientation, it interpreted the condition of American Jewry in a fundamentally global context. The subsection on the United States proved to be particularly revealing in this regard. It began not with domestic events, whether internal to the Jewish community or as they revealed information about the way American Jews interacted with the larger, non-Jewish society.

Rather, the 1929 *AJY* put the travails of the Jewish people outside the geopolitical boundaries of the United States first. Indeed, this section opened with a statement that "the attention of the Jews of the United States was focused during the past year, as in no other since the Peace Conference, upon the situation of their brethren in foreign lands, especially Palestine, Russia, Poland and Roumania," places that then consumed much of the editor's attention. The actual words, the placement, and the amount of space devoted to these events represented a fundamentally global orientation and an understanding among at least the American Jewish elite that the situation of the Jews of the United States could not be understood independent of that of Jews elsewhere.[18]

This global orientation continued through much of the rest of the United States section, inasmuch as the *AJY* repeatedly noted similarities between American Jews and other Jewries, as American Jewry, "like all its sister communities in other countries," experienced the "business depression" as well as reacted to the tumultuous events in Palestine, namely, the Arab riots in Hebron and Jerusalem. Likewise, as the *AJY* chronicled the political dealings of American Jewry, through the activities of the American Jewish Committee, the American Jewish Congress, and other agencies and organizations, it emphasized how much capital it had expended that year in pleading for and representing to Congress, the State Department, other government officials, and various and sundry gentiles of goodwill the needs of Jewish communities in need.

That world Jewish connection served as the bridge between the "Review of the Year 5690: United States" and "Review of the Year 5690: Other Countries." For each of the enumerated countries, the editor made overall comments about the conditions under which Jews found themselves, their economic, political, and religious circumstances, focusing on the activities of the Jews, the activities of the governments and peoples among whom they lived, and the efforts of the Jews of the United States to intervene on their behalf and, it was hoped, to ameliorate their situations where need be. The editors, relying on reports derived from the Jewish press and from the *AJY*'s own correspondents in those places, noted what changes had taken place since the last publication of the *AJY*, what factors seemed to have been constant, and particularly in a number of disturbing places, what portents for the future seemed most ominous. Readers decades later, historians who have found reason to peruse this volume, might have found particularly chilling and prescient the section on Germany. The vast details included there on the rising appeal of the National Socialist Party and its leader, Adolf Hitler, make the *AJY* seem to have been endowed with near clairvoyant powers that proved prescient.

> The National Socialists, led by Hitler, are acquiring a controlling voice in many cities, . . . where small Jewish communities were being boycotted, terrorized and economically ruined. . . . It is from the membership of these "cells" that cemetery vandals and synagogue defilers are recruited. . . . Attacks on synagogues usually followed rallies or meetings addressed by Hitlerist agitators.[19]

Reporting about Thuringia, where a chair in "racial science" had been established at the University of Jena in 1929, the *AJY* described the development of a "pogrom atmosphere . . . where propaganda inciting to the annihilation of the Jews was freely carried on." The editors of the 1929 *AJY* detailed that a group of Hitlerites had boasted to have invented a machine which its inventor, a supporter of the party, "one, Brukhahn, claimed could generate and transmit electric 'death-rays' with which, he averred, he could rid Berlin of all its Jews in three minutes."[20]

The *AJY*'s thoroughness in ferreting out anti-Jewish talk and action around the world and its particular sensitivity to the German situation as it assimilated and transmitted information on the growing threat there emerged as a powerful theme and as an exemplar of its global orientation. It demonstrated American Jewry's understanding of the interconnectedness of the fate of the Jewish people, wherever they may have found themselves.

The *AJY* followed the political news of the Jewish world with a variety of appendices which for all of these places listed notable anniversaries and celebrations ("April 5, 1929, Memphis, Tenn.: Celebration of the seventy-fifth anniversary of the founding of Congregation Children of Israel" or "November 12, 1929. Berlin, Germany: Celebration of seventieth anniversary of the birth of ludwig stein, publicist"), "Appointments, Honors, and Elections" ("Brill, Jeannette (Mrs.), Brooklyn, N.Y., appointed City Magistrate, May 28, 1929"; "Frances, Elijah,

Salonika, Greece, elected Vice-Mayor, August 24, 1929") and "Necrologies," informing readers of the deaths around the world of Jews of note in an array of endeavors. Finally, an appendix appeared which listed major bequests and contributions given by Jews to both Jewish and general projects. Julius Rosenwald, for example, in 1929 donated to the University of Chicago Hospital, to the Museum of Science and Inquiry, for a "Medical Center for Negroes," and to Wellesley College. (All of those combined did not equal his gift to the Jewish Theological Seminary of America.) But then the *AJY* felt the need also to note that Israel Snamirowski of Warsaw bequeathed money for a ritual bath in that city and that Montague Burton of Leeds endowed a chair to Cardiff University to further the study of industrial relations.[21]

From the global back to the national, the *AJY* then turned its attention to the organizational landscape of American Jewry, offering thumbnail sketches of national Jewish organizations, starting with Aleph Zadik Aleph of the B'nai B'rith, giving date of organization, address, date of last national gathering, number of chapters, number of members, purpose, as well as the names and places of residence of its "Supreme Advisory Council," and ending some thirty-five pages later with the Zionist Organization of America, providing the same kind of data. After the national bodies, the *AJY* turned its lenses on the federations, hospitals, old-age homes, child-care facilities, and newspapers of American Jewry, followed by lists of the names of all Jews who had served in the U.S. Congress, as well as those eight (seven men, one woman) who sat with the present, Seventy-First Congress (including three Republicans and five Democrats).[22]

But then, once again, the focus shifted back to the larger Jewish world. The next large chunk of the *AJY* of 5691 had been prepared by H. S. Linfield, a statistician and director of the American Jewish Committee's Statistical Department. Here readers had access to the available figures on Jewish population counts around the world, organized by country and continent. Likewise, they could peruse special sections on Jewish immigration to the United States, as well as to Canada, Brazil, Argentina, and Palestine. Linfield included supplements with closer, more in-depth accounts, based on recently released figures on the demographic and economic conditions of the Jews of Danzig, of Germany, Hungary, the Irish Free State, Northern Ireland, Latvia, and Lithuania.[23]

The blurring of the line between American Jewry and the larger Jewish people continued in the last two sections of the *American Jewish Yearbook*. The annual report of the American Jewish Committee, the sponsoring body which made the reference work possible, constituted the penultimate part of the *AJY*. In this lengthy section, many of the same concerns that had been raised in the "Year in Review" surfaced again—particularly the political and economic problems faced by various sectors of the Jewish people in their many places of residence—although not surprisingly here the *AJY* editors chronicled in even greater detail than before what the American Jewish Committee had done in relationship to those stressful situations. Finally, the *AJY* republished the annual report of the Jewish Publication Society of America, chronicling here some material on the cultural condition of America's Jews, and—of great benefit to subsequent historians—it listed the names of all subscribers to JPS, arranging them by state, city, and country of residence and, in the process, showed that the words and works of American Jewry were being consumed by Jews in Shanghai, Berlin, Belfast, Jerusalem, and Budapest. Like the *AJY* as a whole, this section demonstrated the connections that bound Jews around the world to each other through the United States.

The pages and sections of this relatively prosaic and dry volume, the *American Jewish Yearbook: 5691*, demonstrated the degree to which the Jews of the United States in 1929, at least as reflected in their book of record, saw themselves as being part of a worldwide people and not as an isolated group of women and men, identified only with the land in which they lived. That volume also reflected this transnational self-understanding in the lengthy homage it paid, in its opening section, to the recently deceased Louis Marshall. He dominated the volume. His picture indeed had been prominently placed opposite the title page, and the tribute offered him by Cyrus Adler preceded the conventional opener, the calendar. Adler's tribute to Marshall, the sentiments of which were echoed in the material on Palestine and Poland and on the many other spots around the Jewish world which appeared later in the book, emphasized his powerful role as "a dominant figure in the Jewish affairs of America and of the world." That Marshall died while in Zurich on September 11, 1929, after he had "completed his part of the labor connected with the initiation of the Enlarged Jewish Agency for

Palestine," had a symbolic quality. Here had been a fiercely "American" Jew, who had spent at least two decades playing world Jewish politics. He died, as he had spent those twenty years, operating as a Jew deeply involved in American and American Jewish affairs and as a player on the world Jewish stage. As Adler remarked in bringing his tribute to an end, "he has written himself into Jewish History and in the long and noble annals of the Jewish people, there will always be a place for the name of Louis Marshall."[24]

Marshall, as a hero and exemplar of American Jewry, like the *AJY*, as a text in and of itself, and as a reflector of the sensibilities of much of American Jewry in 1929, drew no sharp distinctions between their domestic concerns and their global ones, between their efforts to integrate into America and their sense of a shared destiny with Jews elsewhere. While historians have emphasized repeatedly how the 1920s reflected the high-water mark of American isolationism, a force which prevailed until the attack on Pearl Harbor on December 7, 1941, American Jews saw the world quite differently. They moved with relative ease from the local to the national on the American scene, and they went from the American to nearly every place around the Jewish world, as they determined what concerned them as Jews. The *AJY* offers a limited, yet clear, testimony to the ways in which American Jewry saw itself as linked to a global Jewish chain. While the Jews of the United States had become increasingly American and Americanized, demonstrated by the American nativity of the majority of them, they did not retreat to a decidedly American-focused engagement with their Jewishness. They remained fixed on the broader, global picture. They evinced a continuing belief that what happened to Jews in other parts of the world impacted upon themselves as well.

NOTES

1. On Marshall and his embrace of a Palestine-based solution to the increasing difficulties of central and eastern European Jewry in the middle of the 1920s, see Oscar Handlin's introduction to *Louis Marshall: Champion of Liberty: Selected Papers and Addresses*, ed. Charles Reznikoff, vol. 1 (Philadelphia: Jewish Publication Society of America, 1957), xxxv–xxxvi.

2. *AJY: 5691*, 21–53; the phrase "at home in America" is derived from Deborah Dash Moore's book of that title, which posited the interwar period as one in which American Jews found ways to carve out comfortable niches for themselves. See

Deborah Dash Moore, *At Home in America: Second Generation New York Jews* (New York: Columbia University Press, 1981).

3. For the implications of that post–World War II transfer of power to American Jewry, see Hasia R. Diner, *We Remember with Reverence and Love: American Jews and the Myth of Silence after the Holocaust, 1945–1962* (New York: NYU Press, 2009).

4. Gary Dean Best, *To Free a People: American Jewish Leaders and the Jewish Problem in Eastern Europe, 1890–1014* (Westport, CT: Greenwood, 1982).

5. Herbert Agar, *The Saving Remnant: An Account of Jewish Survival* (New York: Viking, 1962); Yehuda Bauer, *My Brother's Keeper: A History of the American Jewish Joint Distribution Committee, 1929–1939* (Philadelphia: Jewish Publication Society of America, 1974).

6. See Harry S. Linfield, *Statistics of Jews: 1931* (New York: American Jewish Committee, 1931), 11–16, for a fuller profile of American Jewry as retrievable by numbers.

7. *AJY: 5691,* 232–33.

8. *AJY: 5691,* 219–24; on the significance of the 1920 census and its revelation of an urban majority, see Joseph A. Hill, "Some Results of the 1920 Population Census," *Journal of the American Statistical Association* 18.139 (1922): 350–59.

9. For a fuller portrait of the organizational infrastructure of American Jewry in this period, see Harry S. Linfield, *The Communal Organization of the Jews in the United States, 1927* (New York: American Jewish Committee, 1930).

10. *AJY: 5691,* 161–98.

11. Shelly Tenenbaum, in *A Credit to Their Community: Jewish Loan Societies in the United States, 1880–1945* (Detroit: Wayne State University Press, 1985), discusses the importance of these kinds of financial institutions in the economic life of American Jewry and notes that in 1929 the New York Hebrew Free Loan Society distributed 9,551 loans, amounting to $1,129,850, with each loan amounting to about $118.

12. *AJY: 5691,* 199–207.

13. *AJY: 5691,* 208–12. In 1925, Mordecai Soltes published what is still considered the most important analysis of the Yiddish press, *The Yiddish Press: An Americanizing Agency* (New York: Teachers College, Columbia University, 1925), in which he argued that the press, which reached almost 200,000 readers daily, played a crucial role in fostering the integration of the immigrant Jews into the American polity.

14. Soltes, *The Yiddish Press.*

15. The American Jewish Committee maintained a Statistical Department, and reflecting its understanding of itself as not just an American Jewish organization with concern for the fate of American Jewry, it collected and analyzed data on Jews around the world. See Linfield, *Statistics of Jews,* as a case in point. The volume devoted thirteen pages to American Jews and their statistical profile but over fifty pages to Jews elsewhere.

16. Jonathan Sarna, *JPS: The Americanization of Jewish Culture, 1888–1988* (Philadelphia: Jewish Publication Society of America, 1989), 70–75.

17. *AJY: 5691*, 2–16.

18. *AJY: 5691*, 57.

19. *AJY: 5691*, 95.

20. *AJY: 5691*, 97, 99.

21. *AJY: 5691*, 149–53.

22. *AJY: 5691*, 161–214.

23. *AJY: 5691*, 215–81.

24. *AJY: 5691*, 21–53.

2

Jewish Diplomacy at a Crossroads

DAVID ENGEL

Three personal ends and one institutional beginning that took place within slightly more than a year of one another offer a way of understanding Jewish diplomacy in the year 1929. Those events, when taken together, symbolize the waning of one approach to a fundamental problem of modern Jewish politics and the rise of another to a hegemonic position in which it remains, despite rising doubts of late, to this day. The institutional beginning was the convening in Zürich, on 14 August 1929, of the Constituent Assembly of the Jewish Agency for Palestine, a public body whose formation had initially been ordered seven years earlier in the Mandate for Palestine given to the British government by the League of Nations as a vehicle for "secur[ing] the co-operation of all Jews who are willing to assist in the establishment of the Jewish National Home."[1] The personal ends are the deaths of three towering spokesmen for Jewish communal interests, both in their own countries and throughout the world—Louis Marshall, the New York attorney and president of the American Jewish Committee, who passed away in Zürich on 11 September 1929 (ironically, perhaps, as the result of an illness he contracted while attending the Constituent Assembly of the Jewish Agency); Leon Reich, the newspaper editor and essayist from Lwów (today Lviv, Ukraine), head of the Zionist Federation of East Galicia and chairman of the Jewish caucus in the Polish Sejm, who fell victim to a botched appendicitis operation on 1 December 1929; and Lucien Wolf, the blind British journalist, amateur historian, and secretary of the Joint Foreign Committee of the Anglo-Jewish Association and Board of Deputies of British Jews, who was finally released from deepening physical affliction on 27 August 1930. The fundamental problem of modern Jewish politics for which all three individuals and the new Jewish Agency sought a solution was how best to guarantee the physical security and material well-being of masses of east European Jews in a system of sovereign nation-states governed by majorities from which Jews could be easily excluded. And the transition in approaches to this problem that attained a critical momentum around 1929 was from one that sought to establish the arena of international diplomacy as a countervailing force to that system by using it to limit the sovereignty of nation-states and the prerogatives of governing majorities to one that sought to bring Jews into the dominant system as a sovereign majority in a nation-state of their own.

For all of the ideological differences among them—Reich was a centrist Zionist, Wolf a passionate anti-Zionist, and Marshall a rather unemotional non-Zionist generally ready to cooperate with Zionist interests as long as they did not demand that he profess personal loyalty to the movement—the three Jewish leaders whose lives ended within a year of one another in 1929–30 had all during the previous decade been staunch advocates and architects of the conception that predicated security for Jews on the restriction of state sovereignty by agencies of the international community. All had attended the Paris Peace Conference in 1919 and pressed there for the establishment of an international apparatus of protection for ethnic, linguistic, and religious minorities, anchored in multilateral treaties that would serve, in Wolf's words, as "a really practical Charter of Liberties, not for the Jews alone but for all the mixed populations of Eastern Europe."[2] Shortly following the institution of such a system by the Peace Conference—less, to be sure, thanks to their own efforts as on account of momentary strategic disagreements among the Great Powers that the so-called minorities treaties helped to resolve[3]—Wolf had declared it in glowing tones to be "a perfectly revolutionary limitation on the rights of Sovereignty in both their external and domestic relations."[4] Reich had spoken similarly, following the conclusion of the minorities treaty with Poland on 28 June 1919, of a "new order" created at Paris, one that recognized Jews as a worldwide community (społeczność in Polish) possessing collective legal rights that no individual state could abrogate on its own.[5] Marshall, too, had represented the Peace Conference as having articulated "a new and important principle in international law," according to which "any violation of the rights of a minority is an offense not only against the [offended] individuals but against the law which controls all of the civilized nations of the earth," and an international tribunal was empowered to nullify any and all such violations by sovereign governments.[6] Indeed, the League of Nations and the Permanent Court of International Justice were initially perceived not only by these three but by Jews of virtually all ideological persuasions as what another leading Jewish internationalist, Leo Motzkin, the Zionist chairman of the Paris-based Comité des Délégations Juives, forerunner of the World Jewish Congress, called "the Great Areopagus" of modern times, comparable to the legendary supreme administrative, political, and judicial body of pretyrannical ancient Athens, "a magnificent temple in which humanity, weary of war and strife, may find at last a real bulwark of peace and justice," to which "the great task of safeguarding the rights of national minorities" (and, a fortiori, the security of east European Jewry) had been assigned.[7]

The strategy of entrusting Jewish physical security and material well-being to international instruments stood in considerable tension to the ideological perspectives that Reich, Marshall, and Wolf had brought to its formulation. For Reich (the Zionist), approving the subordination of the will of each nation, as expressed in the state through which it exercised political power, to international regulation came perilously close to delegitimizing the very notion that Zionists asserted in claiming territorial sovereignty for the Jewish people in the form of a Jewish nation-state—that states were properly constituted by preexisting nations and existed first and foremost in order to foster their constituting nations' particular needs and interests. Indeed, the international minorities protection regime inaugurated in 1919 strongly implied that the fourteen signatory states were to be regarded legally as federations of autonomous nationalities, each of which had a proportional claim on state resources—not as nation-states of the type Zionists sought to establish for Jews in an ethnically mixed part of the world. Additionally, the contention that international protection would likely result in substantially enhanced safety and improved material conditions for the Jewish masses of eastern Europe contradicted the bedrock Zionist assumption that conditions for Jews were universally and entirely a function of the exilic situation, in which Jews were everywhere barred

from exercising sovereign power on their own behalf, and therefore could not be effectively ameliorated until exile was ended and
Jews established as a majority in the homeland to which they rightly
belonged. On the other hand, for Marshall and Wolf, who consistently
spoke of themselves as belonging of right exclusively to their American
and British homelands, respectively, the assertion that Jews constituted
a worldwide entity having collective standing of its own in international
law, independent of any individual Jew's status as citizen or subject of a
particular state, transgressed what they took to be a cardinal rule under
which Jews had been admitted to citizenship in the first place—that
loyalties to their non-Jewish countrymen took precedence over loyalties to Jews from other countries. Indeed, some of Reich, Marshall, and
Wolf's ideological associates objected strenuously to the internationalist project precisely because of such conflicts of principle.

In response, the three had asserted, each to his own constituency,
that ideological considerations had to give way to pragmatic ones in
light of actual conditions faced by Jews in the wake of the First World
War. Zionists needed to understand, as Reich explained in September
1919, that Jews were not about to gain a majority of Palestine's population and establish a Jewish state in the country at any time in the
foreseeable future. After all, he observed, "we do not have even the
technical possibilities for large-scale immigration: we lack means of
transportation, housing, and sources of income" for more than a handful of pioneers.[8] Clearly the bulk of east European Jews would need to
find a way to live securely and without want in their present countries
of residence for many years to come. On the other hand, the notion
of a citizenship dependent on ethnicity that characterized most of the
new east European states created by the Peace Conference combined
with the palpable sociocultural differences that set east European Jews
apart from their Polish, Romanian, or Lithuanian neighbors to militate
against those states becoming primary frames of reference with which
Jews of the region could identify. Hence, Wolf affirmed that, in contrast
to the norm in western Europe, "the principle of self-government and
equal rights for all nationalities has taken its place as a necessary cor-
ollary of the principle of individual freedom and equal rights" in the
lands of the former Russian and Habsburg empires, with Jews counting
as a nationality on a par with Ukrainians, Poles, Finns, and Georgians,

entitled to a proportional share of the resources of whichever new states they inhabited.⁹ Marshall, for his part, admonished a colleague troubled by references to the "national rights" of east European Jewry that "we must be careful not to permit ourselves to judge what is most desirable for the people who live [in that region] by the standards which prevail on Fifth Avenue or in the States of Maine or Ohio, where a different horizon from that which prevails in Poland, Galicia, Ukrainia or Lithuania bounds one's vision."¹⁰ In other words, Reich, Wolf, Marshall, and the many Jewish leaders from around the world who joined with them in formulating and pursuing the strategy of seeking protections for east European Jews in the international diplomatic arena regarded neither the Zionist nor the liberal integrationist approaches to adjusting the relations between Jews and non-Jews as immediately applicable to the postwar situation in that part of the world.

In contrast, using the arena of international diplomacy to control the manner in which the new east European nation-states related to their Jewish populations appeared to chime with that situation perfectly. For several decades before the First World War, Jewish leaders in western Europe and the United States had sought to advance the welfare of their east European coreligionists largely by exploiting the political clout of a small number of wealthy Jewish merchant and investment bankers—people like Gerson Bleichröder, Jacob Schiff, the Warburg family, and most famously, the Rothschilds. The leverage that these financiers wielded in the era when they provided much of the glue for the international system, together with their frequent willingness to use that leverage on behalf of Jews living under nonliberal regimes, enabled the organizations entrusted with securing the well-being of those Jews to operate with some success in a diplomatic arena in which Staatsraison and Realpolitik reigned supreme. The war, however, put an end to their international dominance, both because the costs of state operation that they had earlier helped finance now generally exceeded amounts they could underwrite themselves and because during the war governments had learned to raise significant capital on their own through direct sale of state securities to large numbers of small investors. Moreover, a shift in their investment interests, prompted in part by the disruption of the Russian capital market following the Bolshevik revolution, left many of them less concerned with east European Jewish affairs. Jewish political leaders such as Reich, Wolf, and Marshall thus greeted the ethos that animated the creation of the League of Nations as a lifesaver, throwing themselves enthusiastically behind a concept of international order that negated Staatsraison as a legitimate basis for state conduct and sought to replace Realpolitik with international law as the governing principle through which states and peoples related to one another.

Unfortunately, that new international order quickly proved a broken reed. The Great Areopagus remained silent as at least 60,000 Ukrainian Jews were slaughtered in the pogrom wave of 1919–20, while the minorities treaties turned out not to deter the Austrian government from denying citizenship to upward of 50,000 Galician Jewish war refugees and threatening to expel them from Vienna to Poland; the Hungarian and Polish governments from instituting *numerus clausus* restrictions in universities, public employment, and the free professions; or the Romanian government from sitting by as Jewish students at universities in Cluj, Iasi, and Bucharest were beaten and prevented from entering— all cases in which Jewish organizations unsuccessfully sought League of Nations intervention between 1920 and 1928. From the beginning of the decade, the leaders of the Jewish diplomatic effort had thus cast about for ways to activate the international minorities protection system on their behalf. There had been disagreement among them over how best to do so. Some, like Wolf, had concentrated on rectifying what they saw as the system's procedural flaws; others, including Reich, had explored ways of bringing pressure to bear on both the international community and the individual east European states, including forging (or threatening to forge) political alliances with other minorities, organizing systematic press campaigns in various countries to rally public opinion to Jewish causes, and establishing an international Jewish organization that would represent world Jewry in the diplomatic arena with a single unified voice. Marshall had initially oscillated between the two approaches, but as the decade wore on he came increasingly to despair of any possibility that the broken system could ever be fixed. Thus, for example, when in February 1929 Julius Brodnitz, chairman of the German Jewish defense organization Centralverein deutscher Staatsbürger jüdischen Glaubens, contacted Marshall's American Jewish Committee about the possibility of establishing "an international Jewish organization to combat antisemitism," Marshall and his colleague Felix

Warburg "expressed doubt as to the necessity of the Verein's incurring the expense" required to sustain the effort.[11]

Indeed, that the expense of the internationalist strategy did not justify its results, actual or potential, had become common wisdom among Jewish leaders by 1929, even before the Great Depression weakened the financial health of most Jewish organizations throughout the world. During the previous year, both the American Jewish Committee and the American Jewish Congress, which had maintained lobbying offices in Geneva earlier in the decade, had cut off all funds for those operations. The Comité des Délégations Juives, which in late 1928 had warned that declining contributions were jeopardizing its continued existence,[12] was forced to do the same in 1930. Even Wolf, whose Joint Foreign Committee stayed with the diplomatic approach for another few years, had to take note already in February 1928 of "the increasing public discontent in regard to the execution of the [minorities] Treaties and the ineffectiveness of the Guarantee of the League of Nations," which, among other things, made it difficult for him to justify his yearly attendance at the meeting of the League Council.[13]

In this context, Marshall, who, though never regarding himself as a Zionist, had shown keen interest in Palestine as a promising destination for Jews who wished to leave eastern Europe ever since the First World War, concluded that, as he wrote to Jewish educator Heinemann Stern of Berlin on 2 February 1929, "Conditions have so shaped themselves throughout the world in consequence of the war and the misery of the Jews in Eastern Europe has been such that it is but natural that those endowed with the spirit of enterprise should desire to establish themselves under more favorable conditions than those existing in the lands in which they and their ancestors have lived." Moreover, he noted, whereas "the doors of opportunity which for more than a century stood wide open in the United States have been closed to all but a very small percentage of immigrants," and "legislation and the administration of the laws of Western European countries make it practically impossible for Jewish migrants to be received, Palestine . . . offers the hope of relief to those who are possessed of the pioneer spirit and who are willing to undergo hardships in the expectation of attaining a measure of independence."[14] He thus preferred to invest his resources in an organization devoted to easing those hardships and increasing substantially the number of Jews who could find refuge in what he unabashedly termed "the land of our fathers"[15] than in diplomatic and political efforts aimed at combating forces hostile to Jewish interests in the Diaspora so as to reduce the number of Jews who would need to find refuge in Palestine in the first place. Hence, he took the lead in recruiting non-Zionist leaders of Jewish organizations in twenty-seven countries around the world to join in equal measure with the World Zionist Organization in a cooperative, ostensibly nonideological endeavor to support mass immigration of Jews to Palestine, to promote agricultural coloniza-tion based on Jewish labor, to purchase land in the name of the Jewish National Fund, and to foster the development of the Hebrew language and Jewish culture in the Jewish homeland.[16] Those were the expressed aims of the Jewish Agency founded at Zürich in August 1929.

Marshall insisted to his dying day a month later that joining the Jew-ish Agency did not make him a Zionist, because it committed him to neither a Jewish state nor a Jewish majority. It did, however, commit him and his fellow non-Zionists who joined him to substituting settle-ment in Palestine for the international system of minorities protection as the lynchpin of organized Jewish efforts to ameliorate the increas-ingly grave situation of east European Jews. That commitment, how-ever, opened the door wide to de facto Zionization, as it were, for if the new Agency were successful in its stated goals, a Jewish majority in Palestine would eventually be created, and Jews there would be entitled to claim state sovereignty on the basis of the same principle of national self-determination that had worked to their detriment in the east Euro-pean successor states. Certainly the Arab leadership in Palestine under-stood the logic of this situation, and it may well be that news of what transpired in Zürich on 14 August 1929 added to the growing volatil-ity of Jewish-Arab relations, which led to an explosion of violence nine days later. That explosion, in turn, precipitated a crisis in Zionist-Brit-ish relations, one of whose notable effects was to force the non-Zionists who had joined the Jewish Agency to close ranks behind the Zionist leadership and march more and more to its tune. The deaths of Mar-shall, Reich, and Wolf shortly thereafter thus symbolized the end of one era and the beginning of another.

NOTES

1. League of Nations, Mandate for Palestine, Article 4, in *Great Britain and Palestine, 1915–1939*, Royal Institute of International Affairs Information Department Papers No. 20A (London: Royal Institute of International Affairs, 1939), 120.

2. "Speech by L.W. at a Meeting in Connection with the Minorities Treaties of 1919," 8 June 1920, YIVO Archives, RG 348, Box 8, File 82.

3. See David Engel, "Perceptions of Power: Poland and World Jewry," *Simon Dubnow Institute Yearbook* 1 (2002): 17–28.

4. Draft of speech by Wolf, 8 June 1920, YIVO Archives, New York, RG 348, Box 8, File 82.

5. Leon Reich, "Traktaty Polski a przyszłe stosunki polsko-żydowskie," 29 June 1919, Central Archives for the History of the Jewish People, Jerusalem (CAHJP), P83/G308.

6. Texts in Charles Reznikoff, ed., *Louis Marshall, Champion of Liberty: Selected Papers and Addresses* (Philadelphia, 1957), 544, 546.

7. "Letter from the Secretary-General of the Committee of the Jewish Delegations to the Peace Conference," 26 January 1920, League of Nations Council Document G (41/2784/1249).

8. L. Reich, "Przed rozstrygnięciem sprawy palestyńskiej," *Chwila*, 10 September 1919.

9. From an article published in September 1917, quoted in Mark Levene, *War, Jews, and the New Europe: The Diplomacy of Lucien Wolf, 1914–1919* (Oxford: Oxford University Press, 1992), 167.

10. In Reznikoff, *Louis Marshall*, 536.

11. American Jewish Committee, "Minutes of the Meeting of the Executive Committee," 14 April 1929, American Jewish Archives, Cincinnati, Louis Marshall Papers, Box 144, Folder 1929.

12. "Zapiska o sovete zashchity prav evreiskikh men'shinstv," Central Zionist Archives, Jerusalem, A126/686 (handwritten annotation "1928 oder 1929").

13. Wolf to Mrs. H. W. Swanwick, 20 February 1928, YIVO Archives, RG348/91/9524.

14. In Reznikoff, *Louis Marshall*, 775.

15. Ibid.

16. Jewish Agency for Palestine, Constitution of the Jewish Agency for Palestine (London, 1929).

3

The Stalinist "Great Break" in Yiddishland

GENNADY ESTRAIKH

The year 1929 marked the end of a five-year "romantic" period in Soviet Jewish history. This period started around 1924, when the Soviet regime began to deal much more seriously with issues related to Jews, while previously the state and party apparatus responsible for Jewish affairs was involved largely with testing its propaganda function. In the early postrevolutionary period, the Bolsheviks did not formulate any consistent programs for economic and social work among the Jews, because they believed that traditional shtetl life (deemed "parasitic") would quickly lose its footing in a productive socialist environment. This attitude did not reflect a specifically communist analysis of the problems of contemporary Jewish life or of possible ways to rectify them. Rather, the Soviet regime appropriated from Jewish socialists and liberals of various hues (who permeated Soviet Jewish institutions) their plans for the "productivization" of the eastern European Jewish masses.[1]

Of course, productivization of the Jews did not happen with a wave of the Bolsheviks' magic wand, especially since the country's economy had been ruined by wars and social upheavals. Yet although Jewish traders, clergy, and other "unproductive elements" did not turn overnight into miners, steelworkers, and peasants, the social structure of the Soviet Jewish population began to reshape itself, forming into main groups: achievers, temporary beneficiaries of the relaxed economic environment of the New Economic Program (NEP), and "déclassé" individuals. The achievers consisted mainly of members of the Communist Party, its youth organization (the Komsomol), and trade unions. Soviet trade unions were part of the one-party-state apparatus and did little to protect their members' rights, but a trade-union card was a token of acceptance into the Soviet mainstream.

While the number of Jews who achieved access to the most presti-gious and lucrative positions in society was growing rapidly through the 1920s, they remained a minority of the general Jewish population. Thus, even when the party's Jewish membership quadrupled during the years 1922–30 to 76,000, communists made up less than 3 percent of Soviet Jews—or perhaps as much as 10 percent, if one takes into account the communists' spouses and children. The number of trade-unionists (some of whom were also members of the party or Komsomol) was more significant—about 300,000, or over one million if one includes members of their families—but they also represented a minority of the 2.75 million Soviet Jews. In 1926, during a meeting of the Central Com-mittee of the Communist Party, Shimen Dimanshtein, the first commis-sar in charge of Jewish affairs in Lenin's government, had to admit that initially the revolution had brought misfortune to the majority of Jews.[2] That was hardly surprising in a country ruled by a "workers' and peas-ants' government" in which only a small minority of the Jews belonged to the proletariat or peasantry.

It is hard to gauge how many people—predominantly traders and artisans—later succeeded in finding their place in the liberalized but always volatile market economy of the early Soviet Union. The num-ber of Jews who benefited in some way from the NEP could be around half a million. Compare this with the total number of achievers (over one million) and the up to one million Soviet Jews who had an inde-finable vocation and were categorized as "déclassé." Although some of the entrepreneurs, known as "NEPmen," became rich or at least well-off during this period of time, the average self-employed "beneficiaries" earned a very modest income—which did not stop the authorities from disenfranchising them as "bourgeois elements."

For instance, artisans would get twenty to twenty-five roubles a month. Since fifteen to twenty roubles had to be paid for accommo-dation and taxes, such a monthly income consigned them and their families to poverty. The majority of shopkeepers, too, could hardly keep their heads above water.[3] For all that, the artisans and shopkeep-ers were better off than the déclassés, who dragged out a miserable existence and often survived only thanks to American relatives or charities, most notably the American Jewish Joint Distribution Com-mittee (JDC).[4]

In 1924, two agencies responsible for Jewish agricultural colonization were formed in the Soviet Union: the governmental Committee
for the Settlement of Jewish Toilers on the Land (KOMZET) and the
Association for the Settlement of Jewish Toilers on the Land (OZET).
Both Soviet agencies became the government's liaisons to the Jewish population, pursuing two objectives: first, to "normalize" the Jews
within the structure of Soviet peoples, each with its national territory;
second, to find a useful and self-supporting occupation for at least part
of the unemployed shtetl dwellers. In contrast to Palestinian colonization, neither the KOMZET/OZET nor the foreign sponsors of Soviet
projects had to buy land, because it had been nationalized in one of the
first decrees of Lenin's government and later was distributed gratis by
the powers that be. The JDC emerged as the principal sponsor of Soviet
Jewish colonization projects, particularly in the Crimea.[5]

Jewish colonization represented the central project of the "romantic" period. To many Yiddishist cultural activists and enthusiasts about
Jewish colonization, Soviet Russia of the mid-1920s was a happier place
than Palestine, particularly as the design for Soviet Jewish territorial entities in the Crimea and southeastern areas of Ukraine began to
emerge. Many Jewish activists of non-Zionist persuasion were happy
that Yiddish, rather than the "bourgeois-cum-clerical" Hebrew, was
being recognized and sponsored by the state as the language of Soviet
Jews. Boruch Glazman, an American Yiddish prose writer, attempted
to find an answer to the question, how can one explain such enthusiasm on the part of Western Jewish activists toward colonization in the
Soviet Union, especially since colonization meant, strictly speaking,
going from more advanced urban forms of life to a lower step on the
ladder of economic development? Still, Glazman wrote during his visit
to the Soviet Union,

> It is a great joy for all of us, because here, too, our life is being normal-
> ized, because a peasant class is being created among Jews—and not only
> in the Soviet Union but among the whole Jewish people; a peasant class
> that must bring new freshness and new content into our lives. . . .
>
> And show me, incidentally, a Yiddish writer who does not become
> overwhelmed by the wildest, most kaleidoscopic and romantic fever
> when he only begins to imagine the excellent perspectives that are

emerging for the large-scale development of a rich, diverse, healthy and deeply rooted Yiddish literature!

This is exactly the same Yiddish writer who looks with great fear at the new, alien tribe that is now being created, before our very eyes, in Palestine.[6]

The colonization project particularly appealed to the Territorialists, who called for creation of a Jewish statehood outside Palestine. Israel Zangwill, the father of Territorialism, less than six months before he died in August 1926 took part in a meeting held in support of the Jewish colonization movement in Russia.[7] Moshe Katz, a Comintern Yiddish journalist, reported in a memorandum written in September 1926 to the Soviet Foreign Office, "No other campaign of the Soviet government has made such an exceptionally good impression there [in the United States] as it has the settlement of Jews on the land."[8] Among Soviet Yiddish intellectuals, particularly of the Territorialist stripe, colonization was becoming "the most significant factor" in their activities.[9] Moshe Litvakov, a Territorialist-turned-Communist, who edited the Moscow daily *Der Emes* (Truth) starting in 1921, wrote about the Crimea as "our Palestine."[10] Some people even came from Palestine to try their luck in the Crimea.[11]

The Soviet Jewish colonization drive developed in the climate of the NEP, when Russia achieved its pre–First World War GNP and an average worker's salary equaled or even exceeded the prewar level.[12] Many people regarded Joseph Stalin as a moderately authoritarian and a fairly enlightened leader and did not realize that he was already backsliding on the liberalization of the early NEP period. In 1926, Abraham Cahan, editor of the largest New York Yiddish daily, *Forverts* (Forward), was satisfied with the victory of Stalin and his group over the "wild, bloodthirsty tactic and rhetoric of Zinoviev and Trotsky." According to Cahan's delusional analysis, this was a promising development that augured improvements in the Soviet government's relationship with the Socialist movement and the country's entry into the democratic fold.[13] Many intellectuals were misled by the resolution on literature adopted by the Soviet Communist Party's Central Committee in June 1925. It called for the tactful treatment of fellow travelers and refused to allow any literary organization, including the militant proletarian coteries, to speak in the name of the party.[14] 1925 and 1926 were years marked by a record number of returnees to the USSR, including the Yiddish poets Peretz Markish, Leyb Kvitko, and David Hofshteyn, who occupied the Soviet Yiddish literary Olympus. The leading Yiddish prose writer David Bergelson lived in Berlin until 1933, but in 1926 he made public his affiliation with the Soviet literary world; his 1928–29 sojourn in the United States was sponsored by American communists.[15] Joseph Roth, one of the numerous pilgrims to the Soviet Union, wrote in 1926,

> Today Soviet Russia is the only country in Europe where anti-Semitism is scorned, though it might not have ceased. Jews are entirely free citizens—though their freedom may not yet signify that a solution of the Jewish question is at hand. As individuals they are free from hatred and persecution. As a people they have *all* the rights of a "national minority." In the history of the Jews, such a sudden and complete liberation is unexampled.[16]

Yiddish education flourished in Ukraine, Belorussia, and Russia. The number of Yiddish schools increased from 906 in 1927–28 to 1,203 in 1930–31. Teachers' training colleges turned out an ever-growing number of Yiddish teachers. In 1929–30, in Ukraine alone 670 future Yiddish teachers studied at four colleges. More than 2,600 students studied at Yiddish agricultural colleges. In addition, there were, for instance, a Yiddish medical college, Yiddish musical, art, and cooperative colleges, a college for political education in Yiddish, and a Yiddish department at a printing college. Scores of Yiddish scholars worked at the Kiev-based Institute for Jewish Proletarian Culture of the Ukrainian Academy of Sciences and at the Jewish Department of the Belorussian Academy of Sciences.[17]

In November 1926, thousands of Jewish activists were in seventh heaven when Mikhail Kalinin, the chairman of the All-Union Executive Committee and thus the (largely ceremonial) head of the Soviet state, tentatively promised to form a Jewish republic in the Crimea. Henceforth, he was a popular household name among Jews all over the world.[18] An American functionary of the JDC wrote a decade later, "Not a Jew, he has been one of the men who from the beginning believed that a bent Jewish peddler could be transformed into a horny-handed farmer."[19] All in all, by the end of the 1920s, the Soviet Union looked like an astonishing place, at least in the eyes of numerous Soviet and foreign Jewish activists: its 200,000 Jewish farmers exceeded the whole contemporary Jewish population in Palestine at that time;[20] the government had promised to establish a Jewish republic; no other country boasted so many Jewish statesmen and generals; and Yiddish had a high status in society, as it was widely used in various domains of Soviet life.

* * *

In the mid-1920s, the authorities' strategy of solving the Jewish problem in the Soviet Union combined the further resettlement of Jews (to agricultural colonies, most notably in the Crimea, and to various industrial centers) with the "productivization" of the former shtetl, which was no longer acknowledged as a reality of Jewish life in a new ideological, social, and economic environment. With a single stroke of the pen, the ideology-driven bureaucracy removed the shtetl (*mestechko*) from Soviet maps, because in the country of the hammer and sickle it was more appropriate to define these settlements as "towns" or "villages." Nonetheless, rebranding alone could not transform the new town and village dwellers into proletarians and peasants. The shtetl stubbornly functioned as the place where rural and urban, Jewish and non-Jewish components of the economy interacted, trying to survive in the Soviet environment.

At the same time, the notion of "shtetl" continued to be widely used in Soviet academic and popular publications.[21] Furthermore, in keeping with the party's 1924 decision to turn its "face to the countryside," the Jewish apparatus turned its "face to the shtetl." Some Jewish communists even sought to preserve the shtetl.[22] No doubt, many Yiddish *Kulturträger* realized that destroying the shtetl meant, in effect, sawing off the branch they were sitting on, because the shtetl backwater remained the main habitat of Yiddish speakers. As Peretz Markish put it in a 1927 letter to a Warsaw-based fellow writer, "The bit of Yiddishkayt that we have depends entirely on backwardness. The less backwardness remains, the less Yiddish remains."[23]

In 1929, Itsik Fefer, the leading Yiddish poet in Ukraine, included a section with the scatological title "Manure in Full Bloom" (*Bliendike mistn*) in his first *Selected Works*.[24] It was presented as a poetic travelogue about the author's trip to his home shtetl of Shpola, where 5,000 Jews made up 95 percent of the local population. Shpola also boasted one of the first *soviets* (counsels) which functioned in Yiddish.[25] (In the late 1920s, Yiddish *soviets* became a widespread phenomenon.)[26] Fefer, who knew how to trim his sails to the prevailing winds, hailed the Soviet transformation of shtetl. He noticed many signs of change in his shtetl: Young Pioneers and members of the Komsomol, a club for workers of the clothing industry, new houses, and a tannery that provided jobs for local workers. A former dive keeper traded in needlework rather than in liquor and girls, and her only son was in the Red Army. The poet's former *melamed* had died, and his daughter had run away with a *goy*. The *shames* (synagogue sexton) was dreaming about a position as a courier at the local office of the Communist Party. Not very much was left of the "synagogue, goats, shops, and mud" that he remembered.[27]

State support of the shtetl was provided in a series of decrees. On 3 November 1927, the Belorussian government issued a decree about the transformation of the shtetl's economic structure. On 15 December 1928, the Presidium of the Nationalities Council at the Central Executive Committee of the Soviet Union adopted a resolution, which inter alia recommended building new factories in the urban areas inhabited by Jews and helping Jewish artisans organize their cooperatives. On 26 February 1929, the Ukrainian government issued a decree about helping the shtetls' Jewish poor by developing cooperatives.[28]

All in all, the shtetl was granted an amnesty. Significantly, by the end of the 1920s the shtetl problem seemed very different from the way it had looked a decade earlier. First, the shtetl Jewish population had decreased to 530,000 and made up less than 20 percent of all Soviet Jews.[29] Second, the NEP policy allowed the shtetl Jews to find earnings in small producers' *artels*, kolkhozes, and various other cooperatives. Educated people could work in schools and other educational and cultural institutions, both Yiddish and non-Yiddish, in hospitals, and in the state apparatus. Third, the industrial development of some former shtetls also created new jobs. Outmigration of young people helped mitigate the shtetl problem. Furthermore, a new hybrid—Soviet-cum-traditional—Jewish life took root there. It was a predominantly Yiddish-speaking world where a former *shochet* could work in an all-Jewish cooperative, producing chicken products. But the only way he and his pious colleagues knew to slaughter chickens was to make them kosher. Thus, "Soviet meat turned out to be kosher."[30] Children reared on Soviet-and-kosher food would finish a local Yiddish school and then move to a city, leaving the parochial world of their parents behind.

* * *

The climate in society changed radically in 1929, the year of the Great Break (*velikii perelom*), as it was called in Soviet Newspeak following Stalin's speech on the twelfth anniversary of the revolution. The doctrine of a "great break" in industry and agriculture marked the beginning of Stalin's autocracy, which had consequences for virtually all aspects of Soviet life as well as for the atmosphere of the international communist movement. In the beginning of 1929, Leon Trotsky was expelled from the country. The charismatic Soviet ideologist Nikolai Bukharin and his supporters were defeated in July 1929 by the Stalinists, who advocated a more militant and isolationist policy even vis-à-vis Social Democracy, which was stigmatized now as "social-fascism."[31]

The Great Break affected the Jewish population, particularly those who failed or did not want to find a place in the Soviet mainstream. By reducing the private sector of the economy, the government increased the number of Jewish migrants looking for alternative sources of income. The Crimea could not solve the problem of the shtetl by absorbing its excess population, because this republic-in-the-making had limited territorial resources. Two more factors hindered the expansion of the Crimean project: the unhappiness of the surrounding non-Jewish residents, most notably the Tartars, who regarded the Crimea as their ancestral land; and the lopsided—almost exclusively agricultural—character of the economy in the areas of Jewish colonization. At the same time, the convincing success of Crimean colonization had proved that the productivization of shtetl dwellers could bring practical results and, thanks to available foreign aid, did not involve huge investments.

In 1928, the building site for the Jewish republic was moved to the Far
Eastern territory which soon became known as Birobidzhan. At the same
time, Birobidzhan did not receive the same status as other high-profile
projects of the time, such as the building of industrial centers in Mag-
nitogorsk, Zaporozhe, and Komsomolsk. This signaled that Far Eastern
Jewish statehood was to rely on domestic and, more importantly, international fundraising campaigns, rather than on the state budget alone. As it
happened, Birobidzhan created a new divide among sponsors of Soviet
Jewish colonization: it immediately found hot supporters in overtly
communist circles, whereas its richest sponsor, the JDC, took pains to
distance itself from Birobidzhan.[32] The change of the building site for
the future Jewish republic contributed to a mood swing among some
supporters of Soviet Jewish projects. Although the Crimean colonies
continued to exist, the JDC and other foreign charities were extremely
disappointed to have had invested millions of dollars in a more or less
dead-end enterprise.

In general, 1929 marked a "great break" in the receipt of funds from
abroad, because the fundraising targets of the JDC and other relief
organizations could not be realized. The stock-market crash in the
United States limited American Jewry's ability to support humanitarian
projects in other countries. The timing of the Birobidzhan drive was not
good for domestic economic reasons as well: thanks to the large-scale
industrialization of the Soviet Union, destitute shtetl dwellers had a
good chance to find jobs in the growing urban centers of the European
part of the country and did not have to try their luck in a distant and
obscure province.

The beginning of 1929 saw anti-Zionist and antireligious campaigns
in the Soviet Union, triggered by the decision of the party's Central
Committee to leave little leeway for Jewish religious life. In April 1929, a
decree tightened state control over all religious organizations and cler-
gymen, forbidding them to conduct any financial, charitable, or educational activities.[33] In September 1929, *Der Emes* reported that Kapulye,
the birthplace of the classic Jewish writer Mendele Moykher-Sforim,
had become the first former shtetl where the day off was shifted from
Saturday to Sunday. The situation was somewhat different in the agricultural colonies operated under the auspices of the KOMZET, which
was rather reluctant to undertake drastic measures, for fear that they

could damage its relations with foreign sponsors of colonization. Peter Smidovich, the KOMZET's non-Jewish chairman, belonged to the upper echelons of the Soviet leadership and thus had the power to mitigate some of the antireligious campaigns organized by the hypervigilant Jewish Sections of the Communist Party.[34]

In this situation, cooperatives of artisans, or *artels*, created the best refuge for religious people. Indeed, the Soviet authorities saw *artels* as a relatively progressive mode of production—an intermediate stage on the way to mechanized manufacturing. Such cooperatives were able to gain access to scarce raw materials, and their members were not disenfranchised like individual artisans. Significantly, observant people who worked in an *artel* had some leeway in setting up their schedules, so they could keep the Sabbath and observe holidays. The JDC and other foreign Jewish charities, notably the ORT, helped establish hundreds of *artels*, providing them with machinery, tools, and instruction. The religious and political activist Solomon Joseph (Shlomo Yosef) Zevin, then the rabbi of the town of Novozybkov, appealed to the leadership of the JDC:

> The heart of all faithful Jews bleeds at the sight of the new Crimean colonies which lack all Jewish spirit and coloring and have no Kosher meat, no ritual bath, teachers for their children, nor any of the religious necessities that these settlers have been accustomed to all their lives. . . . And it is readily understood that in this manner there will be obliterated the memory of Jewishness from their midst so that our eyes will behold not Jewish settlements but the home of the soulless Jewish bodies. A situation such as this requires a thorough and radical consideration.[35]

He called, in particular,

> to assign sums of money for the teaching of trades and handicrafts. Our Government is granting many concessions to hand workers, so that it would be possible for the devoted public workers to establish in each town *artels* (unions) of laborers in various fields whose members would support themselves in plenty out of fruits of their own labors, and they would not have to wander about from place to place, besides. At present, they are in a pitiable state. The Sabbath is also a drawback to them,

which could be overcome if they were established in labor groups by themselves.[36]

At the same time, communist watchdogs applied more rigid yardsticks to intellectuals. The campaign that came to be known as the "Pilnyak and Zamyatin Affair," which was unprecedented in its virulence and scale, revealed the general change of climate in literary circles. (The pretext was the publication abroad of novels by two Russian writers: Yevgeny Zamyatin's *We* and Boris Pilnyak's *Mahogany*.) Jewish communist functionaries sought to sunder the Soviet and non-Soviet literary milieus. The venerable Yiddish novelist Sholem Asch, the honorary chairman of the Yiddish PEN Club, was torn to pieces in Soviet critical articles following his 1928 visit to the Soviet Union. The castigation of Shmuel Gordon, then a newly hatched Yiddish writer, for sending his poems to the Warsaw weekly *Literarishe Bleter* (Literary Pages) signaled a turning point in the relations between Soviet and non-Soviet Yiddish circles.[37]

Relations with the West became even more confrontational after violence in Palestine in August 1929 was interpreted by communists as a commendable episode in the Arab people's struggle against their British and Zionist colonizers. As a result, Jewish fellow travelers whose national feelings were stronger than their commitment to the communist ideal left the pro-Soviet camp. In fact, the communists' relations with fellow travelers began to deteriorate at the end of 1928. In the beginning of 1929, Moshe Olgin, a founder of the New York communist Yiddish daily *Frayhayt* (renamed *Morgn-Frayhayt*—often spelled *Morg(e)n-Freiheit*—on 17 June 1929, when it changed from an afternoon to a morning newspaper),[38] called a meeting of about thirty hot communist literati without inviting the fellow travelers. Olgin told them that the time had come to form a separate writers' association, because the communist press could rely no longer on halfhearted petit bourgeois authors and needed contributors who could write "with swords in their hands."[39]

Four decades later, Paul Novick, who edited *Morgn-Frayhayt* after Olgin's death in 1939, drew the following lesson from the events of 1929:

> In the months of August–September 1929 the M[orgn-]F[rayhayt] as well as the progressive Jewish organizations were in a crisis in connection with the unrest in Palestine at that time. We came into a head-on

collision with the Jewish community. . . . We paid dearly for our stand, having lost a great many of our readers and having weakened our mass base. Years later we *were criticized for our lack of flexibility*, for our failure to avoid this head-on collision with the community (from which we were ostracized).[40]

Still, many American Yiddish readers and writers remained loyal to communism. On 13 September 1929—a month after the Arab riots, ten days after the fellow travelers' mass departure, and a month before the Wall Street Crash—pro-Soviet American Yiddish literati established Proletpen, which became the largest Yiddish communist literary association outside the Soviet Union. Thus, the Yiddish Red Decade began in America a month earlier than the general Red Decade (between the Wall Street Crash and the Molotov-Ribbentrop Pact). In literary life, Proletpen predated the John Reed clubs of American English-language pro-Soviet writers, which were established in October 1929. The name of Proletpen was coined as an antonym to the Yiddish PEN Club, which professed nonpartisanship in Yiddish literature. Proletpen's spiritual center was in Moscow, at the headquarters of the International Union of Revolutionary Writers. In 1930, the second conference of this literary arm of the Comintern adopted a resolution on Yiddish literature, stressing the importance of Proletpen. Joseph Stalin's interpretation—circa 1930—of Leninism provided the foreign activists with fodder for their ideology of Leninist *Yiddishkayt* or Yiddishness:

Firstly, Lenin never said that national differences must disappear and national languages become fused in one common language within the boundaries of a *single* state, *before the victory* of socialism *on a world scale*. . . .

Secondly, Lenin never said that the abolition of national oppression and the fusion of the interests of nationalities into a single whole is equivalent to the abolition of national differences. . . .

Thirdly, Lenin never said that the watchword of developing national culture under the proletarian dictatorship is a reactionary watchword. On the contrary, Lenin was always in favour of *helping* the people of the U.S.S.R.[41]

From 1929 onward, the communist Yiddish cultural world was generally populated by its own cohort of writers, actors, and other cultural activists who had little contact with noncommunist circles. In New York, the Y. L. Peretz Yiddish Writers' Union expelled those literati who were associated with the communist movement.[42] In fact, the stratum of Jewry associated with the movement was rather narrow. In the United States, it numbered about 40,000 in 1934, with only a few thousand card-carrying communists among them. The others were "sympathizers," often members of front organizations such as the International Workers Order or the Workers Musical Alliance. These sympathizers generously supported the *Frayhayt*; in 1934, for instance, they collected some $60,000 for the paper. However, party leaders were worried that many workers who donated money did not actually read the *Frayhayt*.[43] In April 1934, Bela Kun, a Comintern leader, instructed communist editors to publish "full newspapers" that would fully satisfy all of their readers' interests, diverting them from any temptation to read the bourgeois press.[44] Members of the International Union of Revolutionary Writers, for their part, were required to support all the policies and programs of the Soviet regime.[45]

The Comintern apparatus coordinated and sponsored numerous Jewish cultural projects. Among them was the "theater pamphlet in eleven scenes" *Jim Kooperkop*. Penned between the end of 1928 and the beginning of 1930 by the Soviet writer Shmuel Godiner, the play was staged by the Belorussian State Yiddish Theater and the New York communist-leaning theater Artef. Godiner's fantasy created the two-dimensional image of Rockford, a self-made American millionaire who dreams about replacing his communism-infected workers with uncomplaining, tireless robots. No doubt, Godiner was influenced by Karel Čapek's 1920 play *Rossum's Universal Robots* (better known as *R.U.R.*) or its 1924 Russian interpretation, *The Uprising of Machines* by Aleksei Tolstoy. In the Yiddish play, an inventor named Edward Howard has created a mechanical man, whom he calls Jim Kooperkop. Howard's robot is able to do any operation needed by industry, but it has no brains or heart—the two "harmful emotion-generating centers."[46] Rockford finds it particularly important to use such robots in a multimillion-dollar government contract aimed at producing weapons against the Soviet

Union. However, the workers led by communists are ready to help their Russian comrades.

Yiddish-speaking groups of communist parties continued to cooperate in the framework of the Comintern, despite the fact that, in the beginning of 1930, the Jewish sections were phased out of the structure of the Soviet Communist Party.[47] The sections had been established in 1918, though the Bolsheviks were always reluctant to tolerate separate cohorts in their ranks. After the revolution, however, they had to face the reality of dealing with a society riddled with such "legacies of capitalism" as ethnic and gender inequalities, hence the need to target every particular stratum with a separate apparatus. In 1930, the regime believed that the mission of such specialized agitprop substructures, including the Jewish one, had been accomplished. Some Soviet activists welcomed the closing down of the Jewish sections, which—they argued—had been a breeding ground for turf battles.[48]

In the 1930s, the Far Eastern territorial project was the main focus of the activities of Soviet and non-Soviet Jewish communists. The Jewish Autonomous Region, with its capital Birobidzhan, represented essentially the final product of *yidishe arbet* (Jewish work), which pursued two main objectives: the propagation of Communist ideology in the language of the masses, Yiddish, and nation-building. The first objective lost its domestic importance by the mid-1930s, when the vast majority of Soviet Jews were already able to consume propaganda in Russian, Ukrainian, or Belorussian. By that time, antireligious agitation, an arch-important issue within *yidishe arbet*, had also become much less vital, as Jews turned out to be more pliable than the Christian and Muslim populations.[49]

As for the building of a Yiddish-speaking nation of workers and peasants from the socially amorphous, hidebound shtetl dwellers, Birobidzhan, despite its negligible Jewish population, provided Stalinist dogmatists with the missing link: national territory. "Normalization"— the illusory, never-to-be-achieved purpose of Soviet policy toward the Jews—also dictated Birobidzhan history. The existence of a national territory made the Jews *look* less abnormal, at least according to Stalinist rules for qualifying ethnic groups as nations. As a result of this turn in Soviet politics toward Jews, only Birobidzhan-based Jews would be regarded (at least, theoretically) as a national community, whereas Jews in all other parts of the country were treated as people with very limited Jewish cultural and educational interests. This approach remained the pivot on which the Soviet Jewish life had to turn during the following six decades.

NOTES

1. For various aspects of "productivization," see, e.g., Tamar Bermann, *Produktivier-ungsmythen und Antisemitismus: Eine soziologische Studie* (Vienna: Europa Verlag, 1973).

2. Gennady Estraikh, "The Soviet Shtetl in the 1920s," in Antony Polonsky, ed., *The Shtetl: Myth and Reality* (Oxford, UK: Littman Library of Jewish Civilization, 2000), 201–202.

3. Ibid., 204–205.

4. Nora Levin, *The Jews of the Soviet Union since 1917: Paradox of Survival*, vol. 1 (New York: NYU Press, 1987), 121.

5. See Jonathan Dekel-Chen, "An Unlikely Triangle: Philanthropists, Commissars, and American Statesmanship Meet in Soviet Crimea, 1922–37," *Diplomatic History* 27.3 (2003): 353–376.

6. Borukh Glazman, *Step un yishev: Bilder fun a rayze iber di yidishe kolonyes fun sovet-Rusland un Ukraine* (Warsaw: Kultur-lige, 1928), 226–229. All translations are mine.

7. Joseph Leftwich, *What Will Happen to the Jews?* (London: P. S. King, 1936), 161; Joseph Leftwich, *Israel Zangwill* (London: J. Clarke, 1956), 217.

8. Russian Center for the Preservation and Study of Documents of Most Recent History (hereafter RTsKhIDNI), fond 445, opis' 1, delo 86, 115.

9. See the letter written by Yekhezkel Dobrushin to the American Yiddish poet H. Leivik on Jan. 4, 1927, published in Mordechai Altshuler, ed., *Briv fun yidishe sovetishe shraybers* (Jerusalem: Hebrew University, 1979), 63.

10. Quoted in Levin, *The Jews of the Soviet Union Since 1917*, 146–147.

11. See, in particular, Anita Shapira, "Goralah shel 'kvutsat Elkind' be-Rusya," *Shvut* 1 (1973): 87–94.

12. Alla Chernykh, *Stanovlenie Rossii sovetskoi: 20-e gody v zerkale sotsiologii* (Moscow: Pamiatniki istoricheskoi mysli, 1998), 16.

13. Gennady Estraikh, "The Berlin Bureau of the New York *Forverts*," in Gennady Estraikh and Mikhail Krutikov, eds., *Yiddish in Weimar Berlin: At the Crossroads of Diaspora Politics and Culture* (Oxford, UK: Legenda, 2010), 152.

14. Herman Ermolaev, *Soviet Literary Theories, 1917–1934: The Genesis of Socialist Realism* (Berkeley: University of California Press, 1963), 48.

15. Gennady Estraikh, "Bergelson in and on America," in Joseph Sherman and Gennady Estraikh, eds., *David Bergelson: From Modernism to Socialist Realism* (Oxford, UK: Legenda, 2007), 205–221.

16. Joseph Roth, *The Wandering Jews* (London: Granta, 2001), 107.

17. For a comprehensive survey of Soviet Yiddish academic life, see Abraham Green-baum, *Jewish Scholarship and Scholarly Institutions in Soviet Russia, 1918–1953* (Jerusalem: Hebrew University, 1978).

18. Hersh Smolyar, *Fun ineveynik* (Tel Aviv: I. L. Peretz, 1978), 335, 353. For a panegyric on Kalinin, see, e.g., S. Dingal, "Tsen yor prezident," *Der Tog*, April 25, 1929.

19. Evelyn Morrissey, *Jewish Workers and Farmers in the Crimea and Ukraine* (New York: privately published, 1937), 40.

20. In 1927, the number of American Jews wholly or partly engaged in farming was between 80,000 and 100,000—see Gabriel Davidson, *Our Jewish Farmers* (New York: L. B. Fischer, 1943), 146.

21. Estraikh, "The Soviet Shtetl in the 1920s," 197–212; Deborah Hope Yalen, "'On the Social-Economic Front': The Polemics of Shtetl Research during the Stalin Revolution," *Science in Context* 20.2 (2007): 239–301; idem, "Red *Kasrilevke*: Ethnographics of Economic Transformation in the Soviet Shtetl 1917–39" (Ph.D. dissertation, University of California, Berkeley, 2007).

22. Estraikh, "The Soviet Shtetl in the 1920s," 208.

23. Melech Ravitch, *Dos mayse-bukh fun mayn lebn: Yorn in Varshe, 1921–1934* (Tel Aviv: I. L. Peretz, 1975), 412.

24. Itsik Fefer, *Geklibene verk* (Kiev: Melikhe-farlag, 1929), 329–356.

25. See Jacob Leshtshinsky, *Dos sovetishe yidntum: Zayn fargangenhayt un kegnvart* (New York: Poale Zion-Zeire Zion, 1941), 353.

26. Zvi Y. Gitelman, *Jewish Nationality and Soviet Politics: The Jewish Sections of the CPSU, 1917–30* (Princeton: Princeton University Press, 1972), 352–353.

27. Gennady Estraikh, *In Harness: Yiddish Writers' Romance with Communism* (Syracuse: Syracuse University Press, 2005), 117–118.

28. *Prakticheskoe pazreshenie natsional'nogo voprosa v Belorusskoi Sotsialisticheskoi Sovetskoi Respublike*, part 2 (Minsk: Tsentrail'naia natsional'naia komissiia, 1928), 97–106, 117–118.

29. Leyb Zinger, *Evreiskoe naselenie v Sovetskom Soiuze* (Moscow-Leningrad: Gosudarstvennoe sotsial'no-ekonomicheskoe izdatel'stvo, 1932), 116.

30. Anna Shternshis, "Soviet and Kosher in the Ukrainian Shtetl," in Gennady Estraikh and Mikhail Krutikov, eds., *The Shtetl: Image and Reality* (Oxford, UK: Legenda, 2000), 148.

31. Robert C. Tucker, "The Emergence of Stalin's Foreign Policy," *Slavic Review* 36.4 (1977): 567–568.

32. Yehuda Bauer, *My Brother's Keeper: A History of the American Jewish Joint Distribution Committee, 1929–1939* (Philadelphia: Jewish Publication Society of America, 1979), 91; Alexander Ivanov, "Facing East: The World ORT Union and the Jewish Refugee Problem in Europe," *East European Jewish Affairs* 39.3 (2009): 369–388.

33. E. G. Gimpel'son, *NEP i sovetskaia politicheskaia sistema, 20-e gody* (Moscow: Institut russkoi istorii, 2000), 279.

34. See Gennady Estraikh, "From 'Green Fields' to 'Red Fields': Peretz Hirschbein's Soviet Sojourn, 1928–29," *Jews in Russia and Eastern Europe* 56 (2006): 69.

35. Rabbi Solomon Joseph Zevin's letter, May 1926, 1, American Joint Distribution Committee Archives, collection 21/32, file 208.

36. Ibid., 2.

37. Estraikh, *In Harness*, 128–129.

38. For the early history of *Frayhayt*, see Tony Michels, "Socialism with a Jewish Face: The Origins of the Yiddish-Speaking Communist Movement in the United States, 1907–23," in Gennady Estraikh and Mikhail Krutikov, eds., *Yiddish and the Left* (Oxford, UK: Legenda, 2001), 24–55; Tony Michels, *A Fire in Their Hearts: Yiddish Socialists in New York* (Cambridge: Harvard University Press, 2005), 238–250.

39. Estraikh, *In Harness*, 97.

40. Novick's YIVO archival collection RG1247 (Novick, folder 34); emphasis in the original.

41. Joseph Stalin, *Marxism and the National and Colonial Question* (London: Martin Lawrence, 1936), 257–259; emphasis in the original. See also Alexander Bittelman, *A program farn kiem fun yidishn folk: Di komunistishe shtelung tsu der yidisher frage* (New York: Morgn-Frayhayt, 1947), 27.

42. Naomi Wiener Cohen, *The Year after the Riots: American Responses to the Palestinian Crisis of 1929–30* (Detroit: Wayne State University Press, 1988), 89.

43. RTsKhIDNI, fond 495, opis' 30, delo 3492, 2–3; ibid., fond 495, opis' 30, delo 3993, 19.

44. RTsKhIDNI, fond 495, opis' 30, delo 1014a, 80.

45. RTsKhIDNI, fond 495, opis' 30, delo 988, 17.

46. Shmuel Godiner, *Dzhim Kuperkop* (Minsk: Tsentraler Farlag, 1930); Edna Nahshon, *Yiddish Proletarian Theatre: The Art and Politics of the Artef, 1925–40* (Westport, CT: Greenwood, 1998), 68.

47. Gitelman, *Jewish Nationality and Soviet Politics*, 472–475.

48. Motl Kiper, "A vort tsu der ordenung," *Di Royte Velt* 6 (1930): 94–111.

49. Cf. Valentina Zhiromskaia, *Demograficheskaia istoriia Rossii v 1930-e gody* (Moscow: ROSSPEN, 2001), 211.

4

Permanent Transit

Jewish Migration during the Interwar Period

TOBIAS BRINKMANN

On a night in late April 1929 Benjamin M. Day, commissioner of immigration, attended a Passover Seder at Ellis Island, together with 150 people, many of them Jewish immigrants. According to the *New York Times*, "he instructed all departments to lend every possible hand in permitting the fullest enjoyment of the festival in true holiday fashion."[1] Passover is a joyful Jewish holiday. The parallel between the Exodus from Egypt to the promised land of Israel and the passage from Europe to the land of freedom was emphasized and celebrated at many Seder tables in America on this evening. Why did Day so explicitly ask his staff to cheer up the Jewish participants? Most had certainly looked forward to the 1929 Passover Seder, anywhere in America—but not at Ellis Island. The question why the 1929 Seder at Ellis Island was a rather gloomy affair leads to a larger issue concerning the situation of Jewish migrants after World War I more generally. Why were countless Jewish migrants across central and eastern Europe caught up in a situation best characterized as permanent transit, and what did the United States have to do with it? Before turning to the European and global situation in more detail it is necessary to examine how the momentous changes in American immigration policy after the war affected Jewish migrants and would-be migrants in Europe.

Closing American Gates

In April 1929 Ellis Island was a conspicuously quiet place, compared to its glory days before World War I. The number of about 12,000 Jews who arrived there between January and December pales in comparison to the pre-1914 figures. Between the early 1880s and the beginning of the war more than 2 million Jews from the Russian and Austro-Hungarian Empires and Romania moved to the United States. Smaller groups went to Britain, France, and more far-flung destinations such as Argentina and South Africa. In the year 1907 alone almost 150,000 Jews immigrated to the United States, the overwhelming majority through Ellis Island. These Jews constituted almost 15 percent of the general immigration of 1.3 million in that year. On several occasions in 1907, more than 15,000 immigrants were processed daily at Ellis Island. The general and Jewish immigration declined somewhat in the following years but increased again significantly in 1913 and 1914. In 1914 almost 140,000 Jews came to the United States. This year would have seen a new record in Jewish immigration, if the war had not intervened in early August 1914.[2]

After 1918 the immigration from Europe recovered only slowly. In many places the transport infrastructure was destroyed or not accessible due to various blockades. Across eastern Europe military conflicts, which lasted into the early 1920s, forced several million people to flee; Jews were especially hard hit. A series of targeted pogroms claimed at least 60,000 Jewish lives in Poland and Ukraine in 1918–19 and displaced many more. Boris Bogen, general director of the American Jewish Joint Distribution Committee (JDC), described what he saw on a visit to Galicia in 1919: "The road to Lwoff was a Via Dolorosa of hunger and death and sickness and fear. Jewish refugees were tramping on the highways, going God knows where, living in abandoned barns like cattle, crowded often many in a room in houses that gave them shelter." Many eastern European Jews had already been forced from their homes between 1914 and 1918: the Russian military authorities had deported thousands of Jews (and ethnic Germans), as potential "collaborators," to central Russia; the German occupying forces had recruited Jews (and Poles) as forced laborers; and intense fighting, particularly in Galicia, triggered a massive refugee wave. Most war refugees and displaced persons had to rely on support by various aid organizations such as the JDC. Homeless Jews found shelter in makeshift camps, in cheap hotels, or (as witnessed by Bogen) in ruined buildings. Their situation was often so desperate that a migration to America in the short term was not even imaginable.[3]

In western Europe various restrictions preventing internal and cross-border mobility were only gradually lifted. Apart from these considerable obstacles the fortunate Jews, who had not lost their homes, were affected by severe economic crisis and frequently had to postpone migration plans. The postwar turmoil in central and eastern Europe made it difficult for Jewish aid organizations to raise funds for refugees and survivors of pogroms. Another challenge, explaining Bogen's repeated trips to the region, was to assess the measure of suffering and to locate the victims. Due to the chaotic conditions, only some destitute Jews were supported; it is impossible to ascertain precise numbers of Jewish fatalities and expellees.[4]

Considering these circumstances, it astonishes that more than 100,000 Jews managed to make the journey across the Atlantic in 1921. Already in the following year the Jewish immigration declined sharply to about 50,000.[5] This sudden drop was not limited to Jews but to all migrants hailing from eastern and southern Europe and from Asia. In 1921 the U.S. Congress severely restricted immigration by passing a bill with fixed annual quotas based on citizenship. The new immigration act heavily favored "old stock" northern and western Europeans. The main sending countries of the pre-1914 period, such as Italy, Japan, and Russia, were allocated low annual quotas, which were quickly exhausted and imposed lengthy and excruciating waiting periods on would-be immigrants. It was of course no coincidence that at the moment when the pressure for Jews (and other eastern Europeans) to leave was greater than ever before, the United States closed it gates.[6]

Fears of a Communist takeover and of destitute refugee masses from eastern Europe provided the opponents of immigration with the decisive momentum; anti-Semitism and racism heavily influenced the design of the law. Immigration historian Mae Ngai has stressed the influence of a new kind of nativism behind the national origins quota acts. The late nineteenth-century "cultural nationalism" was replaced by an explicitly racist nationalism. For the new nativists the racial background of certain immigrants precluded any assimilation. The rise of a new and more radical anti-Semitism was an important driving force behind this transition.[7] The turn to massive immigration restrictions was only one issue that highlighted a profound cultural conflict in postwar America. John Higham's term the "Tribal Twenties" aptly describes the deepening divide between urban and rural America. In the three decades before World War I, mass immigration by non-Protestants— Catholics, Eastern Orthodox Christians, and Jews—had boosted the population of America's big cities. As the cities underwent a massive transformation, small-town America appeared as a world apart. "Old stock" rural Americans favored isolationism, despised immigrants, opposed the emancipation of women, supported Prohibition and, in many parts of the country, the Ku Klux Klan. Of course, like other issues, immigration cut across cultural and class boundaries. In the cities unionized blue-collar workers (many themselves immigrants) tended to support immigration restrictions to keep out cheap labor from abroad. Such coalitions help to explain why a majority of voters eventually defeated Prohibition. However, immigration restrictions remained firmly in place until the mid-1960s.[8]

Discriminatory quotas constituted not the only hurdle. After 1921 prospective immigrants had to apply for an immigrant visa at the U.S. embassy or consulate in their home country. Often they had to wait many months for a visa or a negative decision, which they usually could not appeal. For the countries migrants needed to cross in order to reach ports such as Rotterdam or Liverpool, transit visas were required. The 1924 Johnson-Reed immigration act reduced the quotas even more. In 1922, 1923, and 1924 about 50,000 Jews came to the United States annually; in 1925 and the following years only about 10,000 were admitted.[9] Even these declining numbers are still significant, if set against the Third Aliyah, which brought about 35,000 mostly eastern European Jews to Palestine between 1919 and 1923. The Fourth Aliya saw a strong increase, but this was already a consequence of the restrictive American policy: about 70,000 Jews moved to Palestine between 1924 and 1929.[10]

In the context of American immigration restrictions the importance of changes implemented in 1929–30 is frequently overlooked. In March 1929 President Hoover, who in the previous year had campaigned for immigration restrictions but had criticized the rigidity of the quota regime, signed a bill fixing the low ceilings. Congress and the president gave in to enormous pressure by groups favoring restrictions. Thus, the racially prejudiced national origins quota system was cloaked in the mantle of legitimacy. The annual quotas for Poland (6,524), the Soviet Union (2,784), and Romania (295), countries with large numbers of

Jews, Catholics, and Eastern Orthodox Christians desperate to leave for the United States, were conspicuously low, compared with tiny Luxemburg (100), Germany (25,957), or Norway (2,377). The quotas for the large Asian nations were even lower; China, India, and Japan received a quota of 100 each. In late 1930, under the impact of the Depression and mass unemployment, Hoover instructed U.S. consular officials to handle all visa applications as rigidly as possible to curb immigration. Worldwide migration was declining as more and more countries were affected by the Depression. Potential migrants lacked the means for the journey, and the prospects at most destinations looked bleak. Nevertheless, even in 1930 thousands of applications were filed at American consulates and embassies. Yet between September 1930 and March 1931 alone American consular officials turned down almost 100,000 applications, which otherwise would have been processed.[11]

The immigration statistics compiled by the American Jewish Committee illustrate the drastic impact of Hoover's executive order, an immediate and significant decline of Jewish immigration from 12,479 (1929) and 11,526 (1930) to 5,692 (1931) and 2,755 (1932). The number of Jewish immigrants for 1933, 2,372, was even lower. The strict policy of the consulates affected all immigrants; in fact, the share of Jewish immigration actually increased from almost 5 percent in 1929 to over 10 percent in 1933. In the early 1930s more people emigrated from the United States than were admitted as immigrants. Hoover's instructions explain why even low quotas were frequently not exhausted until the beginning of the Second World War. In 1936 Franklin D. Roosevelt revoked Hoover's 1930 executive order. Yet most consular officials continued to adhere to the stricter admission criteria.[12]

It is impossible to assess the exact impact of Hoover's order. The shock of the Great Depression should certainly not be underestimated. But the German case illustrates that immigration restrictions and obstruction by consular officials kept many deserving Jews out. Germany had been allocated a generous quota, which would have promised safe emigration to the United States for over 25,000 people annually. But the quota was fully filled for the first time in 1939, on the eve of the war. Scores of distressed Jewish men and women were turned away at American consulates in Germany and neighboring countries throughout the 1930s. The number of all Jewish immigrants to the United States crossed the

10,000 threshold only in 1937. The 50,000 Jews who immigrated in 1939 constituted more than 50 percent (!) of the general immigration to the United States. The high percentage indicates the almost immeasurable pressure for Jews to escape Nazi terror. But the number also points to a belated, albeit limited opening of the American gates. But already in September 1939 the German attack against Poland blocked the path to the West for most eastern European Jews, even for the majority of those who had obtained an immigration visa to the United States.[13]

Due to changes in American immigration policy after 1921–24, and especially after 1929–30, only a fraction of the Jews who wanted to immigrate to the United States could actually do so. Many deserving migrants were caught in a web of complicated, contradictory, and changing regulations. American restrictions hit eastern European Jews much harder than other groups targeted by the 1921 and 1924 quota laws. Most Italians, for instance, lived in a clearly defined homeland, were not displaced by the war, had valid citizenship papers, and could easily reach the American embassy or consulate in their country. In sharp contrast, many Jews had literally lost their home countries. In the wake of the various military conflicts following the collapse of the large multiethnic empires in eastern and southeastern Europe in 1917–18, Jews had become stateless in large numbers, sometimes without even leaving the ancestral shtetl. The successor states of the Russian, Austro-Hungarian, and Ottoman Empires, such as Poland, Lithuania, and Hungary, often were not willing to give citizenship to unwanted minorities, notably to Jews. A similar fate also affected two other groups: the government of the new Turkish state refused to extend citizenship to many Armenian refugees and genocide survivors, and former citizens of the Russian Empire who opposed Bolshevism could not obtain passports from the new Soviet government—if they actually possessed the courage to step into a Soviet embassy or consulate.

The American national origins quota acts of 1921 and 1924 did not reserve quotas for Jews and other transterritorial Diaspora groups such as Armenians. Of course, there was no quota for stateless persons either. To complicate matters even further, stateless persons did not possess valid or recognized passports and thus could not even apply for a visa or a transit visa to travel across international borders. And it was frequently unclear which consulate or embassy they should turn to. Statelessness literally contained countless Jewish refugees in postwar Europe: they frequently could not go back to their hometowns. Without papers they could not continue their journey across international borders. Many lived on the margins of central and western European cities, sometimes in makeshift camps. In Germany Jewish refugees were tolerated but repeatedly the target of anti-Semitic abuse and even violence. Apart from various Jewish philanthropic associations, such as the JDC or the *Hilfsverein der Deutschen Juden* (Aid Association of the German Jews), and local Jewish communities, no official body represented the interests of Jewish refugees without citizenship in the international arena.

In 1922 the League of Nations high commissioner for refugees, Norwegian explorer Fridtjof Nansen, issued provisional passports to stateless persons from the former Russian Empire and to Armenian refugees from the former Ottoman Empire (but not to refugees from the former Austro-Hungarian Empire). This document made crossing borders easier. But it was not a real passport and did not provide legal protection against deportation. In the novel *Pnin* the Russian-born writer Vladimir Nabokov, himself a stateless migrant living in Berlin during the 1920s, recalled the hurdles facing stateless migrants and refugees in interwar Europe: "the dreary hell that had been devised by European bureaucrats (to the vast amusement of the Soviets) for holders of that miserable thing, called the Nansen passport (a kind of parolee's card issued to Russian émigrés)."[14]

These changes explain why relatively few people came to Ellis Island in 1929. The number of about 12,000 Jews who still managed to immigrate to the United States in that year after difficult passages betrays many more unknown tragedies of migrants who failed somewhere along the way or did not even depart. In December 1929 several Jewish passengers arrived in New York on a ship from the German port Bremerhaven. They had valid papers and immigrant visa and were admitted. A report by the Bremen office of the *Hilfsverein* allows a closer look at the complicated journey of these Jews. The group, consisting of twenty-nine men, women, and children, had come to Bremerhaven six years earlier in 1923. Each migrant had a valid immigration visa issued by the U.S. consulate in the Latvian capital, Riga. The migrants, who hailed from the territory of the Soviet Union, were spared the trip to the Soviet capital because the United States only established diplomatic relations with Moscow in 1933. But after they had spent time waiting at Riga their journey was again interrupted in Bremerhaven because the Russian quota for the year 1923 had been exhausted. The 1924 act complicated their situation (and that of hundreds other migrants waiting at European ports) because the already low quotas were drastically reduced. The *Hilfsverein* workers who had cared for the migrants described their situation as desperate. They had enough food and a place to stay, but their hope had gradually vanished. It was unclear how the waiting list for Russian quota immigrants was administered. In the fall of 1929 the Riga consulate announced in a communication that the twenty-nine Jews would have to wait for an indefinite period. This news had apparently broken several of the stranded migrants. The Bremen aid workers commented, "They suffer mentally, because they have been uprooted and separated from their relatives for years. And they suffer physically, for they are condemned to do nothing [but wait] and they do not know what to do with themselves." One family eventually decided to go to Brazil, but the others did not know where to go. Only the intervention of New York congressman Samuel Dickstein finally made the impossible possible. Dickstein, himself a Jewish immigrant from a town in present-day Lithuania, represented the Lower East Side and emerged as a prominent critic of the restrictions on Capitol Hill in the late 1920s.[15]

Little is known about the fate of stranded migrants who were less lucky. The new American legislation turned legitimate and deserving Jewish and other migrants into unwanted and illegal aliens who were treated like criminals if they came to the attention of state authorities. Thousands of people on the journey to and in some cases already in the United States found themselves on the wrong side of the new regulations. Some tried to find loopholes. A few hundred Jews illegally entered the United States through Mexico during the 1920s, many by crossing the Rio Grande at El Paso. A few came with forged documents— an obvious option for stateless migrants. During the 1920s 8,000 Jews settled permanently in Mexico as legal immigrants. But in 1930 Mexico too enacted restrictive immigration legislation, thus also closing the illegal route to the United States. Tellingly, the U.S. Border Patrol at the Mexican border was established in 1924 primarily to arrest illegal Chinese and European immigrants, not Mexicans, who remained outside the immigration legislation. Indeed, largely as a result of the American restrictions against European and Asian immigrants, Mexicans became a source of cheap and easily disposable temporary labor, especially in the large agricultural estates in California and Texas.[16]

Nowhere was the change in American immigration policy more symbolically felt than at Ellis Island. The entrance gate to America reversed its function and transformed for many potential immigrants into a one-way exit, with no possibility of return. Already when the United States entered the war in 1917, suspicious immigrants and enemy aliens were detained on the island. One of the most famous involuntary migrants was anarchist Emma Goldman, who in 1919 was stripped of her U.S. citizenship, detained, and deported from Ellis Island to Soviet Russia, together with her partner, Alexander Berkman, and dozens of left-wing radicals. After 1924 fewer immigrants arrived, and due to the massive checks imposed before departure to obtain a visa, they passed the inspection without much hassle. But now immigrants often came to Ellis Island from the American mainland, in order to be deported.[17]

Passover Seders for Jewish immigrants had been celebrated at Ellis Island probably already during the 1890s.[18] Before 1914 most participants of Ellis Island Seders were recently arrived immigrants detained for various reasons. Some had been diagnosed with contagious illnesses such as the eye disease trachoma; others, such as single women with children, were deemed "likely to become a public charge" or had violated the immigration laws. Detained migrants were deported or eventually admitted, especially if relatives or Jewish aid organizations formally promised to take responsibility for them. Such interventions on behalf of migrants judged to be problematic became more difficult after 1921, and the new legislation deemed such persons illegal immigrants because they violated certain regulations. Because of the poignant parallel between the theme of the celebration and the real experience of passage in reverse, Passover Seders at Ellis Island were depressing affairs for all Jews involved: for the migrants anxious and uncertain whether they would be admitted or desperately awaiting the final stage of their deportation, for the members of the Hebrew Sheltering and Immigrant Aid Society (HIAS), which arranged the Seder, for the rabbis who led the ceremony, and for compassionate bystanders. In the previous year (and very likely in 1929) Immigration Commissioner Day had generously promised to suspend the deportation of the 150 Jewish participants for the duration of the Passover holiday. The deportees were reprieved for a few days to "enjoy the holiday before they start back to their native lands."[19]

The stringent American restrictions permanently excluded an unknown but very substantial number of Europeans and Asians. The pioneering Jewish migration scholars Alexander and Eugen Kulischer pointed in 1932 at the contradiction between America's self-image as home for the oppressed and its closed-door policy:

> With this catastrophe [the First World War] the era of large anarchic and free migration has come to an end. . . . The Gate of the Promised Land, which presented itself as asylum of the poor and persecuted of this world, has closed with a loud bang, and it is ever more tightly locked. But at the same time, many new immigration restrictions and work restrictions have been enacted along many old and new borders in Europe.[20]

Alternative Destinations and Dead Ends

To gain a more detailed understanding of Jewish migration in 1929, it is indeed necessary to look at the wider European and global context. Some countries such as Canada or Mexico raised the bar for immigrants to exclude migrants looking for alternatives and alternative routes to the United States. Several others such as Britain never lifted the stringent wartime regulations excluding foreign migrants. Migration restrictions were a global phenomenon highlighting the crisis of the international system that emerged from the Paris peace settlement. The League of Nations could never sufficiently address the plight of millions of refugees and stateless persons across Europe. The rise of the passport and the visa as the new "currency" of movement across borders and the fate of the stateless, who did not possess "papers," illustrates the loss of trust between nation-states.[21] The situation of stateless Jewish migrants and refugees who found themselves almost literally between the postwar borders, lacking any international protection, highlights paradigmatically the transition or relatively free global migration before 1914 to a system of state restrictions against "unwanted" aliens, who were categorized and treated as "illegal" migrants.

Eastern European Jews were particularly vulnerable because they lacked protection as a group. Before 1914 their safety had depended largely on the integrity of the large multiethnic empires. In postimperial eastern Europe the new territorially defined nation-states almost literally fenced out transterritorial Diaspora communities such as Jews and Armenians. The successor states treated Jews as an unwanted national minority whose loyalty could not be trusted and placed various restrictions on them. Anti-Semitic quotas discriminating against Jewish university students are only one example. The Hungarian *numerus clausus* forced many young Hungarian Jews to move to foreign universities during the 1920s, among them the physicists Edward Teller and Leo Szilard. Both studied and worked in Germany before escaping to the United States after 1933.[22]

* * *

To whom could Jewish refugees, stranded migrants, and would-be migrants turn for help in the post-1918 "broken world"? And more importantly, where could they actually go? As Carol Fink has shown in her study *Defending the Rights of Others*, the limited political influence of established western Jews and Jewish aid organizations that lobbied on behalf of Jewish minorities across eastern Europe and of Jewish refugees withered quickly after the Paris peace accords. Long before 1933 governments around the world showed little interest in protecting the rights of Jewish minorities and refugees across eastern Europe. Nevertheless, in more than a few cases Jewish aid organizations were able to support refugees. The *Hilfsverein* published a detailed biannual newsletter that was distributed across eastern Europe. It carried updates on the immigration policies of countries around the world and described alternative destinations for Jewish immigrants. In the early 1920s a number of eastern European Jews led by Zionist leader Leo Motzkin established *Emigdirect*. This organization closely cooperated with existing Jewish associations such as the *Hilfsverein*, HIAS, the Jewish Colonization Association (ICA), and the JDC to find new homes for Jewish migrants, especially in South America and South Africa. As the doors to America were gradually closing, several new options for eastern European Jews came into play: the Soviet Union,

Palestine, France, Germany—and returning home or postponing migration.[23]

In the first years after 1918 the first destination for many war refugees and stranded migrants was the German capital, Berlin. Soon after the war had ended in the West, Berlin became one of the main theaters of a European refugee drama, a consequence of the emerging new order in eastern Europe. Berlin was an obvious choice because of its location in relative proximity to the eastern war zone. Political turmoil and economic crisis in the huge city created small niches for foreign transmigrants and refugees without papers. In Berlin even a little money in foreign currency represented a small fortune, at least until the end of the hyperinflation in early 1924. Berlin was also home to one of Europe's largest and wealthiest Jewish communities. Even under severe economic pressure the Berlin *Gemeinde* cared for destitute refugees. Berlin's vibrant cultural and intellectual scene only added to its attraction. Eastern European refugees and transmigrants, many of them Jewish, made lasting contributions as artists, writers, university students, scholars, and scientists. The democratically elected government of the Weimar Republic, unlike its imperial predecessor, explicitly tolerated refugees from eastern Europe on its territory. Several thousand eastern European Jews even received German citizenship (only to be made stateless by the Nazi regime in 1933). Berlin was, however, not an easy or particularly welcoming place. Especially in the early postwar period and after 1929 with the rise of the Nazi party Jewish transmigrants faced public abuse and occasional violent attacks by right-wing extremists.[24]

For a few years after the war Berlin served as a vital center of the Yiddish-speaking Jewish Diaspora. Dozens of Yiddish periodicals were edited in Berlin; Europe's leading Yiddish theater troupes performed repeatedly in the German capital in front of large Jewish audiences; numerous Jewish writers and surprisingly many Jewish spokespersons and scholars lived for some time in the city. The Jewish Scientific Institute (YIVO) was founded in Berlin in 1926. Yet none of this was permanent. For most Jews from eastern Europe Berlin was a transit city. Most of the periodicals only existed for a few months, and no Yiddish theater was established in the city. Jewish migrants and refugees formed a disparate community on the move. By the mid-1920s most Jews had moved on with other eastern European émigrés to Paris, which partly replaced America as a destination for many eastern (and southern) Europeans barred by the American immigration restrictions, much further to destinations such as Harbin or São Paulo, and not least back home, to countries that had not existed when they had left.[25]

In postimperial Europe Berlin was not just an important stopover for Jews but also a place for reflection on the condition and prospects of the Jewish Diaspora. Several scholars who were significant pioneers of migration studies spent time in the city: Mark Wischnitzer, who was the main manager of the *Hilfsverein* and wrote what is still the best overview of modern Jewish migration history in 1948; the famous Jewish historian Simon Dubnow; the demographers Alexander and Eugen Kulischer, who coauthored a pioneering account of global migration in 1932; the demographer and YIVO cofounder Jacob Lestschinsky; the Zionist leader Leo Motzkin, an important institution builder and representative of the interests of the Diaspora on the international level; and several others. An intimate observer of the Jewish transmigration was the Galician-born author Joseph Roth, one of the most famous journalists and rising writers of the Weimar Republic.

In Roth's remarkable 1927 essay *The Wandering Jews*, he deplored the desperate situation of the much-despised *Ostjuden* on the move. Through the subchapters of *The Wandering Jews* Roth developed an intriguing topography of Jewish migration during the mid-1920s: from the Shtetl to Berlin, Vienna, Paris, London, New York, and the Soviet Union. Each one of these places stood for an option. In the East, where the Jews came from, they could not stay. In Vienna they were not welcome. In Paris, America, and the Soviet Union they could stay—if they managed to get in—but the price was assimilation. Palestine, as Roth conceded in a short passage, really was the "only way out," but for him Zionism represented a dead end. Berlin was the place of passage, a gloomy waiting room between East and West:

No eastern Jew comes to Berlin voluntarily. Who, after all, comes to Berlin voluntarily? Berlin is a thoroughfare, where one stays longer because one is forced to. Berlin has no ghetto. It has a Jewish quarter. Jewish emigrants come here, on their journey to America via Hamburg and Amsterdam. Quite often, they are stuck here. They have not enough money. Or their papers are not sufficient. (Of course, the papers! Half a Jewish life is wasted by the useless struggle against the papers). . . . Berlin equalizes differences and destroys distinctive traits. This is why Berlin has no large ghetto. There are some small Jewish streets near the *Warschauer Brücke* and in the *Scheunenviertel*. The most Jewish street in Berlin is the sad *Hirtenstraße*. No street in the whole world is so sad.[26]

The *Ostjuden* did not come to stay; they came to go. Berlin had no "ghetto"—a space of Jewish life, at least partly tolerated and accepted by state and society—for Berlin suppressed difference. Jewish life was characterized by the experience of transition and mobility. Roth was especially interested in the epistemology of Jewish mobility: "Many return. More move on. The *Ostjuden* have no *Heimat* [home] anywhere, but graves on every cemetery."[27]

The topography in *The Wandering Jews* also had a temporal dimension: the world of the Shtetl, as Roth imagined it, had passed with the empires— Paris, America, and the Soviet Union represented gates to a future. Jews could enter, but they had to leave their Jewish past behind. Palestine was (for him) an Utopia in the literal sense: an imagined place, which could not exist in reality. The space that was constructed in Roth's texts existed in the past, but its emblems persisted and were represented by the Jewish migrants: the transnational sphere of the empires and the world of the shtetl, which was tied to the imperial space. The experience of the wandering Jews *in between*, who did not really arrive anywhere, intrigued Roth because of the relationship between the preservation of a transnational diaspora identity in time and space with elements of mobility.

Admittedly, Roth's essay was no scholarly analysis. But his piece highlights the drawbacks of the alternative destinations which replaced America. In a different way than the United States the Soviet Union and Palestine were not just destinations but also destinies. For Jews who were not willing to sacrifice their religious beliefs, political orientations, and even their careers, for an uncertain future in a completely new and unknown environment where they would have much less agency over their own future than in America, neither the Soviet Union nor Palestine was a viable options. The 1929 Hebron pogrom, Soviet support for the Arab cause, and the early stages of collectivization and mass deportations in the Soviet Union in the late 1920s forced even committed

Communists and Zionists to reconsider the decision to migrate. Indeed, the Fourth Aliyah was hardly a one-way street. Declining economic prospects forced thousands of Jews to leave Palestine years before the Depression: in 1926 around 13,000 Jews from Europe immigrated, but 7,300 went the other direction; in 1928 the official net immigration was a mere 10. The Immigration and Travel Section of the British authorities in Palestine registered 2,178 Jewish immigrants and 2,168 Jewish emigrants.[28]

This left other far-flung destinations, especially South America—often the last resort for stranded migrants. Argentina raised the hurdles for legal immigration already in 1922. Brazil, however, admitted more than 55,000 Jews between 1921 and 1942, primarily from Poland, and during the second half of the 1930s, from Germany. Officially Brazil too restricted immigration in the early 1920s. But Jewish aid organizations, as Jeffrey Lesser has shown, sponsored Polish Jewish immigrants and managed to win the trust of the Brazilian government. Brazil represented one of the few remaining options, as migration within Europe became difficult with the onset of the Depression.[29]

More unusual destinations were Danzig and Shanghai. Their status as extraterritorial cities in the interwar period made them attractive for stateless refugees. As an international treaty port Shanghai was more easily accessible for refugees than territories belonging to a state. Hundreds of Jewish migrants from the former Russian Empire completely transformed Shanghai's small Jewish community in the early 1920s. The status of the Chinese port city also explains why it served as one of the last safe havens for German Jewish refugees after 1939.[30] In the immediate aftermath of the First World War widespread travel restrictions across central Europe turned Danzig into an important launching pad for transatlantic migration. In 1920 Danzig became a League of Nations mandate. No passport was required to cross from Poland into the "Free City" Danzig, and the League of Nations protected refugees against an involuntary expulsion to Germany or Poland. For Polish Jews Danzig was the first stop on their way to a better future overseas. Some were stranded for years in the city and required support from the Danzig Jewish community.[31]

By the late 1920s Jews were returning to eastern Europe in sizeable numbers. In an overview article on the *Hilfsverein* its general secretary,

Mark Wischnitzer, mentioned that in the first nine months of 1929 more than 30,000 "emigrants and return migrants," some non-Jewish, had been supported by the *Hilfsverein* at the Silesian train station, Berlin's main gateway to the East.[32] Many more Jews gave up their plans to migrate, as they learned about the economic problems and violence in Palestine, the effects of America's restrictive immigration policy, and the impact of the Depression. This background explains the difficulties faced by German Jewish emigrants after 1933. Most neighbor countries gave these emigrants shelter, notably France, Belgium, the Netherlands, and Britain, but the migration to overseas destinations was difficult, and almost impossible after 1939. The situation of eastern European Jewish migrants in post-1933 Europe is often overlooked. The anti-Semitic German policies were mirrored in other countries, notably in Romania and Hungary. In 1935, following the death of longtime ruler Józef Piłsudski, Poland too imposed severe restrictions on its large Jewish population. For eastern European Jews, not to mention stateless Jews, poverty, state discrimination, and the restrictive American quotas made it even more difficult to leave than for German Jews. In fact by the 1930s especially Jews in smaller Polish communities depended on remittances and support by relatives who had managed to move abroad.[33]

The fate of the Jewish migration scholars mentioned earlier illustrates how perilous the situation became for Jews who remained on the European continent. Simon Dubnow, who had moved from Petrograd with a short stop in Kovno/Kaunas to Berlin in the early 1920s, fled to the Latvian capital, Riga, in 1933. In December 1941 the SS murdered the eighty-one-year-old historian during an "Aktion" to clear the first Riga Ghetto for Jewish deportees from Germany. The Kulischer brothers headed west, first to Paris and then to the unoccupied zone of France. There Alexander was arrested by Vichy authorities and deported, very likely to Auschwitz. Eugen managed to escape to the United States in 1941 and worked for the Library of Congress in Washington, DC; in 1948 he published an important overview of European migration after 1918, *Europe on the Move*. Mark Wischnitzer and his wife, the art historian Rachel Wischnitzer, moved to Paris in 1938. While Rachel obtained a visa for the United States in 1940, her husband moved to the Dominican Republic and could only join her in New York in 1941. In 1948 Wischnitzer wrote an excellent overview of Jewish migration history during the nineteenth and twentieth centuries, *To Dwell in Safety*, which is still unsurpassed. Jacob Lestschinsky also emigrated to America and continued to publish on Jewish migration matters. Leo Motzkin had already died in 1933 in Paris, where he had moved in the early 1920s. Joseph Roth fled to the French capital in 1933 and wrote for a German-emigrant weekly. Deprived of his large audience, he died a broken man in May 1939, eleven months before the German occupation in 1940.[34]

In hindsight the year 1929 proved to be a turning point for the worse—in an already difficult period for Jewish migrants. Hundreds of thousands had been displaced during the war and in its aftermath; many became stateless and were thus deprived of agency over movement across countless new borders—and of legal protection. Immigration restrictions were a global phenomenon and an expression of the insta-bility of the postwar international "order." The situation of unwanted refugees, who found themselves literally outside the new system, on the margins of European societies, often in makeshift camps, symbolically highlights the weakness of the "broken world." Many years before the Nazi regime occupied large parts of Europe and implemented its "Final Solution" many Jewish migrants and refugees were literally exposed because they were caught in permanent transit and a legal gray zone without protection against discriminatory state policies. The hopeless situation of many Jewish migrants only highlights the unknown trag-edies of countless would-be migrants who were desperate to leave but encountered dead ends wherever they turned, often many years before they faced forced deportation and death.[35]

NOTES

1. "'Seder' Joy Shared by Aged and Needy," *New York Times*, 25 April 1929.
2. *American Jewish Yearbook* 30 (1928–29): 258–59; Philip Cowen, *Memories of an American Jew* (New York: International, 1932), 187–88.
3. Aristide R. Zolberg, *A Nation by Design: Immigration Policy in the Fashioning of America* (Cambridge: Harvard University Press, 2006), 246–47; Michael R. Mar-rus, *The Unwanted—European Refugees in the Twentieth Century* (Oxford: Oxford University Press, 1985), 52–80; Carole Fink, *Defending the Rights of Others: The Great Powers, the Jews, and International Minority Protection, 1878–1938* (Cam-bridge: Cambridge University Press, 2004), 101–30; Boris Bogen, *Born a Jew* (New York: Macmillan, 1930), 190; Eric Lohr, *Nationalizing the Russian Empire: The Campaign against Enemy Aliens during World War I* (Cambridge: Harvard Uni-versity Press, 2003); see also Peter Gatrell, *A Whole Empire Walking: Refugees in*

Russia during World War I (Bloomington: Indiana University Press, 1999); David Rechter, *The Jews of Vienna and the First World War* (London: Littman, 2001).

4. Mark Wischnitzer, *To Dwell in Safety: The Story of Jewish Migration since 1800* (Philadelphia: Jewish Publication Society, 1948), 141–51.

5. *American Jewish Yearbook* 30 (1928–29): 259; Arthur Ruppin, *Die Soziologie der Juden*, vol. 1 (Berlin: Jüdischer Verlag, 1930), 138.

6. Daniel Tichenor, *Dividing Lines: The Politics of Immigration Control in America* (Princeton: Princeton University Press, 2002), 142–46.

7. Mae M. Ngai, *Impossible Subjects: Illegal Aliens and the Making of Modern America* (Princeton; Princeton University Press, 2003), 23; John Higham, *Strangers in the Land: Patterns of American Nativism, 1860–1925* (New York: Atheneum, 1977), 277–86.

8. Higham, *Strangers in the Land*, 264–99; Roger Daniels, *Coming to America: A History of Immigration and Ethnicity in American Life* (New York: HarperCollins, 1991), 281.

9. *American Jewish Yearbook* 42 (1940–41), 618; Ngai, *Impossible Subjects*, 21–55, esp. 34–35; Zolberg, *A Nation by Design*, 243–92.

10. Ruppin, *Soziologie der Juden*, 147.

11. Zolberg, *A Nation by Design*, 267–70; *American Jewish Yearbook* (1929–30): 29; Ngai, *Impossible Subjects*, 34–35; Roger Daniels and Otis L. Graham, *Debating American Immigration, 1882–Present* (New York: Rowman and Littlefield, 2001), 25; John T. Woolley and Gerhard Peters, "Herbert Hoover," in *The American Presidency Project* (online), University of California, Santa Barbara, http://www.presidency.ucsb.edu/ws/?pid=21838 (accessed 11 February 2008).

12. *American Jewish Yearbook* 42 (1940–41): 618; Daniels, *Coming to America*, 294–95.

13. *American Jewish Yearbook* 42 (1940–41): 618; for an impressive personal account of a successful last-minute attempt to reach the United States (by bribing a U.S. consular official) see Abraham Ascher, *A Community under Siege: The Jews of Breslau under Nazism* (Stanford: Stanford University Press, 2007).

14. Isabel Kaprielian-Churchill, "Rejecting 'Misfits:' Canada and the Nansen Passport," *International Migration Review* 28 (1994): 281–306, esp. 282–85; Heinrich Engländer, *Die Staatenlosen* (Vienna: Mantsche Verlags- und Universitätsbuchhandlung, 1932), 9–30; Vladimir Nabokov, *Pnin* (Garden City, NY: Doubleday, 1957), 46.

15. Hilfsverein der Deutschen Juden, *Jahresbericht für 1929* (Berlin: Hilfsverein der Deutschen Juden, 1930), 24; on the effect of the 1924 immigration act on stranded migrants with immigration visas at European ports see "7,100 Aliens Stranded," *New York Times*, 19 December 1924.

16. Hollace Ava Weiner, *Jewish Stars in Texas: Rabbis and Their Work* (College Station: Texas A&M University Press, 1999), 102–20; Clifford Alan Perkins, *Border Patrol: With the U.S. Immigration Service on the Mexican Boundary, 1910–1954* (El Paso: Texas Western Press, 1978), 89–92; Zolberg, *A Nation by Design*, 266; Ngai, *Impossible Subjects*, 127–66.

17. Richard Drinnon, *Rebel in Paradise: A Biography of Emma Goldman* (Chicago: University of Chicago Press, 1982).

18. "Passover at Ellis Island," *New York Times*, 31 March 1904; "Passover Starts Tonight," *New York Times*, 10 April 1914; "Jews to Celebrate Passover Tonight," *New York Times*, 17 April 1916; "Passover at Ellis Island," *New York Times*, 3 April 1920.

19. "Halt Deportation of Jews," *New York Times*, 3 April 1928; for a personal memoir of a Jewish immigration official at Ellis Island see Philip Cowen, *Memories of an American Jew* (New York: International, 1932), 143–88.

20. Alexander Kulischer and Eugen Kulischer, *Kriegs- und Wanderzüge: Welt-geschichte als Völkerbewegung* (Berlin: de Gruyter, 1932), 201–2 (author's translation).

21. John Torpey, "The Great War and the Birth of the Modern Passport System," in *Documenting Individual Identity: The Development of State Practices in the Modern World*, ed. John Torpey and Jane Caplan (Princeton: Princeton University Press, 2001), 256–70.

22. Tibor Frank, "Station Berlin: Ungarische Wissenschaftler und Künstler in Deutschland 1919–1933," *IMIS Beiträge* 10 (1999): 7–39.

23. Raymond J. Sontag, *A Broken World, 1919–1939* (New York: Harper and Row, 1971); *Bericht über die Tätigkeit im Jahre 1924* (Berlin: Hilfsverein der Deutschen Juden, 1925), 10–18; Fink, *Defending the Rights of Others*; Marrus, *The Unwanted*, 28–29.

24. Tobias Brinkmann, "From *Hinterberlin* to Berlin: Jewish Migrants from Eastern Europe in Berlin before and after 1918," *Journal of Modern Jewish Studies* 8 (2008): 339–55.

25. Delphine Bechtel, *La Renaissance culturelle juive: Europe centrale et orientale, 1897–1930* (Paris: Belin, 2001), 201–51; Clifford Rosenberg, *Policing Paris: The Origins of Modern Immigration Control between the Wars* (Ithaca: Cornell University Press, 2006), 85; Marion Neiss, *Presse im Transit: Jiddische Zeitungen und Zeitschriften in Berlin von 1919 bis 1925* (Berlin: Metropol, 2002).

26. Joseph Roth, *Juden auf Wanderschaft* (Berlin: Die Schmiede, 1927), 65–68 (author's translation).

27. Ibid., 14.

28. *Korrespondenzblatt des Centralbüros für jüdische Auswanderungsangelegenheiten des Hilfsvereins der Deutschen Juden* (Berlin, March–April 1927); *Jahresbericht für 1928* (Berlin: Hilfsverein der Deutschen Juden, 1929), 30; on Jewish migration to Soviet cities see Gabriele Freitag, *Nächstes Jahr in Moskau! Die Zuwanderung von Juden in die sowjetische Metropole 1917–1932* (Göttingen: V&R, 2004).

29. Jeffrey Lesser, "The Immigration and Integration of Polish Jews in Brazil, 1924–1934," *Americas* 51 (1994): 173–91; idem, "In Search of Home Abroad: German Jews in Brazil, 1933–1945," in *The Heimat Abroad: The Boundaries of Germanness*, ed. Krista O'Donnell, Renate Bridenthal, and Nancy Reagin (Ann Arbor: University of Michigan Press, 2005), 167–84.

30. Marcia Reynders Ristaino, *Port of Last Resort: The Diaspora Communities of Shanghai* (Stanford: Stanford University Press, 2001), 21–53.

31. *Jahresbericht der Jüdischen Centralwohlfahrtsstelle im Gebiet der Freien Stadt Danzig 1. April 1927 bis 31. März 1928* (Danzig: Jüdische Centralwohlfahrtsstelle, 1928), 3–4.

32. Mark Wischnitzer, "Programm und Werk des Hilfsvereins der Deutschen Juden," *CV-Zeitung*, 8 November 1929.

33. Samuel Kassow, "The Shtetl in Interwar Poland," in *The Shtetl: New Evaluations*, ed. Steven T. Katz (New York: NYU Press, 2007), 121–39, esp. 132.

34. Sophie Dubnov-Erlich, *The Life and Work of S. M. Dubnov: Diaspora Nationalism and Jewish History* (Bloomington: Indiana University Press, 1991); Eugene Kulischer, *Europe on the Move: War and Population Changes, 1917–47* (New York: Columbia University Press, 1948); Wischnitzer, *To Dwell in Safety*; Claire Richter Sherman, "Rachel Wischnitzer: Pioneer Scholar of Jewish Art," *Woman's Art Journal* 1 (1980): 42–46; Gennady Estraikh, "Jacob Lestschinsky: A Yiddishist Dreamer and Social Scientist," *Science in Context* 20 (2007): 215–37; Frank Nesemann, "Minderheitendiplomatie—Leo Motzkin zwischen Imperien und Nationen," in *Synchrone Welten: Zeiträume jüdischer Geschichte*, ed. Dan Diner (Göttingen: V&R, 2004), 147–71.

35. Sontag, *A Broken World*; for the desperate yet unsuccessful attempt of a Jewish family to leave Poland months *before* September 1939 see, for instance, Daniel Mendelsohn, *The Lost* (New York: HarperCollins, 2006).

5

Polish Jewry, American Jewish Immigrant Philanthropy, and the Crisis of 1929

REBECCA KOBRIN

It was a particularly cold morning on December 12, 1930, when thousands lined up in front of the Bank of United States on Orchard Street to withdraw their savings. Founded in 1913 by Jacob Marcus, the Bank of United States stood as a celebrated symbol of Jewish economic success. Holding over $268 million in deposits, the Bank of United States embodied the promise of America to four hundred thousand working-class Jews who entrusted their money, and their organizations' savings, spanning from large enterprises such as the International Ladies' Garment Workers Union to the smaller Brisker Relief Committee and other *landsmanshaft* (Jewish immigrant hometown) associations, which all held accounts with this institution. But several bad investments forced the Bank of United States to close its fifty-seven branches. As the fourth-largest deposit bank in New York City, its closure marked a watershed moment in American economic history. While many scholars and popular writers discuss the role this bank's closing played in the onset of the Great Depression, few have commented on the havoc it wrought for New York's Jewish community and those Jewish communities that had grown dependent on money from New York.[1] Jewish immigrants in 1930s New York, as Sam Levenson has described, had to rethink their commitments and obligations. Despite the pleas they received from relatives and friends still in Europe, they no longer could send money to relatives abroad because they themselves "never made money."[2]

This chapter examines the impact the economic turmoil of 1929 had on the philanthropic ties forged between Jews in Poland and the United States during the 1920s. While the flow of money from America to Europe never totally ceased, it did pale in comparison to amounts sent during the 1920s, when immigrant Jews funded and shaped the local effort to "reconstruct the nation" throughout Poland and Lithuania.[3] Like most immigrant groups, eastern European Jews in the United States sent remittances back to eastern Europe even before the war.[4] But the complete devastation of the First World War prodded these recent arrivals to collect and distribute close to $100 million between the outbreak of the First World War and the stock-market crash of 1929.[5] Many scholars discuss the philanthropic efforts of organizations such as the Joint Distribution Committee (JDC), which established banks and hospitals in Poland in the 1920s,[6] but few have analyzed the efforts of the smaller *landsmanshaft* organizations that sent hundreds of "delegates" to distribute millions of dollars on the local level. These American Jewish immigrant organizations, which kept their funds in institutions such as the Bank of United States, believed that they were not merely relieving economic distress; they saw themselves as also furthering Wilsonian diplomacy by helping Polish Jews establish themselves in the new Second Polish Republic. Indeed, their efforts and funds often unleashed a complex array of unintended dynamics throughout Poland.[7]

American Jewish immigrant philanthropy not only transformed Jewish life in eastern Europe, but it also radically altered its donors' lives. During the 1920s, the collection of money for eastern Europe offered immigrant Jews an opportunity to redefine for themselves what it meant to be an American Jew. To be sure, the tradition of giving charity has long played a central role in Jewish communal praxis; but mass fundraising drives that linked the giving of money to new modes of cultural production, in particular the production of postcards, were distinctly early twentieth-century phenomena.[8] This chapter mines Yiddish postcards and publications to provide a glimpse into American Jewish immigrants' "inner world," recounting not only what they experienced but also the worldview through which they experienced it.[9] Immigrant Jews in America saw their identities as Americans as entwined with their ability to send money abroad, appreciating, to use the words of historian Derek Penslar, that "the application of Jewish power was primarily economic in nature and was expressed chiefly through the distribution of money."[10] The power their dollars brought them in eastern Europe enabled immigrant Jews to reenvision themselves as powerful leaders, not struggling foreigners who faced rising anti-immigrant sentiment and anti-Semitism.

The stock-market crash of 1929 that ultimately led to numerous bank failures transformed the lives of immigrant Jews in America—who relished defining themselves in the crucible of their foreign charitable efforts—as well as Jews in Poland who were dependent on American aid. To be sure, the cessation of donations took place against a backdrop of an increasingly complicated economic and political situation in Poland, but Polish Jewish communal life was drastically altered on the local level by the practical evaporation of American funds. Individual families could no longer fund their relatives' businesses in Poland. *Landsmanshaft* organizations closed their overseas philanthropic groups. Jews in Poland, with their lifeline pulled, were forced to search for new survival strategies, as immigrant Jews in America were forced to rethink what it meant to be an American Jew in a land, to use the words of historian Beth Wenger, filled with "uncertain promises."[11]

War, Revolution, and the Polish Jewish Welfare Crisis: The 1920s and the Creation of a Polish-American Jewish Philanthropic Brotherhood

Shlomye Etonis's memoir of his experiences in the city of Minsk during the First World War was typical for thousands of Jews living in cities nestled in the Pale of Settlement, precariously perched on the First World War's eastern front. As he recalled, "everyone was frightened and anxious."[12] Forced to live in a cellar because of the fierce battles being fought in the street, Etonis described what he found afterward: "When the Red Army finally retreated . . . our town lay in ruins. Here, a broken window pane; there a wall full of holes, . . . dead bodies lying in the street like garbage, lying in their own blood as if it were dirty water."[13] Indeed, the First World War was terrifying for Jews throughout the former Pale of Settlement, as thousands of Jewish civilians lost their lives, businesses, and homes. In Brisk (Russian: Brest-Litovsk; Polish: Brzec nad Bugiem), a city of close to sixty thousand residents before the war (where Jews constituted two-thirds of the population), only eighteen hundred families returned after the war. Eighty percent of these families were unemployed since they no longer could earn their livings from commerce, trade, and tax collection as they had before the war. When

Irma May visited Brisk on behalf of the American Joint Distribution Committee in 1920, she described the city as "a picture of misfortune!" "Hundreds are forced [to live] in cellars, anti-rooms and alleys of the old synagogues," she reported. "They huddle together like wild beasts, twenty and thirty in one room. . . . [It is like] hell on earth."[14]

Thus, it comes as little surprise that hundreds of Jews queued up in 1920 on Brisk's potholed streets to speak to Phillip Rabinowitch, "Herr Delegat" from America, because they believed he "could save [them], as well as their fathers, mothers, sisters and brothers in Brisk from certain death."[15] Rabinowitch had been sent to Poland by the United Brisker Relief society of New York to ensure that remittances sent by immigrant Jews in New York reached their relatives in Poland.[16] Indeed, as Jacob Finkelstein, the executive secretary of United Brisker Relief who had sent Rabinowitch to Poland, realized, the "rehabilitation" of Brisk would only take place with the help of "relief from America."[17]

In the city of Bialystok (Russian: Belostok; Polish: Białystok), a few hundred miles away, a similar drama unfolded: as the headline of the city's most popular Yiddish newspaper proclaimed, "Our American brothers and sisters have not forgotten us. . . . We will not die . . . [because we have been delivered] salvation by David Sohn after days of sorrows and despair." David Sohn, a resident of New York, went to Bialystok charged with a mission by the Bialystoker Relief to distribute $200,000 in aid to needy individuals and communal institutions. Using the vast funds at his fingertips, Sohn provided critical financial support to both individual Jews and Jewish communal institutions and to bribe local officials to release imprisoned Jewish leaders. Indeed, such American interventions were common as Jewish immigrants—and Hugh Gibson, the American minister to Poland, estimated there were three hundred of them wandering around Poland in 1920—inserted themselves into local politics, challenging traditional authorities and partisans of the new Polish nation-state.[18]

American Jewish immigrant philanthropists' intervention in local politics was critical in the 1920s, as Jews struggled, like other minority groups in Poland, to create governing bodies, schools, and charitable organizations according to the stipulations of the Polish Minority Treaty.[19] As Poland became mired in recession, government funding for Jewish schools and organizations never materialized.[20] The newly established *kehile* (democratically elected Jewish municipal council; plural: *kehilos*) became crippled by political divisions, as a result of its economic limitations and corrupt leadership. In Bialystok, elected officials embezzled communal funds to help pay for a summer vacation in 1920, prompting the local Red Cross to refuse to give the *kehile* funds for Jewish poor relief.[21] In Brisk, the elected religious and secular Jewish leaders were so divided that one aid worker was unable to distribute funds because no one could agree on how to allocate funds. Poland's economic woes also saw the rapid deterioration of Polish-Jewish communal relations.[22]

So it was against this backdrop of acute poverty, interethnic strain, and Jewish communal corruption that *landsmanshaft* organizations such as United Brisker Relief decided to send representatives to distribute money both to sustain individual families and to revive Jewish communal life. Indeed, American Jews were invited to see the dire situation themselves: Yitzhak Zev Solovetchik (known as Reb Velvele) wrote in an impassioned letter to Jacob Finkelstein in New York City, "Of the 1800 homes in the city, only 800 were left and of the 40 shuls, only eight were left. . . . Half [of 21,000 Jews in the city] were completely pauperized."[23] Relying on the stature and authority that his father, the Brisker Rav, possessed before the war as the leading rabbinic authority in the region (Hayim Solovetchik [1892–1918]), Yitzhak Zev Solovetchik assumed he would be immediately granted "monthly support for each family," which he could personally distribute. But this did not happen because Solovetchik and socialist Jewish leaders were so bitterly split that United Brisker Relief representatives were unable to distribute all their funds. Socialist Jewish parties condemned American "imperialist" charitable aid, demanding that philanthropy should only be given to organizations that would treat equally all segments of the population, such as public kitchens, schools, and clinics. Solovetchik, on the other hand, requested more funds be allocated for individual assistance because respectable bourgeois Jews who had been impoverished by the war would not go to such venues. When Jacob Finkelstein finally arrived in 1921, he found a community ready to implode. He used his power as the dispenser of dollars to force a wide spectrum of communal leaders to create a new united relief committee. To be sure, before the war, a rabbinic figure of Yitzhak Zev Solovetchik's stature would rarely have acquiesced to a building contractor from Staten Island such as Jacob Finkelstein; but the tides had shifted by 1921 for all Jewish leaders, who now had to follow all of Finkelstein's demands. If any Jewish leader wanted to receive any more money from America, Finkelstein told them, "all would have to work together with him in a larger effort to rebuild the city." He used his influence to help Mordecai Drachle launch the local Yiddish newspaper, *Poleser stime*.[24] To cement this coalition, Finkelstein organized a mass rally at Sarver's Theatre, the city's largest public venue, to illustrate Jewish communal unity to local Jews and to Poles as well.

Similar controversies erupted in Bialystok, a city whose Jewish population plummeted from over 70,000 in 1914 to 37,186 in 1921. After the war, most Jewish workers were unemployed, and those with secure jobs worked only three days a week.[25] Thus, the Bialystoker Relief Committee's distribution of over $5 million made a deep imprint, as it enabled Jewish welfare organizations, hospitals, and libraries to expand their services while their Polish counterparts closed their doors.[26] The integral role played by David Sohn in his distribution of money from the Bialystoker Relief Committee earned him an honorary position on the city's *kehile*, which bestowed on him an elaborate pin at a formal ceremony to recognize his courage and contribution to the community.

Such attention lavished on émigrés by Jewish communal leaders made a deep impression on these American visitors. They were not merely generous immigrant donors, but their charitable acts had transformed them into important and powerful figures in local Polish Jewish communal life. As they doled out financial support, American Jewish immigrants demanded that Polish Jewish organizations adopt and incorporate new "more American" standards of operation.[27] Bialystok's largest Jewish orphanage, Ezras Yesomim, offers an illustrative example: after receiving a large grant, the director, Rachel Rachmanowitz, was pushed to make her institution more "worthy" of American contributions. As a result, in the following year, Rachmanowitz divided all her charges by age, established a formal curriculum for them, and purchased uniforms for them. She also modernized her institution's annual report. Steps were taken to illustrate how Ezras Yesomim was an efficient "American-style" charity worthy of more American support.[28] *Dziennik Bialystoki* (Bialystok Daily News), a Polish daily newspaper, railed against local Jews for their reliance on foreign money and for agreeing to American Jews' outlandish demands: Eugene Lifshitz, a member of Bialystok's *kehile*, was sharply criticized after he went to New York to raise money for a new bank for the city that would grant loans to small businesses. While Lifshitz successfully collected $40,000 (close to half a million dollars in 2012 dollar values), he failed to contest his American donors' demands that the bank only loan money to Jews, a stipulation most Poles found outrageous.[29]

Transforming Immigrants into Philanthropists: Fundraising and the Forging of the New American Jew

Immigrant Jews' need to raise vast sums to send to Poland propelled the development and production of new cultural forms during the interwar period. As scholars of twentieth-century American Jewish life have long pointed out, philanthropy emerged as the definitional organizational sphere through which Jews expressed their affiliations and articulated the boundaries of their communal identities.[30] While the tradition of giving charity played a central role in Jewish communal praxis for centuries, interwar mass fundraising drives in the American Jewish immigrant community produced new myths and symbols that stood in stark contrast to traditional models of Jewish charity. The most significant difference involved the public celebration of giving charity in place of the traditional stress on discretion and secrecy.[31] Immigrant Jews embraced seeing themselves as the wealthy benefactors and patrons of eastern Europe and saw charity as providing a means through which to demonstrate their newly achieved financial status and American identities. While these Jews may have been struggling immigrants in America, they quickly understood when they looked across the Atlantic that those who gave away dollars were anything but powerlessness.[32]

The dozens of postcards produced during the early 1920s provide a fascinating visual source through which to view the shifting inner worlds, hopes, and desires of immigrant Jews in the United States. These postcards were part of a larger American postcard "craze" that reached its zenith in the 1920s, with millions of Americans buying, sending, and collecting postcards.[33] In the Jewish immigrant world, Yiddish postcard production was a booming transnational business, with designers working in the United States and Europe and printers producing these cards in Germany and Poland for the growing number of Yiddish-speaking customers in the United States and Latin America.[34]

The shifting imagery presented on two Jewish New Year postcards produced by the Williamsburg Art Company (headquartered in New York but producing all its materials in Germany) before the First World War and in the 1920s eloquently captures the impact that overseas philanthropy had on Jewish immigrants' vision of their identities as Americans as well as their place in the larger fabric of Jewish life. One can find a host of different scenes displayed on New Year's cards—the most popular genre produced by Jewish printers—but most common was the festive holiday meal, perhaps to remind loved ones of their former shared celebrations. The main message emblazoned across a 1910 card, aside from "Happy New Year" in Yiddish and English, is an untranslated Yiddish missive reading, "Holiday joy, holiday cheer, so much good fortune you bring to us." Depicting a traditional and piously dressed family, the card creates a most solemn atmosphere, infused with piety, as it displays a group of men and one little girl sitting around the table, with the holiday candles burning bright. With an apron-donning woman in the corner standing ready to serve the group enjoying a festive meal underneath an array of rabbinic pictures, the card conveys the pensive mood of this holiday season, when all—both senders and recipients of holiday cards—contemplate whether they will be inscribed in the book of life.

In contrast to the overwhelming mood of piety, a mid-1920s postcard illustrates immigrant Jews' enjoyment of dramatizing the dependence of eastern European Jews on their dollars. On the cover of a card produced by the Williamsburg Art Company in the 1920s, one does not find a solemn festive meal but rather a messenger holding a card that reads, "Dollar check." With everyone's arms outstretched to welcome this check into their home like an esteemed visitor, the caption reads, "A letter, a greeting, a check in dollars! / Arrived from the New World / Quickly the table is cleared / Hurry, hand over the check." Indeed all on this postcard, except for the little girl at the center, sit entranced by the messenger and the money he brings from America. As the family abandons the traditional holiday meal once they see money from America, the postcard intimates that Jews in America believed that their compatriots in eastern Europe imagined salvation not in the form of prayer or devout observance of the festival rituals but rather as checks from America. Even this well-dressed, seemingly acculturated family was sustained by remittances from America, a reassuring thought to immigrant Jews evaluating their lives during the season of the High Holidays. English-language New Year cards from the same period demonstrate that even Americanized immigrants enjoyed celebrating their economic success and showcasing the transformational power of their dollars as they reflected on their fates and achievements over the past year. "Bank Note" Rosh Hashanah postcards became widely popular in the early 1920s. On these cards, senders would "transfer" to their friends and family members "assets" from "the unlimited capital" of the "Bank of Joy," just as they sent check or money orders to Europe.

Postcards produced by *landsmanshaft* associations demonstrate even more boldly the extent to which eastern European Jews' Americanization took place in the crucible of their transnational philanthropy. Only once these immigrants set foot in Poland could they display how "American" they had become, as well as their relative economic security, which enabled them to dispense money in eastern Europe. A fabricated image appeared on one postcard, commemorating the visit of "delegate" Morris Sunshine to Bialystok in 1920. Sunshine emigrated from Bialystok to New York in the 1890s, founded Sunshine's Cleaners, a dry-cleaning business on the Lower East Side, and dedicated himself to maintaining the Bialystoker Synagogue in the neighborhood. Technically, this postcard was a combination of two photos: a group photograph of eight men assembled haphazardly in front of the mausoleum of the former chief rabbi of Bialystok, taken by an anonymous visitor from America, with a man superimposed on the lower left corner. The looming figure to the left is Morris Sunshine, who was sent to Bialystok by the Bialystoker Relief Committee with over $250,000 in 1920. As in other portraits of American Jews visiting eastern Europe, the display of disheveled, disorganized, and poorly dressed eastern European Jews accentuated the attire of the American visitor.[35] To be sure, Sunshine had not actually dressed in such ostentatious attire, because, as he reported when he returned to America, he faced great peril trying to reach his former home. With Bolshevik and Polish armies battling for control of the region, Sunshine feared he might be arrested or killed for all the money he was carrying, so he stuffed all the cash he was given into his socks, coat pockets, and suitcase.

So why does Sunshine create such an image of himself on this post-card as visiting Bialystok in elegant formal attire, shiny shoes, a cane in hand, and a bowler hat on his head? First and foremost, it demonstrates Sunshine's understanding that his philanthropic work on behalf of Bial-ystok enhanced his stature in American society since philanthropy had long been a marker of upper-class status in America.[36] Indeed, it was unlikely that Sunshine, as the owner of a small dry-cleaning business on the Lower East Side, had the resources to be a major revered philan-thropist in the United States; but he could enact this part of his aspired American identity only by traveling to Bialystok. Moreover, Sunshine's lack of engagement with the group reveals his understanding of his class stature and power as an American patron of Bialystok. Wearing a costume reminiscent of a British diplomat, Sunshine transformed himself on this postcard from a dry-cleaner with cash-stuffed pockets into a powerful ambassador, underscoring that part of what fueled émi-gré involvement in Bialystok was a sense of empowerment. Sunshine and other interwar delegates saw their philanthropic encounter with their former homes as part of America's imperial mission, spreading its riches to less fortunate parts of the world and transforming both Amer-ica and Europe in the process.

Such philanthropic encounters with Jews in eastern Europe incul-cated into immigrant Jews the critical role that public display and public recognition played in the act of giving charity. Just as some American-izing immigrants demonstrated their wealth through the public con-sumption of goods, others metaphorically acquired status by traveling to eastern Europe and publicly dispensing funds there. Such sentiments shaped immigrant fundraising newsletters, such as those published by the Bialystoker Relief Committee, which urged, "Pity your fellow Bialystoker on the other side of the ocean . . . whose suffering requires our immediate and whole-hearted assistance." If pity was not enough, however, the Bialystoker Relief Committee promised, "the names of all the people who have sent in their contributions will be made public through the press."[37] Indeed, *landsmanshaft* associations often dedicated the bulk of their publications to listing each donor and the amount they gave. The *Grodner veker* (Awakener of Grodno), a publication of the socialist Workmen's Circle association of Jews from the Polish city of Grodno, even provided lists of "collectors" who raised the most money for other donors.[38] Such an overt inversion of the traditional Jewish paradigm to give charity discreetly allowed Jewish immigrants to demonstrate publicly both their commitment to their former home and the extent to which they had succeeded in their new homes (as evidenced by their generous donations).

The sale of certificates and tablets was another innovative method deployed by immigrant fundraisers to achieve their goals. Playing on the desire inculcated in immigrant donors for public recognition, the *Bialystoker Shtime* implored its readers to "purchase a certificate" that proclaimed that they were lifetime members of their respective organizations. With each donation of ten dollars, the Bialystoker Center sent donors an ornately embellished certificate to hang on their walls.[39] Understanding the harsh economic times, the Bialystoker Center allowed its donors to pay for their certificates in installments, as one did when purchasing a washing machine. Like any shrewd marketer selling a product, David Sohn, executive director of the Bialystoker Center, realized that not everyone would be attracted to "purchasing" a bargain, so he concluded by stressing that the certificates were really a necessity for any self-respecting Bialystoker home and that "within a few weeks, there will be no house . . . in [any] Bialystoker colony where the walls will lack the decoration of an honorary certificate."[40] As part of the effort to raise funds for a new orphanage on the outskirts of Grodno, the United Grodno Relief offered donors the chance, for only one hundred dollars, "to perpetuate their names by having [them] engraved [on] tablets over the beds in the pavilion."[41]

By the late 1920s, the postcards, posters, and newspapers popular in the immigrant Jewish community conveyed the ways in which immigrant Jews forged their identities as Americans by engaging eastern Europe. The centrality of a commercial imagery to Yiddish fundraising appeals and postcard culture bespoke its members' newfound sense of power as they became economically successful and were able to send money back to Europe. Despite all the problems they may have been facing in America, with debates raging over immigrant restrictions that proclaimed Jews "a menace to society," their ability to send funds to eastern Europe, where their largess was eagerly awaited, made them still believe that the sacrifice and trip was worthwhile.

The Crisis of 1929 and American Jewish Immigrant Overseas Philanthropy

American Jewish immigrants' economic success, however, became a distant memory by 1930, leaving few with extra money to send to either loved ones or Jewish institutions in Europe. Few eastern European Jewish immigrants in New York were speculators directly impacted by Black Thursday in October 1929, but the ensuing credit crisis sent ripples throughout the American Jewish community, as exemplified by the December 1930 failure of the Bank of United States. The bank's closing remained front-page news for over a year; its directors went to jail, and thousands of Jewish organizations, spanning from small *landsmanshaft* groups such as the United Brisker Relief to the Industrial Council of Cloak, Suit and Skirt Manufacturers, lost much of their savings, making it virtually impossible for individuals to send money overseas. In this era of financial crisis, New Year's cards, which had benefited from the technological advances in color print reproduction, reverted back from celebrating New York Jews' ability to send money abroad to depicting the religious rituals of the High Holidays. Widely circulated cards depicted Jews attending synagogue as well as performing acts that allowed them to atone for their sins through rituals other than giving charity.

Vividly echoing the themes raised in postcards concerning the immense impact of 1929 are the 175 poignant letters written by Wolf Lewkowicz in Lodz to his nephew Sol Zissman in Chicago. Throughout the interwar period, Lewkowicz wrote to his nephew in America to seek financial aid, as his businesses failed and his family's financial predicament grew desperate.[42] Whereas in 1921, 1925, and 1926, Zissman sent large sums totaling over $1,000 to his uncle in Lodz to help him establish himself as a partner in a garment business (which ultimately failed), by 1930, Lewkowicz's request for funds to establish an automated bakery was refused because Zissman had no extra funds to offer. Instead, Zissman offered to sponsor a visa for Lewkowicz's son Yosef. In the end, however, Lewkowicz could not afford to allow Yosef to immigrate, because Lewkowicz was unemployed, and he and his family in Poland depended on Yosef's meager salary for survival.

As American Jewish immigrants such as Zissman watched their personal fortunes evaporate and their synagogues, community centers, and philanthropic organization plunge from prosperity to near bankruptcy, they feared for their own future. But the situation was even more distressing for Jews still living in Poland, who faced an increasingly bleak economic future. To be sure, the worldwide depression and the rise of Hitler to power, along with a host of other factors, molded Jewish life in 1930s Poland, but diminished American Jewish immigrant philanthropy had a direct and devastating impact on local Jewish life. With virtually no financial support from the Bialystoker Center, which closed its relief committee in 1932, Jewish welfare institutions in Bialystok drastically cut the types of services they offered, even though the ranks of the Jewish poor grew each day. Between 1932 and 1939, fifteen regularly published newspapers, weekly magazines, and monthly periodicals were forced to cease publications because of funding issues.[43] The new poverty of the Jewish community exacerbated tensions between Jews and Poles, as their respective welfare institutions were forced into fierce competition for limited municipal funds.[44] The *kehile*, deriving most of its power from the funding it received from the Bialystoker Center, could do little to remedy the situation, provoking less than 8 percent of the eligible electorate even to turn out for its 1938 elections.[45] Instead, Bialystok Jews sought to address their concerns in Bialystok's municipal authority, electing Vincente Hermanovski, a local Jewish pharmacist, who allotted Jewish organizations a greater share of municipal funds.[46]

Even anti-Jewish violence in Poland did not force American Jewish immigrants to shift their focus away from their own shrinking fortunes, as events in Brisk vividly illustrate. By 1930, an almost bankrupt United Brisker Relief merged with the International Workers' Organization, designating itself a "Brisker branch."[47] Yet few funds were sent to Poland, allowing the fragile coalitions initially forged by Jacob Finkelstein and his promises of money to fall apart. On May 13, 1937, a pogrom erupted in Brisk in which two Jews were killed, hundreds were injured, and over a million zlotys worth of property was destroyed. Jews in Brisk were shocked by their American brothers' silence and failure to respond, as cartoonist William Grapier evocatively captured in his caustic depiction

of old, tired, and worn-down Brisk knocking at America's door screaming, "Now Brisk is knocking! Will Jews in America hear him?" as fellow
beleaguered "neighbors" of Vilna, Lemberg, and Warsaw look on. While
a relief effort was launched by a revived United Brisker Relief in June
1937, it collected only $15,000, leaving the Jews of Brisk, like most of east-
ern European Jewry, out in the cold. The aftershocks of the seismic economic shifts of 1929 left most American Jewish immigrants more concerned with their own financial prospects than with the needs of their
friends, families, and loved ones in Poland knocking on their doors.

Conclusion

The year 1929 marked a turning point for the transatlantic Polish-Jewish
community, created by the dispersal of migration but maintained by the
collection and distribution of charity. While the coalitions formed and
constituencies served by philanthropy in the 1920s spanned national
boundaries, they were nevertheless shaped by the specific needs of both
the donors and recipients, who were both struggling to come to terms
with their radically new political and economic situations. In eastern
Europe, the political and economic chaos of the postwar years placed
immense strain on Polish Jewry's already drained communal resources.
With thousands of impoverished Jews, corrupt Jewish leaders, and an
unresponsive Polish government, Jews in Poland found themselves in
desperate need of help. Their cries were heard by émigrés living in the
United States who still saw themselves as foreigners, intimately linked
to their former homes and forced to struggle to reestablish themselves.
Combining innovative images and publications with fundraising ral-
lies, parades, and balls, immigrant Jewish philanthropies introduced
distinctly new methods of fundraising that fundamentally reshaped
the practice of giving charity from a private affair to a public celebration. During the 1920s, when America's economic expansion appeared
unstoppable, immigrant Jews assumed the mantle of Wilsonian idealism
as they raised and distributed money to rebuild eastern Europe. Forcing
Polish and Jewish leaders to create new alliances, immigrant Jews began
to see themselves as Americans and to appreciate their economic power.[48]

But this world of American economic supremacy was turned on
its head in the 1930s. When *Fortune* magazine reported on American

Jews' apprehension in 1936, its editors focused on Jews' fears about rising anti-Semitism.[49] To be sure, this was a growing concern for Jews, as leaders such as Father Coughlin grew in popularity. But it should not obscure, as *Fortune*'s editors failed to capture, that the anxiety prevalent among American Jews in the 1930s was far more complex than simply external threats of anti-Semitism. For a population composed mainly of immigrants and their children, the previous years of economic hardship forced many to question the promise of America and their choice to abandon eastern Europe.[50] Was all the upheaval worthwhile when they could not even earn enough money to support their families? What did it mean to be an "American Jew" when one could not send money overseas? Tragically, by the time immigrant Jews regained their footing, the total decimation of Polish Jewry left few to recall how philanthropy provided the answers to these questions, transforming in the process the contours and content of Jewish life on both sides of the Atlantic.

NOTES

1. Many scholars have commented on the role the failure of the Bank of United States played in setting in motion the economic panic that led to the Great Depression. See Milton Friedman and Anna Schwartz, *A Monetary History of the United States, 1867–1960* (Princeton: Princeton University Press, 1963); Elmus Wicker, "A Reconsideration of the Cause of the Banking Panic of 1930," *Journal of Economic History* 40 (September 1980): 571–83; Paul Trescott, "The Failure of the Bank of United States, 1930," *Journal of Money, Credit and Banking* 24:3 (August 1992): 384–98; Joseph Lucia, "The Failure of the Bank of United States: A Reappraisal," *Explorations in Economic History* 22 (October 1985): 402–16. On the impact it had on the Jewish community, see Beth Wenger, *New York Jews and the Great Depression: Uncertain Promise* (New Haven: Yale University Press, 1996), 10–14.

2. Sam Levenson, oral history, 2, William Weiner Oral History Library, part of the Jewish Division of the New York Public Library.

3. Timothy Snyder, *Reconstruction of Nations* (New Haven: Yale University Press, 2004).

4. Jose Moya, "Immigrants and Associations: A Global and Historical Perspective," *Journal of Ethnic and Migration Studies* 31:5 (2005): 833–64; on the increased ease of transferring money from America to Europe, see Gary Magee and Andrew Thompson, "The Global and the Local: Explaining Migrant Remittance Flows in the English-Speaking World, 1880–1914," *Journal of Economic History* 66:1 (March 2006): 177–202.

5. There are many monographs on the history of interwar Jewish aid. See Steven Zip-perstein, "The Politics of Relief: The Transformation of Russian Jewish Communal Life during the First World War," *Studies in Contemporary Jewry*, vol. 4, *The Jews and the European Crisis, 1914–1921*, ed. Jonathan Frankel (Oxford: Oxford University Press, 1988), 22–40; Ezra Mendelsohn, *Zionism in Poland: The Formative Years, 1915–1926* (New Haven: Yale University Press, 1981), 46–49.

6. Joseph Hyman, *The Activities of the Joint Distribution Committee: A Summary Report* (New York: American Jewish Joint Distribution Committee, 1931), 38; Zosa Szajkowski, "Private and Organized American Jewish Overseas Relief (1914–1938)," *AJHQ* 57:1 (September 1967): 103; Zosa Szajkowski, "Private and Organized American Jewish Overseas Relief (1914–1938)," *AJHQ* 57:2 (December 1967): 246.

7. Magdalena Opalski and Israel Bartal, *Poles and Jews: A Failed Brotherhood* (Hanover, NH: Brandeis University Press, 1992); Alina Cała, *Asymilacja Żydów w Królestwie Polskim, 1864–1897* (Warsaw: Państwowy Instytut Wydawniczy, 1989); Frank Golczewski, *Polnisch-Jüdische Beziehungen, 1881–1922: Eine Studie zur Geschichte des Anti-Semitismus in Osteuropa* (Wiesbaden, Germany: Steiner, 1981); Jan Gross, *Neighbors: The Destruction of the Jewish Community in Jedwabne, Poland* (Princeton: Princeton University Press, 2001).

8. For more on how modern Jewish philanthropy differs from traditional forms of Jewish charity, see Jonathan Woocher, *Sacred Survival: The Civil Religion of American Jews* (Bloomington: Indian University Press, 1985), 1–22. Michael Berkowitz argues in his study of the Zionist movement in western Europe that philanthropic organizations and their fundraising materials played a central role in shaping how European Jews envisioned their identities. Michael Berkowitz, *Zionist Culture and West European Jewry before the First World War* (Cambridge: Cambridge University Press, 1993), 161–87.

9. This study was greatly influenced by several exemplary models of this type of examination. See Ewa Morawska, *For Bread with Butter: Lifeworlds of East Central European Immigrants in Johnstown, Pennsylvania, 1890–1940* (Cambridge: Cambridge University Press, 1985); Robert Orsi, *The Madonna of 115th Street: Faith and Community in Italian Harlem, 1880–1950* (New Haven: Yale University Press, 1985).

10. Derek Penslar, *Shylock's Children: Economics and Jewish Identity in Modern Europe* (Berkeley: University of California Press, 2001), 3.

11. Wenger, *New York Jews and the Great Depression*, 2.

12. "S. Etonis," in *Awakening Lives: Autobiographies of Jewish Youth in Poland before the Holocaust*, ed. Jeffrey Shandler (New Haven: YIVO Institute for Jewish Research, 2002), 6.

13. Ibid., 8–9.

14. Irma May, "Synagogues of Brest-Litovsk: An Inferno of Human Suffering as Told by Miss Irma May," transcript, RG 898, box 2, folder 1, 1–2, YIVO Institute for Jewish Research.

15. Philip Rabinowitch to Jacob Finkelstein, June 28, 1920, RG 898, box 2, folder 11, YIVO Institute for Jewish Research.

16. Jacob Finkelstein, "Fifty Years United Brisker Relief," in *Fiftieth Anniversary Journal of United Brisker Relief* (New York: Brisker Relief, 1965), 4.

17. Ibid.

18. See Rebecca Kobrin, "Contested Contributions: American Jewish Money and Polish-Jewish Relations in Inter-War Poland, 1919–1929," *Gal-Ed*, Fall 2005, 49–62; Rachel Rojanski, "Hashpata shel yehadut artsot-ha-brot 'al hakamat mer" (American Jewry's Influence upon the Establishment of the Jewish Welfare Apparatus in Poland, 1920–1929), *Gal-Ed* 11 (1989): 59–86; Yehuda Bauer, *American Jewry and the Holocaust: The American Jewish Joint Distribution Committee, 1939–1945* (Detroit: Wayne State University Press, 1981), 22. Such subversive behavior is common among many dispersed migrant groups. See William Safran, "Diasporas in Modern Societies: Myths of Homeland and Return," *Diaspora* 1 (1994): 83–84; Robin Cohen, *Global Diasporas: An Introduction* (Seattle: University of Washington Press, 2000), 26. Jews had long been aware, Derek Penslar argues, that the application of Jewish power was economic in nature. Penslar, *Shylock's Children*, 3.

19. The authority of the *kehile* (democratically elected Jewish municipal council) was based on the stipulations of the Polish Minority Treaty, which required Poland to set up institutions to protect the rights of all minority groups living within its borders. Concerned after the pogroms of 1918 and 1919, the League of Nations required Poland to set up separate governing bodies and schools for non-Polish nationals in order to maintain their independence. For more on the Polish Minority Treaty (including a translation of the treaty itself), see I. Lewin, *A History of Polish Jewry during the Revival of Poland, 1918–1919* (New York: Shengold, 1990), 167–205, 207–11.

20. See Antony Polonsky, *Politics in Independent Poland, 1921–1939: The Crisis of Constitutional Government* (Oxford, UK: Clarendon, 1972), 119–22; Pavel Korzec, *Juifs in Pologne* (Paris: Presses de la Fondation Nationale des Sciences Politiques, 1980), 142–150; Lewin, *A History of Polish Jewry during the Revival of Poland*, 175–76.

21. *Dos Naye Lebn*, October 3, 5, 20, 31, 1919, and December 11, 1919.

22. Space does not enable me to fully discuss the long and complex development of Polish-Jewish relations. Several insightful treatments of this large topic can be found in Opalski and Bartal, *Poles and Jews*; Cała, *Asymilacja Żydow w Krolestwie Polskim*; Golczewski, *Polnisch-Jüdische Beziehungen*; Gross, *Neighbors*.

23. Yitzhak Zev Solovetchik to Jacob Finkelstein, July 25, 1919, RG 898, box 3, folder 2, YIVO Institute for Jewish Research.

24. There is extensive correspondence between M. Drachle to Jacob Finkelstein in the 1920s. See in particular M. Drachle to Finkelstein, March 18, 1926; M. Drachle to Finkelstein, August 27, 1926; and M. Drachle to Finkelstein, February 2, 1927; all in RG 898, box 1, folder 13, YIVO Institute for Jewish Research.

25. Piotr Wróbel, "Na równi pochyłej. Żydzi Białegostoku w latach 1918–1939: Demografia, ekonomika desintegracja, konflikty z Polakami," *Studia Podlaskie*

(Bialystok, 1989), 175; B. Goldberg, "Bialistoker Textil Industria," *Unzer lebn*, October 8, 1937, 8; Abraham Herschberg, *Pinkes Bialystok: Grunt materyaln tsu der geshikte fun di Yidn in Byalistok* (The Chronicle of Bialystok: Basic Material on the History of the Jews in Bialystok) (New York: Bialystok Jewish Historical Association, 1949), 30–33; Tomasz Wisniewski, *Jewish Bialystok: A Guide for Yesterday and Today* (Ipswich, MA: Ipswich, 1998), appendix 3.

26. See Budżet Miasta Białegostoku na rok 1927/8 and Budżet Miasta Białegostoku na rok 1929/30, Archiwun Państwowe w Białymstoku, Akta Miasta Białegostoku, sygnatura 116, 117, 121. See Ezras Yesomim, *Ezras Yesomim, 1917–1920* (Bialystok: Ezras Yesomim, 1921) and Ezras Yesomim, *Report fun Ezras Yesomin, 1923–1927* (Bialystok: Ezras Yesomim, 1928). Both these booklets can be found in M-14, folder 17, Bund Archives/YIVO. In this collection, one can also see the influence of American representatives in the bulletin of the Sholom Aleichem Library in Bialystok from 1927 and 1939 (Bialystok, February 1927 and May 1938).

27. Shaul Stampfer notes that the need to raise funds in America provoked many informally run institutions of Jewish education to formalize their curricula and to publish newsletters, balance sheets, and annual reports. See Shaul Stampfer, "Hasidic Yeshivot in Inter-War Poland," *Polin* 11 (1998): 3–25. Also see Rojanski, "Hashpata shel yehadut artsot-ha-brot 'al hakamat mer."

28. It is fascinating to compare the financial reports of Ezras Yesomim in Bialystok from the period before 1920 and the period following the intervention of Morris Sunshine, one of the representatives of the Bialystoker Relief Organization in Bialystok. See Ezras Yesomim, *Ezras Yesomim, 1917–1920*; and Ezras Yesomim, *Report fun Ezras Yesomin, 1923–1927*. The impact that the requirements of American philanthropists had on institutions can also be clearly seen through the comparison of the reports of Ezras Yesomim with the Peretz Children's Home and Work School's 1920 handwritten report of its activities from the period between 1919 and 1920.

29. *Bericht fun Payen Bank in Bialistok* (Bialystok, 1926); David Sohn, "A Half Century of Bialystoker Activity in America" (manuscript, 1928), Tel Aviv University Archives, A-18/67, 5. The conversion to approximate 2012 dollar values is derived from www.measuringworth.com or from eh.net/hmit.

30. Woocher, *Sacred Survival*, 1–63.

31. Moses Maimonides, *Hilchot Matanot La-evyonim*, chapter 7:12.

32. For more on how modern Jewish philanthropy differs from traditional forms of Jewish charity, see Woocher, *Sacred Survival*, 1–22; Berkowitz, *Zionist Culture and West European Jewry*, 161–87.

33. Shalom Sabar, introduction to *Past Perfect: The Jewish Experience in Early 20th Century Postcards*, exhibition catalogue (New York: Jewish Theological Seminary of America, 1997), 6.

34. Sabar Shalom, "Between Poland and Germany: Jewish Religious Practices in Illustrated Postcards of the Early Twentieth Century," in "Jewish Popular Culture and Its Afterlife," special issue, *Polin* 16 (2004): 144–56.

35. It is interesting to note that none of the Jewish men in Bialystok have beards, a trope which was common in these photos to highlight the clean-shaven modern attire of the visiting American Jews. For more on these photos, see Jeff Shandler and Jack Kugelmass, *Going Home: How American Jews Invent the Old World* (New York: YIVO Institute for Jewish Research, 1989).

36. For more on the links between philanthropy and class status in the United States, see Mary P. Ryan, *Cradle of the Middle Class: The Family in Oneida County, New York, 1790–1865* (New York: Cambridge University Press, 1981); Andrew Herman, *The "Better Angels" of Capitalism: Rhetoric, Narrative, and Moral Identity among Men of the American Upper Class* (Boulder, CO: Westview, 2000).

37. "Appeal to the Bialystoker Fellow Countrymen in America," *Bialystoker Shtime* 13 (March 1926): 10.

38. *Grodner veker* 330 (1936): 4–5.

39. "Durk a 10 dolar 'certifikeyt' vert a member fun bialistoker moshav zekanim far ire ganzen lebn," *Bialystoker Stimme 28* (May 1931): n.p.

40. David Sohn, "At the Present Time," *Bialystoker Stimme* 28 (May 1931): 2.

41. "Pavilion 'TOZ' Kolonia," United Grodno Relief, RG 996, folder 2, YIVO Institute for Jewish Research.

42. The collection of letters from Lewkowicz to Zissman provides an illustration of the immense impact these funds made on individual lives. With the $150 Lewkowicz received in 1923—he was able to get 33,500 Polish marks for each dollar—he was able to become a partner in his brother-in-law's garment business. See "Letter 5: Wolf Lewkowicz to Sol Zissman," February 10, 1923, archived at http://web.mit.edu/maz/wolf.

43. *Dos naye lebn* was the only major newspaper until September 1939. For a list of all the newspapers, periodicals, and magazines published in Bialystok during the interwar period and their dates of publication, see Marian Fuks, "Prasa żydowska w Białystoku, 1918–1939," *Żydowskiego Instytutu Historycznego w Polsce* 145–46 (1988): 150–52.

44. Menakhem Linder, "Der khurbn funem yidishn handel in bialistoker rayon," *Yidishe ekonomik* 1 (1937): 17.

45. Whereas in 1918, more than half of the Jews in Bialystok voted in the *kehile* election, by 1938, only 3,511 of the 39,165 eligible Jewish voters participated in the elections, which is less than 8 percent. See Herschberg, *Pinkes Bialystok II*, 227–30, 269–79; Wróbel, "Na równi pochyłej," 183–86.

46. "Vitsenti Hermanavski," *Bialistoker almanakh* (Bialystok, 1931), 308–9.

47. Yakov Finkelsteyn, "Va'ad ha-Seuah ha-meyuhad le-Brisk-de-Lita," in *Entsiklopedyah shel galuyot: Sifre zikaron le-artsot ha-golah ve-'edoteha*, vol. 2 (Jerusalem: Ḥevrat Entsiḳlopedyah shel galuyot, 1954), 563.

48. Several notable studies of the centrality of Zionism to eastern European Jewish immigrant life in America are Mark A. Raider, *The Emergence of American Zionism* (New York: NYU Press, 1998); Sarah L. Schmidt, *Horace Kallen: Prophet of American Zionism* (New York: Carlson, 1997); Melvin Urofsky, *American Zionism*

from Herzl to Holocaust (Lincoln: University of Nebraska Press, 1995); and Matthew Frye Jacobson, *Special Sorrows: The Diasporic Imagination of Irish, Polish and Jewish Immigrants in the United States* (Cambridge: Harvard University Press, 1995).

49. "Jews in America," *Fortune* 13 (February 1936): 79.

50. Woocher, *Sacred Survival*, 1–63.

6

Jewish American Philanthropy and the Crisis of 1929

The Case of OZE-TOZ and the JDC

RAKEFET ZALASHIK

It is very hard to convince the people here in Europe that the J.D.C. is at the end of its work; they still believe that by sending appeals and delegations to the States they can go on drawing money from the J.D.C.
—Bernard Kahn, head of the JDC's European office, writing to the home office in New York[1]

Introduction

"It is very beautiful for Lord Rothschild, Sir Samuel Intone and other Europeans to pass the buck to us," wrote Louis Marshall to Joseph Hyman. Marshall, the vice president of the Joint Distribution Committee and chairman of the Agro-Joint, continued in this letter to Hyman, the JDC's vice chairman, "It would not do them much harm if they took off their coats and opened their purses to help people who are just as near to them as they are to us, instead of putting the entire burden upon the United States and to add to our numerous obligations at home, which they totally ignore."[2] These words came in reaction to an appeal sent that same year to Marshall by English Jewish philanthropists requesting that the JDC support the medical work of the two Societies for the Protection of the Health of the Jewish People, the one OZE (in Russian, Obshchestvo Zdravookhraneniia Evreev) and the other TOZ (in Polish, Towarzystwo Ochrony Zdrowia Ludności Żydowskiej), both of which operated in eastern Europe.

Accusations charging the Jews of western Europe with not participating vigorously enough in the reconstruction of postwar Jewish communities in eastern Europe had been heard earlier[3] but became more frequent in 1929, the year in which OZE and TOZ faced their biggest crisis, brought about by the start of the Great Depression.

The crisis of 1929 strained the relationship between the JDC and OZE. It not only brought forth accusations of lack of care but crystallized problems fundamental to the ways these organizations operated. Indeed the financial crisis showed how the strategy of the JDC to support local organizations for a limited period of time and only until they could function independently never could be realized in the case of OZE and TOZ.

Yet the 1929 crisis also revealed the degree to which the JDC depended on OZE and TOZ. This became particularly clear in 1929, when the JDC's status as the main body responsible for raising funds and distributing them to needy Jewish organizations in eastern Europe weakened. The JDC came to fear that the weak showing of independent fundraising campaigns by these organizations in their respective countries not only would damage their ability to raise substantial sums but would also harm the JDC's reputation within the American Jewish community.

In this era American Jewish relief agencies wanted to transfer the "American way" to the Jews of Europe. Through their financial support and the management of construction projects, these philanthropies saw their investments as ideally of limited duration, aimed to stimulate self-help, which the recipients would undertake on their own.[4]

But the case of OZE-TOZ in 1929 presented an even more complex picture of relationships between the JDC as a Jewish American philanthropic organization and two eastern European organizations than the usual story of "givers" and "takers," of the "dependent" and the "independent." It sheds a light on the development of Jewish American philanthropy in eastern Europe, which had been in operation through the interwar period but which in 1929 became particularly sharp.

The 1929 clashes between the JDC and OZE-TOZ also reflected broadly the nature of the relationships between one of the biggest American Jewish philanthropic bodies and eastern European welfare organizations and the tensions such cooperation created, regarding institutional, organizational, and financial issues. It demonstrates the inherent disjunction between the expectations the JDC maintained about the eastern European organizations it supported and those of the "takers," the recipients of the aid. On the one hand, the JDC encouraged them to become financially independent by over time decreasing their funds. On the other had, it restricted their attempts to raise funds among American Jewry, practically the only community at that period which had some resources. This conundrum tied the hands of OZE but at the same time made it impossible for the JDC to fulfill its own expectations.

In order to understand the complicated and contradictory relationship which developed between the JDC and OZE-TOZE and the deleterious impact of 1929, a look backward is in order to the history of the beneficiary organization. OZE had been established in 1912 in St. Petersburg to improve the health of eastern European Jewry, based on a historical understanding of the physical evolution of the Jews, Jewish medicine, hygiene, and sanitation.[5] Modeled on the Russian *zemstvo* (local self-government) system,[6] it envisioned becoming a Jewish health organization that would take over the health system for the Jewish population in Russia. However, the outbreak of World War I, the increase in the number of Jewish refugees who faced a myriad of problems,[7] and the collapse of the Russian Empire put OZE on a different path. It moved from being an organization aimed at providing social and preventive medicine to Russian Jewry to one which expanded its activity to include the Jews of other eastern European countries. It established local branches around eastern Europe and saw itself as providing both rescue and rehabilitation as a result of the war and its dislocations. In 1921 OZE branches in Poland took the name TOZ, and this change stemmed directly from the cooperation which flourished between the local activists and the JDC, as they worked together in a fight against contagious diseases common among local Jews and refugees.[8]

OZE-TOZ received most of its funding from the JDC, which had been founded in 1914 in New York by American Jews concerned about the fate of their coreligionists in the war-torn zones of Europe. Both organizations operated with an understanding that an improvement of the Jewish situation should include public health and social determinants of health. OZE-TOZ provided the local base for these activities, while the JDC provided the money, but both agreed with the need for an autonomous Jewish health system. The leaders of OZE-TOZ hoped to change the health situation among the Jews in order to enhance the political situation of the Jews as a discriminated minority.[9] The JDC aimed to act as an external philanthropic organization providing seed money for local initiatives that would eventually sustain themselves by means of local resources. It wished to help the Jews in the eastern part of the "old continent" and to promote their assimilation to modern life. The common interests of these organizations, solidified by the crisis of eastern European Jewry during World War I and later the Russian civil war, brought them together and allowed them to join forces.[10]

The hopes of both partners foundered on changing political realities. In the autumn of 1921 the Soviet government liquidated OZE.[11] Thus, after nine years of activity in Russia, OZE ceased to exist in the country of its founding but continued its activities in the places where it had created branches. In March 1922 OZE moved its offices to Berlin, which soon emerged as the headquarters of the organization. Within the next year OZE transformed itself into a federation, the Union for Preserving the Health of the Jews, and expanded its activity to include Jewish communities all over eastern Europe, including in Latvia, Lithuania,[12] Bessarabia, Danzig, Galicia, and Bukovina. In addition, it established support committees in London, Paris, Berlin, and Belgium headed by prominent Jewish scientists and philanthropists such as Albert Einstein and Redcliffe Nathan Salaman.[13]

Despite the expulsion from Russia, OZE reappeared there as a result of the work of the JDC. The JDC played a crucial role in the reactivation of the Russian OZE. Starting in the autumn of 1922, OZE actually managed to reestablish in part its activity in Russia through the Nansen Mission, and from 1923 onward it acted through the Soviet-based offices of JDC. Soviet authorities allowed for these activities under a JDC-OZE committee, supervised by the Soviet health authority (Narkomzdrav). JDC and especially its representative Boris Bogen tried to gain OZE a legal status in the Soviet Union in order to allow it to act independently. It hoped that this would enable the JDC to withdraw its direct involvement. But this did not happen, and despite all attempts to secure the medical welfare activities of an independent OZE in the Soviet Union, the effort failed, and the JDC had to remain a central actor. These tensions became only more acute as the world economy collapsed.

The Crisis of 1929

In 1929, as a result of the crash of the American stock market and its worldwide reverberations, OZE experienced its biggest financial crisis ever. The JDC, the central financer of its medical activity, sharply reduced its support for OZE and TOZ. Whereas in 1927 the funding agency had allocated OZE $48,000 and in 1928 OZE got $32,000 and TOZ got $40,000, in 1929 Bernard Kahn, the head of the JDC's European office, reduced funding to OZE to $500 per month, or $6,000 in total, and $20,000 to TOZ.[14]

This drastic cut in JDC funding and change in policy toward OZE and TOZ in fact derived from a shift in American Jewish philanthropy, at the same time that it reflected the impact of the crash.[15] As a result of the economic situation, American Jewish philanthropists considered the need to return to their pre–World War I model of "charity begins at home" and radically reduced their support for Jewish needs outside the United States. In addition, Europe had to share the largess of American Jewish philanthropy with Palestine. In this context, in 1929 the World Zionist Organization established the Jewish Agency, which assumed responsibility for immigration and settlement of Jews in Palestine.[16] This new actor, an umbrella organization created to raise donations for the Zionist cause from Western Jews who did not affiliate with Zionist parties, drew the attention and resources of American Jewry away from a purely eastern European focus. The Jewish Agency became a central partner of the JDC in fundraising, working together until 1935. Thus, the main problem faced by OZE and TOZ, which had become service agencies and no longer humanitarian relief organizations that responded to urgent crisis, now trying to implement long-term plans of social medicine, involved a dwindling ability to attract potential donors. 1929 only made this situation more acute.

In March 1929 Solomon Jacobi, a civil engineer came to the United States representing the OZE-TOZ organization. He hoped to find in America solutions for the financial crisis that the organization faced. He intended to put pressure on the leadership of the JDC and to search for alternative sources of funding among American Jewry.

OZE had previously sent delegates to the United States. On April 1925, for example, it sent a three-person delegation headed by Dr. Moses

Gran to the United States to try and raise funds for the Jews in eastern Europe, due to the prolonged and indeed constant crisis they were experiencing.[17] This fundraising strategy contradicted the previous pattern of relationships between OZE and the JDC. Until then OZE communicated and received its budget from the JDC European office headed by Kahn and had no direct contact with the JDC offices in New York. Approaching the headquarters directly endangered the longstanding relationship between the giver and the taker, although Joseph Rosen, the head of the Russian JDC office,[18] in fact supported this radical step. Despite Rosen's support, this move threatened the status quo inasmuch as it reflected the fact that it expressed a dissatisfaction and mistrust on the part of the Europeans with the Americans' policies and activities.

The plan of the 1925 delegation to carry out a separate fundraising campaign in the United States did in fact lead to deterioration in the relationship between OZE and the JDC. OZE defied the JDC, and on that American trip its representative contacted other philanthropists and American Jewish organizations such as the Federation of Jewish Charities of Philadelphia, as well as individuals within the medical circles of New York and Boston. Gran also met with members of the Jewish community in Los Angeles, attended the annual meeting of the Workmen's Circle,[19] and delivered public lectures in various cities, informing the Jewish public about the activities of OZE in the field of social and preventive medicine, providing information unknown in the United States.

This step represented a serious deviation according to the JDC, for two reasons. First, the JDC perceived itself as the main body that allocated funds from American Jewry and distributed them in eastern Europe. Only it could, it believed, decide on priorities. It saw any independent action on the part of European bodies, potential recipients, to be a violation of a long, albeit unwritten, agreement. Second, the OSE visit in the spring of 1925 to the United States coincided inconveniently with the JDC's own fundraising campaign. The JDC feared that the OZE campaign would not only reduce donations to the JDC but would put it in a bad light. After all, by making a pitch to American Jews, OZE indirectly accused the JDC of failing to distribute money collected from American Jewry to needy organizations in eastern Europe that were involved in providing direct service.

Ultimately Felix Warburg, a major American Jewish philanthropist, got involved. He helped resolve the fundraising crisis. He brokered a compromise which integrated OZE into the JDC campaign, but the former had to promise to stop its campaign aimed at the American Jewish public.[20]

OZE drew several conclusions from the 1925 disputes with the JDC, which it kept in mind as it faced the financial crisis four years later. First, in 1929, when the JCC needed help, it mobilized TOZ to join its effort in the United-States, rather than OZE. After all, in contrast to OZE, TOZ had been established directly by the JDC, which had funded it extensively for many years. The JDC preferred TOZ because during the 1920s TOZ had been very active among eastern European Jewry, much more so than OZE. OZE had decided with the crisis of 1929 to enlarge its collaboration with TOZ, hoping that that move would enhance its chances of receiving money from the JDC and other American sources.

Second, OZE declared emphatically that it had no intention of carrying out any independent campaigns to fundraise. In a meeting between Jacobi and Joseph Hyman the former clarified that "it is not his desire, not that of the group which he represents, at this time to organize any campaign or to make a nationwide appeal for funds so long as the JDC remain in active operation."[21]

But at the same time Jacobi planned to establish an American OZE committee with 2,000 local Jewish physicians. The membership fees would, he expected, create another source for OZE's activities in eastern Europe, and the committee's tasks involved informing American Jews about OZE-TOZ activities and supporting OZE's applications to additional American foundations. These applications to American foundations reflected yet another new pattern in OZE's attempts to find a substitute for the JDC's financial support and to release itself from full dependency on the organization.

Within a few weeks of this activity in the United States Jacobi managed to secure the support of prominent Jewish activists for OZE and TOZ and to establish an American committee with Milton Rosenau, a physician who played a crucial role in the field of preventive medicine and hygiene in the United States, as the chairman; Jacob Golub as vice chair; and Emanuel Libman, a famous heart physician from Mount Sinai hospital, also on board. Others who joined the committee's board included Lee Frankel, Herman Bernstein, Jacob Billikopf, Solis-Cohen, Louis Harris, Mrs. Alexander Kohut, Golub, Julius Levy, Rattnoff, Bela Schick, Mrs. Estelle Sternberger, Judge Horace Stern, Baruch Charney Vladek, Morris Waldman, and Israel Wechsler. However impressive the list and the activities, the JDC viewed this new initiative with great skepticism. According to the JDC, "The result of such an attempt would be to muddy the waters of the JDC without realizing anything substantial or worthwhile in behalf of the OZE."[22]

Undeterred, Jacobi went one step further, asking the JDC leaders to join the American OZE committee as members while ignoring JDC statements about the conflict in purposes. The OZE-TOZ group, for example, had approached Louis Marshall, a JDC activist, hoping to bring him into this new project. Marshall, however, replied not only that he could not join the committee but that he thought that "separate campaigns by European organizations are doomed to failure,"[23] since the expenses involved negated any money the group would raise. Instead, he promised Jacobi that the needs of OZE would be taken into consideration when the JDC campaign of that year began. Moreover, with the failure of a similar campaign by ORT, Marshall explained to Hyman, "It would be perfectly ridiculous for those associated with the JDC to unite in any other campaign for European relief. It was unfortunate that some of other members became associated with the ORT campaign. . . . If a man contribute $100 to OZE and $100 to ORT he will say to the JDC that he has given so much to other causes of a similar nature that all that he can give us is $100, when we would otherwise be able to get $1000."[24]

Whereas Jacobi managed to recruit prominent American Jews to support the activity of OZE and TOZ in eastern Europe, attempts to raise money from American foundations essentially failed. OZE applied through its national American committee to the Rosenwald Fund, which rejected it. A representative of the Fund justified its rejection by noting, "At the present at least it will restrict its activities to this country. . . . We are not engaged on a broad international program. Our funds are relatively small and we feel that only by restricting sharply their use will we be able to accomplish results of measurable values." In addition, the representative stated, "Mr. Rosenwald personally has made substantial gifts to the work of the Joint Distribution Committee. If that Committee takes up again the health work, Mr. Rosenwald's previous gifts may help somewhat in the general cause which you present to me."[25]

The rejection validated Marshall's objection raised earlier that year against OZE's independent efforts in the United States because of patterns of giving among American Jewry. The rejection by the Rosenwald Fund proved his negative assessment of separated fundraising campaigns to be correct.

OZE also applied for assistance to the Rockefeller Foundation, which played an important role in the development of public health, nursing, and social work in the "new" countries in Europe during the interwar period.[26] Thus, although the Rockefeller Foundation did not deal specifically with the Jewish population, OZE-TOZ conformed to the type of activity which the foundation supported, and it worked in precisely those locations in central and eastern Europe. This should have made the application particularly appealing to the Rockefeller Foundation and made the Foundation an appropriate substitute for the JDC. But in October 1929 the Foundation rejected the application, explaining that it cooperated only with state and national governments in the public health field. It could not consider OZE to be a truly official organization, despite the fact that it worked with some government agencies.[27]

This reasoning went to the core of the conflict between OZE and the JDC and reflected OZE's essential problem as an organization. The JDC had supported its activities in Russia for many years because it hoped that OZE would gain legal status and would in the process replace it. But OZE could not be legalized because it lacked the resources and therefore could act only under the name of the JDC. However, in 1929, the chances of OZE becoming a formally recognized organization in the Soviet Union barely existed, on the one hand, and on the other, the JDC found itself in a crisis and had little interest in continuing to finance OZE.

The use of TOZ's name in the campaign in the United States also proved to be a source of conflict between OZE and the JDC. The request letter sent in October 1929 by the American National Committee of OZE to the JDC to appropriate OZE-TOZ $44,000 for the year 1930, out of the total sum of $150,000 per year, or $450,000 for the next three years, for their activities in Lithuania, Latvia, Romania (Bessarabia and Bukovina), Danzig, Poland, and Russia[28] caused the JDC to blame OZE for having made statements that were "inaccurate and tend[ed] to be misleading." The JDC charged that by presenting the members of the committee to the American Jewish public, OZE had offered a false picture of its activities and identity.[29] The JDC claimed that OZE had never been responsible for TOZ's work and that the only reason it had used TOZ's name grew out of the fact that OZE had been very inactive as an organization and had wanted to use TOZ's name to show some results in the medical field among eastern European Jewry. Additionally, although many members of the committee had been OZE members, JDC money had enabled their initiatives. The JDC charged that "all the work that OZE had conducted in Russia since 1923 is simply and solely JDC work conducted with JDC funds. It gives them no right to claim this work as theirs."[30] Rosen, the JDC representative in Russia, has permitted OZE to put the activities in the Odessa district under its name, although Agro-Joint had funded the project. He had done so to strengthen the OZE's position and to justify its claims. The JDC also pointed out that OZE had no legal status in Russia, nor would it likely attain such status. The JDC had negotiated with the Russian government to help OZE gain a legal status in the Soviet Union; however, this has failed. Therefore, it could not take over the work of the JDC in Russia, and the allotment of such sums to OZE were not practical.[31]

In response to the first of these accusations, OZE Berlin presented the OZE-TOZ resolution from November 17, 1929, which had given OZE the permission to carry out campaigns in the United States in the name of TOZ, under a joint OZE-TOZ committee.[32] According to the agreement, TOZ would get 20 percent of every sum OZE would succeed in having allocated from the United States.

Amid all of this sparring between the JDC and OZE over fundraising and jurisdiction, practical concerns loomed large. In December 1929 the state of OZE became very critical. Growing deficits had accumulated over the course of two years. It could not pay the salaries for medical professionals working in its institutions, and it seemingly had no prospects of any external American funds.

It seemed as though OZE would face 1930 with no budget. It had to turn to the JDC. Jacobi wrote to Hyman, "The JDC seems to be our only hope."[33] However, despite this critical situation, as late as December 20, the JDC had not answered OZE as to the upcoming year, claiming, "The entire question of budgetary allotments for 1930 is bound up with the problem of our campaign, the date of which has not yet been determined."[34]

The OZE-JDC relationship became particularly complicated by the fact that in 1929 JDC strove to mount a joint campaign with the Jewish Agency in order to secure funds, so that it no longer had to be the single actor in the sphere of Jewish American philanthropy. It postponed launching a campaign until it had reached a signed agreement with the Jewish Agency.

The pressure on OZE-TOZ's fate grew at the end of 1929. Albert Einstein wrote a letter of support to Bernard Flexner, the head of the JDC health and relief work, asking him to allocate funds for "the important activity of the organization in the field of preventive medicine among the Eastern European Jewry."[35] Rosenau wrote to Warburg asking him to interfere as he did in the crisis of 1925 and to approve an immediate sum of $25,000 to OZE, clarifying that "the OZE and TOZ . . . find themselves in a serious impasse. They have been unable to secure appropriations from existing foundation, and at the same time are interdicted from launching upon an independent fund-raising. They are impaled on the veritable horns of a dilemma which . . . threatens the very existence of a number of their activities."[36] Finally, on January 20, 1930, Warburg agreed to allocate $7,500 to OZE and $10,000 to TOZ via Kahn's European office and to deduct those sums from the future budget of 1930.[37]

The JDC had found a partial solution on January 1930, as it entered into a new agreement, through the work of Rosen in Russia and OZE, when the JDC accepted the suggestion, hammered out in December, according to which the JDC would secure OZE resources for expanding its activity of infant welfare and sanitary education not only in Odessa but also in the rest of the country.[38] This included work in the fields of maternity consultation and infant welfare centers; feeding undernourished children; leading a campaign against rickets, trachoma, ringworm, and malaria; and health education.

Despite the relatively positive ending of the 1929 crisis, the crisis itself underscored the essential problem in the relationship between the JDC and OZE-TOZ. While in the short run the agreement enabled the two eastern European organizations to survive and even to expand their activity helping Jews, who had been totally neglected with regard to public health, in the long run, the problem continued. It deepened the involvement of the JDC in Russia and the dependency of OZE on the JDC, although both tendencies contradicted JDC's original rationale of operation. This outcome awakened a general discussion in the Jewish world about relief organizations in eastern Europe and the dependency of Jews there on Jewish American resources. Kahn, the longstanding director of the JDC in Europe, located the problem not in the economic crisis of Jewish communities in eastern Europe but in their inability to unite forces and to work in the field of public health and welfare. For him, sending more allotments without a substantial reform would not benefit the organizations and the people they took care of. Moreover, since the work did not cover all the needs of the Jewish population, the JDC had to remain a crucial factor in the life of eastern European Jewry.

Thus, 1929 proved to be a symptom and not a cause of the problem. It revealed the inherent problems in the relationships between OZE-TOZ and the JDC, problems that in earlier years, under better economic conditions, could be handled more easily and bureaucratically. The financial crisis of 1929 made manifest the underlying weaknesses in the relationship. New strategies had to be developed to deal with new conditions.

NOTES

1. Bernard Kahn to the secretary of the JDC in New York, 1 April 1924, AR 19–21 #25, Joint Archive, New York.
2. Louis Marshall to Joseph Hyman, 17 April 1929, AR 21–32 #102A Organizations: OSE NY 1.29–11.29, Joint Archive, New York.
3. Zosa Szajkowski, "Budgeting American Jewish Overseas Relief (1919–1939)," *American Jewish Historical Quarterly* 59 (1–4) (1969–1970): 90.
4. Susan Gross Solomon and Nicolai Kremntsov, "Giving and Taking across Borders: The Rockefeller Foundation and Russia, 1919–1928," *Minerva* 39 (3) (2001): 265–98.
5. Lisa Epstein, "Caring for the Soul's Home: The Jews of Russia and Health Care 1860–1914" (Ph.D. dissertation, Yale University, 1995), 255; Michel Virginie, "L'action medico-sociale de l'OSE Paris dans les annes trente," *Archives Juives* 39 (1) (2006): 111.
6. Terence Emmons and Wayne S. Vucinich (eds.), *The Zemstvo in Russia: An Experiment in Local Self-Government* (Cambridge: Cambridge University Press), 1982; T. E. Porter, *The Zemstvo and the Emergence of Civil Society in Late Imperial Russia, 1864–1917* (San Francisco: Mellen Research University Press, 1991).
7. Peter Gatrell, *A Whole Empire Walking: Refugees in Russia during World War I* (Bloomington: Indiana University Press, 1999), 17–19.

8. On the struggle against typhus see Nadav Davidovitch and Rakefet Zalashik, "'Air, Sun, Water': Ideology and Activity of OZE during the Interwar Period," *Dynamis* 28 (2008): 140–45.

9. L. Wollman (ed.), *In the Struggle for Health of the Jewish People (50 Years OSE)* (New York: World Union OSE and the American Committee of OSE, 1968), 298–99.

10. AR 21–23 #235 Countries: Lithuania Subject Matter Medical 1921–1929, Joint Archives, New York.

11. Nokhum Shtif, "Di tsen-yerike geshikhte von OZE," *Volksgezunt* 2–3 (1923): 1–2.

12. For OZE in Lithuania, see Rakefet Zalashik and Nadav Davidovitch, "Taking and Giving: The Case of the JDC and OZE in Lithuania 1919–1926," *East European Jewish Affairs* 39 (1) (2009): 57–68.

13. "Di grindung farzamlung fun «OZE» in London," *Buletin fun zentral-Byuro fun der geselshaft far farhitn di gezuntheit fun der yidisher bafelkerung «OZE»* 2 (June 1923): 10.

14. AR 21–32 #102A Organizations: OSE NY 1.29–11.29, Joint Archive, NY.

15. Szajkowski, "Budgeting American Jewish Overseas Relief," 83–88.

16. Menachem Kaufmann, *An Ambiguous Partnership: Non-Zionists and Zionists in America, 1939–1948* (Detroit: Wayne State University Press, 1991); Yigal Elam, "Hasokhnut heYehudit: Shanim Rishonot 1919–1931," 1990, Zionist Library.

17. OSE to the Executive Committee, Joint Distribution Committee, 4 April 1925, AR 19–21 #253 localities, Joint Archive, NY.

18. A cable from Rosen to JDC, 8 April 1925, reads, "Gran and Bramson of our medical committee are excellent fully reliable workers. . . . Suggest pluck any possible allocation." AR 19–21 #253 localities, Joint Archive, NY.

19. AR 19–21 #253 localities, Joint Archive, NY.

20. Felix Warburg, Memorandum, 10 November 1925, AR 19–21 #253 localities, Joint Archive, NY.

21. Protocol of a meeting between Hyman and Jacobi, 13 March 1929, 1–2, AR 19–21 #253 localities, Joint Archive, NY.

22. AR 21–32 #102A Organizations OSE NY 1.29–11.29, Joint Archive, NY.

23. Marshall to Jacobi, 17 April 29, AR 21–32 #102A Organizations OSE NY 1.29–11.29, Joint Archive, NY.

24. Marshall to Hyman, 16 April 29, AR 21–32 #102A Organizations OSE NY 1.29–11.29, Joint Archive, NY. From a letter to Jacobi in May it is clear that this was also the strategy of the Zionist Organization. "This is the same mistake that was made by the Zionist organization, so that today there are many of money collecting Zionist agencies in America with the result that while people are not tired of giving, they are certainly tired to being asked over and over again for what seems to them to be the same work." AR 21–32 #102A Organizations OSE NY 1.29–11.29, Joint Archive, NY.

25. Edwin Embree, Julius Rosenwald Fund, to Dr. Rosenau, 4 December 1929, AR 21–32 #102A Organizations OSE NY 1929–1932, Joint Archive, NY.

26. Paul Weindling, "Health and Political Stability: The Rockefeller Foundation in Central and Eastern Europe between the Two World Wars," *Minerva* 31 (3) (1993): 253–67; Benjamin Page, "The Rockefeller Foundation and Central Europe: A Reconsideration," *Minerva* 40 (2002); Marta Balinska, "The Rockefeller Foundation and the National Institute of Hygiene, Poland, 1918–45," *Studies in History and Philosophy of Science* 31 (3) (2000): 419–32.

27. G. Vincent, president of the Rockefeller Foundation, to Dr. Frankel, a member of the American National Committee of OZE, 1 October 1929, AR 21–32 #102A Organizations OSE NY 1.29–11.29, Joint Archive, NY.

28. American National Committee to the JDC, 28 October 1929, AR 21–32 #102A Organizations OSE NY 1.29–11.29, Joint Archive, NY. For the detailed budget, see "Jahresbudget des Verbandes 'OSE' in den Randstaete für das Jahr 1930," 30 October 1929, AR 21–32 #102A Organizations OSE NY 1.29–11.29, Joint Archive, NY.

29. Hyman to David Bressler, 11 November 29, AR 21–32 #102A Organizations OSE NY 1929–1932, Joint Archive, NY.

30. Ibid.

31. Memorandum written by Hyman, 11 November 1929, AR 21–32 #102A Organizations OSE NY 1929–1932, Joint Archive, NY.

32. OZE Berlin to Jacobi, 29 November 1929, AR 21–32 #102A Organizations OSE NY 1929–1932, Joint Archive, NY.

33. Jacobi to Hyman, 11 December 1929, AR 21–32 #102A Organizations OSE NY 1929–1932, Joint Archive, NY.

34. JDC to Jacobi, 20 December 1929, AR 21–32 #102A Organizations OSE NY 1929–1932, Joint Archive, NY.

35. Einstein to Flexner, 2 December 1929, AR 21–32 #102A Organizations OSE NY 1929–1932, Joint Archive, NY.

36. Rosenau to Warburg, 31 December 1929, AR 21–32 #102A Organizations OSE NY 1929–1932, Joint Archive, NY.

37. Warburg to Rosenau, 20 January 1930, AR 21–32 #102A Organizations OSE NY 1929–1932, Joint Archive, NY.

38. The suggestion was made in a letter from Jacobi to Hyman, 9 December 1929, AR 21–32 #102A Organizations OSE NY 1929–1932, Joint Archive, NY.

7

Territorialism and the ICOR "American Commission of Scientists and Experts" to the Soviet Far East

HENRY SREBRNIK

Most of the world remembers the year 1929 for the New York stock-market crash at the end of October, ushering in what became known as the Great Depression. For American Jewish Communists, though, there were other issues that same year perhaps more significant. Writing in May 1943, in the midst of World War II, Abraham (Ab.) Epstein, a prominent Jewish Communist, still remembered their effects:

> The year 1929. The whole capitalist world is enveloped by an economic crisis. Our own country is the hardest hit. The collection of money for relief becomes harder. This is one side of the coin. On the other hand, the economic situation in the Soviet Union improves. But immediately the attacks against the Soviet Union grow stronger, . . . Under such circumstances [our efforts] now changed over to propaganda, to the defense of the Soviet Union.[1]

Epstein was the national organizer for the Association for Jewish Colonization in the Soviet Union (*Gezelshaft far Yidishe Kolonizatsye in Sovyetn-Farband*), or the ICOR, an American Communist "front" group founded in 1924 to support Jewish agricultural colonization in the new Soviet Union. He was referring to the intensified attacks on the Soviet state as Joseph Stalin consolidated his power and the increased pressure felt by Jewish Communists due to their opposition to Zionism and the building of a Jewish national home in Palestine. Yet the ICOR managed not only to survive but also to thrive during the 1930s. Why did this Communist "front" group not collapse after 1929? The answer, in a word, was Birobidzhan.[2]

The Birobidzhan project itself is probably best understood in the context of that form of Jewish nationalism known as Territorialism, a proto-Zionist doctrine that preached the formation of a sovereign Jewish collective in a suitable territory anywhere in the world, and not necessarily in the Land of Israel. The solutions included immigration to and settlement in rural, agricultural areas in Argentina, Australia, Canada, and the United States, among many other places, and even the creation of a Jewish polity in part of Uganda and Kenya. Territorialists sought safe havens for the economic "rehabilitation" of the Jewish people, who, in their view, needed to "normalize" through the pursuit of agricultural and industrial labor, rather than remain "nonproductive" middlemen and traders. So the proposal of a Jewish entity in Birobidzhan, in the Soviet Far East, would arouse wide interest among those who sought in Jewish colonization projects a solution to statelessness.

In the wake of the dislocations caused by the Russian Revolution, millions of Jews in the USSR had found themselves bereft of jobs, businesses, or even homes. Two agencies were created to step into the breach and settle Jews on the land: the Committee for the Settlement of Jewish Toilers on the Land (KOMZET in Russian, KOMERD in Yiddish), a government agency attached to the Presidium of the Soviet of Nationalities and chaired by Peter G. Smidovich; and the ostensibly nongovernmental Association for the Settlement of Jewish Toilers on the Land (OZET in Russian, GEZERD in Yiddish), soon chaired by the noted Jewish Bolshevik Shimen Dimanshtein of the *Evsektsiia*, the Jewish Sections of the Soviet Communist Party.

The Bolsheviks did their utmost to encourage the creation of Jewish agricultural collectives in areas of heavy Jewish population destined to become autonomous regions. But land was in great demand in these European areas of the USSR, and very often Jews faced hostility from native Tatars and Ukrainians.[3] So the *Evsektsiia* and the GEZERD began to look for larger, more remote areas in which to settle Jews. On March 28, 1928, the Soviet government approved the choice of Birobidzhan, a sparsely populated area of 13,895 square miles (36,490 square kilometers) in the Amur-Ussuri district of the Far Eastern Territory of the USSR, for Jewish settlement.[4] Jews in Birobidzhan were to possess their own administrative, educational, and judicial institutions and would function in their own language, Yiddish; ideological care would be taken to distinguish the enterprise from Zionist ideology. For the Jewish Communists, whose ideological homeland was the USSR, the creation of a "new" Jew would occur in the Soviet Far East, rather than in Palestine. Birobidzhan would mesh nicely with the subterranean but very powerful secular nationalist sentiments of the Jewish Communist movement.[5]

The Formation of the ICOR

On December 21, 1924, a conference was held in New York City with the participation of 480 delegates representing 24 branches of trade unions, 122 branches of the Workmen's Circle, 94 *landsmanshaftn*, 4 Jewish National Workers Alliance branches, 60 Communist Party branches, and 10 cultural organizations. At these meetings, the ICOR, a nonpartisan mass organization, was founded.[6] The ICOR's first secretary was Dr. Elias (Elye) Wattenberg, then a Left Labor Zionist, but he was replaced first by Leon Talmy in 1928 and then by Shlome (Sol) Almazov in 1932; both were members of the Communist Party. Ab. Epstein, a former president of the Workmen's Circle who had turned to Communism, became the national organizer, and Barnet Brodsky, the treasurer. Among the founding members of the ICOR were Jacob Mordecai Budish, Melech Epstein, Shakhno Epstein, Dr. Joseph Glassman, Abraham Moses Kuntz, Professor Charles Kuntz, Kalmen Marmor, Moissaye (Moshe) Olgin, Ruben Saltzman, and Abraham Victor. Professor Kuntz, a former *maskil* who had studied at the University of Vienna before coming to the United States, soon became the titular head of the organization.

On April 30–May 1, 1925, 122 delegates from thirty-two cities met in New York for the ICOR's first national convention. The convention ratified an agreement between the ICOR and the KOMERD allowing the ICOR legal rights and privileges in the Soviet Union to buy and supply goods and building materials, to open bank accounts, to make credit available, to bring in supplies from outside the country without paying duty, to allow entrance and exit to and from the USSR by foreign citizens working for the ICOR, and otherwise to provide material help to the Jewish agricultural colonization projects.[7]

At first, the ICOR insisted that it was a nonpartisan organization not engaged in the "spread of any social or economic ideal or 'ism.'" Such extremes as Zionists and avowed Communists, quite aside from all the parties and factions that stand midway betwixt these extremes, regularly attend its conferences and are represented on the various committees of the *Icor*."[8] The organization's letterhead in those years incorporated an illustration of a Jewish farmer behind a plough pulled by two horses, rather than more standard Communist iconography. In its first five years of existence, it declined to condemn Jewish colonization in Palestine, for fear of alienating those socialist Zionists favorably disposed to the USSR. It preferred to stress its "socialist territorialism," rather than pro-Soviet politics. Even so, few non-Communists accepted the ICOR's early facade of nonpartisanship, save for a sprinkling of pro-Soviet intellectuals and Labor Zionists.

When the Soviets in 1928 selected Birobidzhan as a new and much larger site for Jewish colonization, the ICOR immediately fell in behind the plan. The new general secretary, Leon Talmy, praised the decision and said that the KOMERD had acted at the request of the Jewish masses in the country. Nor, he wrote, did they fear Birobidzhan's distance from European Russia or the great efforts that would be required there. Thousands of families, Talmy declared, had already expressed their willingness to take up the hard life of pioneers. Talmy predicted that in Birobidzhan both agriculture and industry would develop and a rich culture would result. All this would lead eventually to a Jewish republic. This would be a massive and historic undertaking, but the Jewish masses were ready to meet the task. With help from America and elsewhere, the difficulties might be mitigated.[9]

The well-regarded journalist B. Z. Goldberg of the Yiddish daily *Der Tog* also favored the Birobidzhan idea. He poked fun at the idea that the ICOR was nothing more than a Communist-organized "front." He had been at ICOR meetings where there was a mix of bourgeois Jews, Communists, Labor Zionists, Territorialist-socialists, and Jews simply interested in helping other Jews. What did they have in common? They approved of Jews returning to the land, and they loved the Yiddish language. The work in Russia was immense, much greater than the colonization in Argentina and Palestine. "Herzl almost took Uganda in the wilds of Africa. What would Herzl and Zangwill have said had the tsar offered them Birobidzhan, and on such terms!"[10]

Jacob Levin, a member of the national executive, called Birobidzhan "the Jewish new-land." Something that had been only "a hope for such a long time" was now becoming "realized before our very eyes." But more than just economic rehabilitation was planned: there was also the ideal of a Jewish cultural revitalization, to strengthen and broaden Jewish culture and to create a new Jewish spirit. This land north of the Amur River, drained by the rivers Bira and Bidzhan, with very few inhabitants, would be suitable for large-scale Jewish colonization. Millions of Jews could settle it, and there would be no possibility of them being assimilated into some other culture. The enthusiasm for this venture would grow among the Jewish masses, Levin was certain, and they would "with all their heart" help make this project a reality.[11]

At an ICOR plenum held on June 24, 1928, in New York, Talmy stated that Birobidzhan and the ICOR had become an inseparable combination, and the ICOR now had approximately 10,000 members. Talmy noted that the executive had formed a special commission that had recommended to the national executive that the ICOR send to the new Jewish district machinery and technical expertise to help the new settlers with the building of nascent industries. The national executive placed on the agenda the possibility of sending to Birobidzhan a fact-finding mission to examine the possibilities and potential of the region.[12] Some Jewish settlers had begun moving to Birobidzhan, and various communes and collectives, including Waldheim, Icor, and Birofeld, were established. Kuntz had already gone to Birobidzhan to coordinate the ICOR's work with that of the GEZERD and had inspected the settlements.[13]

In November, the organization put out a call "to the Jewish masses in America" to further help the Jewish colonization projects. Birobidzhan, it stated, was a huge area, with arable land, forests, and rivers full of fish, and one that required the pioneering spirit that developed the American West. Such an undertaking "demands a big response from the Jewish working class in America. And the only organization in America that stands side by side with those who will build the new large Jewish community in Birobidzhan is the ICOR." The ICOR called on sympathizers to help build "a healthy, free and bright future for our brothers in the Soviet Union."[14]

Leon Talmy introduced the Birobidzhan plan to a wider, English-speaking audience with an article titled "A Jewish State in the Soviet Union" in the July 11, 1928, issue of the *Nation*. It was a project of "historic significance," he wrote, one that would mark "a momentous turning-point in the life of the Jewish population of the Soviet Union." Talmy described the region's natural resources and its potential for agriculture, forestry, mining, and industry, which could enable it to "absorb a population of 1,000,000 or more." Although some 80,000 Jews had been settled on land in Belarus, the Crimea, and Ukraine since 1924, those areas were now too small and too densely populated to allow for the resettlement of some 600,000–800,000 "déclassé" Jews still without a livelihood, who needed speedy relief. What made the new project special was "the possibility of the ultimate formation of a Jewish autonomous republic," since Jews would eventually form a majority there. "The difficulties with which the first settlers will have to contend will be many. But with modern American technical methods and facilities the task can be made much easier," explained Talmy.[15]

The ICOR published a pamphlet in January 1929 that attempted to answer the question "Why Birobidzhan?" It described the attributes of the region and suggested that it had such "colossal" possibilities that it could eventually evolve into a Jewish republic. It noted that the GEZERD and the KOMERD, after detailed examinations conducted in 1927, had determined that Birobidzhan was suited to mass colonization. And, added the authorities in Moscow, it had to proceed quickly. "The best guarantee that the district will belong to Jews is—to settle it!"[16]

At the January 20, 1929, national executive's plenum, Jacob Levin remarked that the ICOR should not ignore problems relating to settling Birobidzhan but should not overemphasize them either. He pointed out that although the climate was harsh, there were areas in Canada just as cold, and that had not prevented successful development. So the question was, he said, "how can we help out with the work in Birobidzhan?" It was an unsettled country, and there were no existing models to follow. Levin suggested sending a team of experts to Birobidzhan to explore the situation and to prepare a detailed plan on how to go about colonizing the area.[17]

The Experts Commission

Most American Jews remained wary of the Birobidzhan project. The Ukrainian-born journalist Abraham Revutsky warned the readers of the *Menorah Journal* in February 1929 that "current rumors describing Bira-Bidzhan [*sic*] as a sort of new Eldorado are greatly exaggerated." He noted that "winter and summer are both colder than Winnipeg" and that the clay soil was not very good. "It is not desirable for Jewish colonization," he concluded, and those "who have rushed Jewish settlers into this enterprise without proper investigation and preparation have not acted in a thoroughly impartial and scientific manner."[18]

Given this continued skepticism, the national executive made plans to send a delegation to Birobidzhan to report on the feasibility of the region for mass settlement in advance of the fourth national convention scheduled for the end of 1929. The commission would familiarize itself with the conditions in Birobidzhan and its potential for mass colonization, help draw up plans to make certain the work would proceed along modern technical lines, and upon its return publicize the project to the American Jewish community.

In the spring of 1929, the American Commission of Scientists and Experts left for the USSR. It was led by Franklin S. Harris, an agronomist and president of Brigham Young University in Utah. Harris was one of the country's leading soil scientists, an expert on colonization in the United States, Canada, and Mexico, and director of the American Society of Agricultural Engineering. He had for many years had practical experience on a ranch in Alberta, "where the climate and conditions were similar to Birobidzhan," and had in 1926 visited Palestine, Egypt, and Manchuria to investigate agricultural problems. Other members included J. Brownlee Davidson, head of the Department of Agricultural Engineering at Iowa State College, who had worked for the U.S. Department of Agriculture; Kiefer B. Sauls, a purchasing agent at Brigham Young; and Benjamin Brown, a Salt Lake City marketing specialist and director of the Utah Poultry Producers Cooperative Association. Charles Kuntz, Leon Talmy, and Elias Wattenberg represented the ICOR. Talmy and Brown left New York on May 18, the other commissioners on June 21.[19]

Upon arrival in the Soviet Union, the commission members met with various Soviet academics and government representatives who briefed them on conditions in Birobidzhan. On July 19, they left Moscow by train; nine days later, the group was welcomed by KOMERD and GEZERD officials in Khabarovsk. The commissioners were impressed by the treatment they received; the Soviets even put a special railcar at their disposal. After a few days, they went on to Birobidzhan; the commission spent the next six weeks in actual field investigations, traveling by train, boat, wagon, and on horseback, throughout the region.

Arriving in Tikhonkaia (later to be renamed Birobidzhan City), they were impressed by the hustle and bustle of the town, with buildings going up at a rapid pace. Their first stop was the Icor commune, where they braved rain, flies, and mosquitoes. The Waldheim collective seemed more prosperous. It had been founded by a group of merchants; it was hard to believe, reported Leon Talmy, that these were former businesspeople. In Birofeld, they inspected the local hospital, administrative buildings, beehives, machine shops, and experimental station. Then it was on to the hot springs at Kuldur, known for their therapeutic qualities. The commissioners felt this area could support many settlers.

Using Obluchye as a base, the group, having procured provisions, guides and pack animals, headed into the Khingan hills, an undeveloped region of 15,000 square kilometers. Entering a valley, Brown noticed the lush grass and tall oak trees. This would make excellent agricultural land, he told Talmy. He also pointed out the wild grapes growing there. "When we report this, we will probably not even be believed," he said. They reemerged at Pompeevka, a small settlement on the bank of the Amur; from there they boarded a ship downriver to Amurzet. Talmy noted that the river was the border between "two countries—two worlds." As they left Birobidzhan, Talmy saw a wilderness "beginning to breathe with new life. It is the future being born here. The Soviet future, the socialist life, of which the first shoots were beginning to sprout in this raw earth." The commissioners returned to New York October 22 and were met with a grand reception three days later. They also reported to the ICOR plenum that met October 25–27.[20]

The Experts Commission issued its detailed report, published in both English and Yiddish, in 1930. The document summarized the economic and historical background of Jewish colonization in the Soviet Union and then provided an overview of Birobidzhan: first, the history of its conquest by tsarist Russia and the subjugation of its aboriginal population, followed by a series of chapters describing its geography and geology; climate; natural resources including timber, animals and fish, minerals, and coal and peat; and its water resources. The commission had studied the region's agricultural and industrial potential, its transportation and communications links, and the housing and sanitation situation.[21]

The commissioners noted that most of Birobidzhan lay between the 48th and 49th parallels north latitude—the same latitude as the northern United States and European countries such as France and Germany. It had short, warm, and wet summers and dry, clear, and severe winters; they compared it, topographically, to Ontario and Michigan. Given the types of soil and availability of water, they determined that "all crops possible of cultivation in the temperate zone could be successfully grown in Biro-Bidjan," including wheat, rye, barley, oats, and buckwheat. The climate was also favorable to root crops, soybeans, and rice. In addition, they concluded that Birobidzhan had "minerals of considerable industrial and commercial importance."[22]

At the time of the commissioners' visit, some 28,000 people lived in Birobidzhan, about half of them Koreans and other peoples native to the region, the rest Slavic descendants of earlier colonists. By then, some 1,300 Jews had also already settled in the region. The commissioners were agreed that "the Jew presents untried material as a colonist," since "the tilling of the soil" is to him "a long forgotten art." But the predictions by some pessimists that Jews were "physically incapable and psychically unwilling to go back to the land" had been proved false by the success of the colonies in the European parts of the country.[23]

Shimen Dimanshtein had predicted that, with the help of "Jewish overseas proletarian organizations, above all ICOR in America," all things were possible.[24] After having spent six weeks in the area, the Experts Commission agreed, stating that it had confidence in the possibilities of Birobidzhan and calling it "a vast empire in the making." There seemed to be no reason "why this region should not develop into a well-populated area and its settlers into a prosperous people." Notwithstanding the difficulties of pioneering conditions, it concluded, there were no problems in Birobidzhan "which may not be overcome by diligent work and the intelligent application of modern technical organizational methods."[25]

In a radio address titled "Jewish Colonization in Biro-Bidjan," broadcast over Washington, DC, radio station WOL on October 29, 1929, Harris told listeners, "Never, in all history has yet such an opportunity dawned upon the toiling Jewish people" for the building of "a creative productive community and building it on the basis of real equality of opportunity." The commission had found a region with ten million acres of fertile land, abundant sunshine, and a growing season similar to that of the northern United States. It was also well adapted to the livestock industry, particularly dairy farming. There was an abundance of mineral resources and forest products. As for transportation, the Trans-Siberian Railroad served the region, and the rivers flowing into the Amur would allow transportation by water to the Pacific Ocean. Harris's address was included in a pamphlet that called on American Jews to join the ICOR and to "share in the burden, responsibilities and joy of this really creative work." Every dollar contributed "will bring nearer the day of the formation of the Jewish Socialist Soviet Republic there."[26]

Birobidzhan, exclaimed another pamphlet, is no "romantic dream, no accident, no political maneuver, but the logical outcome of the work that the Soviet state is carrying out in the process of rebuilding Jewish life on new, healthy and productive foundations." Two years earlier, no one had heard of Birobidzhan, "but today it carries the message of an historic renewal, of new possibilities of creating and constructing." The enemies of the Soviet Union had tried to counter this news through lies and misrepresentations. They tried to frighten the public with their cry of "Siberia," claiming that Birobidzhan had an impossibly harsh climate and was infested with flies and mosquitoes. This was designed to prevent the Jewish masses in America "from stretching out their brotherly hand to the Jewish poor in the Soviet Union and involving themselves in the great historic task." It was up to the Jewish masses in America to help lay a strong foundation for a Jewish socialist republic in the Soviet Union. "Do your part to ensure the success of this great historic task!"[27]

The national executive of the ICOR in November 1929 published a pamphlet addressing some of the issues that had been brought up in the Yiddish press which, they noted with some sarcasm, was at last acknowledging Birobidzhan's reality, rather than calling it a

"Communist illusion," an "adventure," a "catastrophe," at the very best a "dream" which would never be realized. Skeptics

> are now realizing that the news from Birobidzhan is positive, as reported by the Experts Commission of the ICOR earlier in the year. The area is fit for mass colonization, it is a land full of natural resources and is superbly adapted for agricultural and industrial development. The report of the commissioners, learned and non-partisan American scholars, had put an end to all the libels and misrepresentations spread about Birobidzhan.
>
> The project to settle large masses of Jews in Birobidzhan and to create a Jewish autonomous territory has been so well received that simply opposing the colonization is no longer an option. No longer can detractors say it will not work and ask "who will build it?"

The Jewish masses in America "understand that only in the Soviet Union, where there reigns the power of work, where the proletarian state concerns itself with the fate of Jewish poverty," is it possible for a great piece of land, rich in possibilities, to be set aside for the creation of an autonomous Jewish Soviet republic.[28] Shlome Almazov asked every member of the ICOR to study the report carefully, as its conclusions were "a slap in the face" of the enemies of the Soviet Union and could be used to counter the lies spread about the project.[29]

The fourth national ICOR convention met in New York, December 27–29, 1929. Kuntz told the delegates that the Experts Commission had learned that Birobidzhan was as suitable both agriculturally and industrially for colonization "as are some of our north-western states." The colonization there was assuming "a type of empire building unprecedented in history." The "primitive peasant methods of work" were being discarded and replaced by an "Industrial Plan." All productive activities, including farming, would be "industrialized on the basis of the modern machine and scientific management." The ICOR was supplying "the missing link, notably the appropriate machinery and the expert specialist."[30]

Benjamin Brown related his experience in Birobidzhan. The climate was suitable for people and domestic animals and particularly for the cultivation of rice. The land had remained uninhabited because the soil was too hard to farm using old methods. "It awaited a time when it could be cultivated by modern methods. It would have to be conquered through collectivization. The commission recommended that machinery and technical help be sent to Birobidzhan and in this the 'Icor' can play an important role. Now is not the time to play politics. Whatever our ideological ideas, all of us can completely trust the Soviet government."[31]

The next day, the national secretary, Leon Talmy, delivered his report on the activities of the ICOR since the previous convention two years earlier. The American organization in 1929 alone had sent $150,000 worth of agricultural and industrial equipment to Birobidzhan. "The role that these machines have already played in the first year and a half of the colonization in Birobidzhan has already been assessed, by the people on the ground, by the Soviet authorities, by our own Experts-Commission, who had seen the machines at work." Everywhere the commission went, it had been warmly received and was able to gain an objective overview of the situation. Talmy stated that the $13,000 that it had cost the ICOR to send the commission to Birobidzhan had more than repaid itself in full. The commission's report created a "deep impression" and inspired ever more interest among the broadest sectors of the Jewish world. It "will be strong ammunition in our hands in the fight against all the enemies of our work." Following the sessions, the delegates greeted "with joy and enthusiasm" the building of a socialist Jewish Birobidzhan and proclaimed March 28, the date Birobidzhan had been declared a district for mass Jewish colonization, to be an annual ICOR holiday. The convention closed with the singing of the "Internationale."[32]

Conclusion: Looking Back on 1929

In May 1943, the ICOR published an *Almanac* that included an article by Ab. Epstein on the history and goals of the ICOR. He detailed the immense amount of help the ICOR had provided to the settlers in Birobidzhan over the years. The 1929 Experts Commission, in particular, had convinced many Jews in the United States that Birobidzhan was a viable enterprise.[33] Charles Kuntz, in the same publication, wrote that Birobidzhan was being celebrated because it was the "grand offspring" of a revolution that had "brought peace and goodwill to One Sixth of the earth" and had "rebuilt society on the solid foundation of social-ist economy which precludes exploitation of man by man and oppres-sion of nation by nation." To acknowledge Birobidzhan during this time of war was to commemorate the grandiose achievements of the Soviet Union, "the universally acknowledged bulwark of historic progress."[34]

The ICOR held its last national convention in March 1946, before it merged with the American Committee for the Settlement of Jews in Birobidjan (Ambijan); the combined organization would be known as the American Birobidjan Committee until its demise in 1951. Abra-ham Jenofsky, the last national secretary, told the ICOR delegates that the time had come to create a united organization to consolidate the strength of the movement and to attract the widest array of Jewish members and supporters, to take part in the work on behalf of Birobid-zhan and to help those who had suffered in the war.

It was now eighteen years since Birobidzhan had been designated an area for Jewish colonization, "a date which should and will become marked in the history of Jews as the beginning of a new epoch in the life of a great portion of our people." Soviet nationality policy had made Jews fully equal with the other people of the Soviet Union. Birobidzhan would assume great importance in postwar plans for the development of the Far East.[35]

But a mere decade later, when Nikita Khrushchev's "secret speech" at the twentieth congress of the Soviet Communist Party exposed Stalin and his henchmen as mass murderers, it had also become obvious that the Birobidzhan project had proved a failure, if not indeed a hoax. But by then, Ambijan had collapsed, and few people could—or would—recall the glory days of the ICOR in 1929.

Why did the Experts Commission return with such a positive report regarding Birobidzhan's potential? Clearly, given the members' politi-cal attitudes toward Jewish colonization and their pro-Soviet sympa-thies, they interpreted what they saw and heard in the most favorable manner possible. This was their implicit mandate. After all, the Soviet authorities hoped their report would induce American Jewish organi-zations to raise money on behalf of Soviet Jewry. And settlement of the region by Jews loyal and devoted to the Soviet regime would safeguard the area from land-hungry Chinese peasants and from the designs of Japanese imperialists.

As well, the ICOR needed, very quickly, to counter the unfavorable publicity generated by events in Palestine that year. Pogroms took place in Jerusalem, Tel Aviv, Safed, Hebron, and a number of smaller locales in the British Mandate. Altogether, eighty-three Jews were killed and hundreds wounded; in Hebron, sixty-seven Jews were murdered on August 23.[36] The Palestinian Arab perpetrators were denounced by almost all American Jewish groups. However, Moscow described this as a revolutionary struggle against British imperialism, and the New York Communist Yiddish daily the *Morgn Frayhayt* and other Jewish Communist institutions were forced to dutifully follow suit—though a number of famous Yiddish writers such as Abraham Reisin, Halpern Leivick, and Isaac Raboy left the paper in protest. The Jewish community was horrified by the stance taken by the Jewish Communist movement, and there was considerable dissension within the ICOR itself.[37] The organization found itself in the embarrassing position of having a resolution passed on September 11, 1929, by its management committee, by eight votes to four, condemning the anti-Zionist position. A period of turmoil followed before the CP leadership overturned the verdict and regained the upper hand. Birobidzhan henceforth served as the socialist-territorialist project that would stand in opposition to the "imperialist" enterprise in Palestine.[38]

So, had the commission brought back any other verdict, the ICOR leadership would have done everything in their power to suppress it. But it is unlikely they even contemplated such a result.

NOTES

1. Ab. Epstein, "Akhtsn yor ikor," in Isaac E. Rontch, ed., *Ikor Almanakh: Lekoved 25 yor Sovyetn-farband un 15 yor Biro-Bidzhan / ICOR Almanac: On the Occasion of the 25th Anniversary of the U.S.S.R. and of the 15th Anniversary of Biro-Bidjan* (New York: ICOR, May 1943), 48–49 [Yiddish section].

2. The name is today transliterated as *Birobidzhan*, but in the 1920s it was usually spelled *Birobidjan* or *Biro-Bidjan* in English.

3. See Allan Laine Kagedan, *Soviet Zion: The Quest for a Russian Jewish Homeland* (New York: St. Martin's, 1994), 73–93.

4. An excellent overview of the entire project is provided by Robert Weinberg, *Stalin's Forgotten Zion: Birobidzhan and the Making of a Soviet Jewish Homeland: An Illustrated History, 1928–1996* (Berkeley: University of California Press, 1998). See, as well, the entry "Birobidjan," written by Avrahm Yarmolinsky, then head of the Slavonic Division of the New York Public Library, in

the *Universal Jewish Encyclopedia of 1941* (1941; repr., New York: Ktav, 1969), 372–78.

5. Henry Srebrnik, "Diaspora, Ethnicity and Dreams of Nationhood: North American Jewish Communists and the Soviet Birobidzhan Project," in Gennady Estraikh and Mikhail Krutikov, eds., *Yiddish and the Left* (Oxford, UK: Legenda, 2001), 80–108.

6. "In di shtet," *ICOR* 1 (March 1925): 14; "Barikht fun sekretar E. Vatenberg," *ICOR* 2–3 (April–May 1925): 7; *"Icor" Bulletin* 1 (April 1925): 8; Ab. Epstein, "Zibn yor ikor-geshikhte," *Ikor Yor-bukh / ICOR Year Book 1932* (New York: National Executive Committee of the ICOR, 1932), 46 [Yiddish section].

7. "Natsionale konferents fun 'ikor' dem 30tn april un 1tn may in nyu-york," *ICOR* 1 (March 1925): 3; "Barikht fun sekretar E. Vatenberg," *ICOR* 2–3 (April–May 1925): 6–9; "Barikht fun der rezolutsyonz komite," *ICOR* 2–3 (April–May 1925): 26–27; "Barikht fun der nominatsyonz komite," *ICOR* 2–3 (April–May 1925): 28; Epstein, "Akhtsn yor ikor," 47 [Yiddish section].

8. *"Icor" Bulletin* 1 (April 1925): 11.

9. L. Talmy, "Tsum oyfboy fun a yidish land," *ICOR* 1.1 (May 1928): 1.

10. B. Z. Goldberg, "Tsvishn 'ikor'-mentshn," *ICOR* 1.1 (May 1928): 2–4. Goldberg was referring to Theodor Herzl's 1903 proposal to settle Jews in East Africa. The Anglo-Jewish activist Israel Zangwill, following the Zionist rejection of the "Uganda proposal," led the Territorialists out of the World Zionist Organization and established the Jewish Territorialist Organization.

11. Jacob Levin, "Biro-bidzhan—dos yidishe nayland," *ICOR* 1.1 (May 1928): 5–6, and *ICOR* 1.2 (July 1928): 6–8.

12. "'Ikor' far biro-bidzhan," *ICOR* 1.1 (May 1928): 9; "Tsu a breyter masn-organizatsye," *ICOR* 1.2 (July 1928): 1; "Plenare zitsung fun der nats. ekz.," *ICOR* 1.2 (July 1928): 11–16. The ICOR had already received a letter from the GEZERD on May 7, 1928, in which the latter had approved of the idea of sending a team of American experts to Birobidzhan. "'Ikor' informatsye-briv numer 2," June 8, 1928, 1, in Group II, Box b, folder 27, "Brainin & the USSR—ICOR—Reports, Minutes," Reuben Brainin Collection, Jewish Public Library Archives, Montreal.

13. Charles Kuntz, "Briv fun biro-bidzhan," *ICOR* 1.3 (November 1928): 2–4.

14. "Far der yidisher kolonizatsye in sovyetn-farband," pamphlet published in November 1928, in United States Territorial Collection, RG 117, Box 57, folder "Icor" 17/16, YIVO Institute for Jewish Research, New York [hereafter cited as USTC/YIVO].

15. Leon Talmy, "A Jewish State in the Soviet Union," *Nation* 127.3288 (July 11, 1928): 51–52.

16. ICOR, *Di ershte trit fun biro-bidzhan* (New York: ICOR, January 1929), 3–6, 16–18, 30–32.

17. "Plenare zitsung fun der nats. ekzekutive," *ICOR* 2.2 (February–March 1929): 18.

18. Abraham Revutsky, "Bira-Bidzhan: A Jewish Eldorado?," *Menorah Journal* 16.2 (February 1929): 158–68.

19. "Icor Experts Sail Today," *New York Times*, June 20, 1929, 17; "'Ikor' shikt ekspertn-komisye keyn biro-bidzhan," *ICOR* 2.4 (June–July 1929): 6–7; circular letter from Ab. Epstein, national organizer, and Abraham Olken, secretary of the New York Committee, New York, April 30, 1929, in the Kalmen Marmor Papers, 1873–1955, RG 205, Microfilm group 495, folder 544 "Ikor-korespondents, 1925–1929," YIVO Institute for Jewish Research, New York.

20. "Vos es vert gezogt vegn der 'ikor'-ekspeditsye keyn biro-bidzhan," *ICOR* 2.5 (August–September 1929): 7–11; "Groyser kaboles-ponem far der 'ikor' ekspedit-sye keyn biro-bidzhan," *ICOR* 2.5 (August–September 1929): 16; "Americans Support Bira-Bidjan [*sic*] Project," *New York Times*, October 13, 1929, sec. 3, 8; Leon Talmy, *Oyf royer erd: Mit der 'Ikor'-ekspeditsye in biro-bidzhan* (New York: Frayhayt, 1931).

21. The 94-page English version, *Report of the American Icor Commission for the Study of Biro-Bidjan and Its Colonization*, and the 111-page Yiddish version, *Barikht fun der amerikaner ikor ekspertn-komisye*, were both published in 1930 (New York: ICOR), with print runs of 1,000 and 3,000 copies, respectively. There is a photo of the commissioners in the *Ikor Yor-bukh / ICOR Year Book 1932*, 146 [Yiddish section]. A short film, *A Scientific Expedition to Birobidzhan*, is in the YIVO archives.

22. ICOR, *Report of the American Icor Commission*, 25, 35, 46, 61–63. They noted that Japan, "which has very little iron ore of its own, . . . is a sure prospective cus-tomer" for iron from Birobidzhan, as well as for dairy products and timber (ibid., 44, 71). Of course, this was written before the Japanese had conquered Manchuria and became a threat to the Soviets in Asia.

23. ICOR, *Report of the American Icor Commission*, 22–23.

24. Shimen M. Dimanshtein, "Di yidishe oytonomye in biro-bidzhan," *Ikor Yor-bukh / ICOR Year Book 1932*, 44 [Yiddish section].

25. ICOR, *Report of the American Icor Commission*, 85, 89.

26. ICOR, *Biro-Bidjan and You* (New York: Astoria, [December 1929]).

27. ICOR, *Tsu der arbet far der yidisher kolonizatsye, far biro-bidzhan!* (New York: National Executive of the ICOR, [1929]).

28. ICOR, *Take—ver vet boyen biro-bidzhan?* (New York: National Executive of the ICOR, November 1929).

29. S. Almazov, "Der barikht fun der amerikaner 'ikor' eksperts-komisye," *ICOR* 3.2 (May 1930): 11.

30. Chas. Kuntz, "The Biro-Bidjan Project and the 'Icor,'" *ICOR* 3.1 (January–February 1930): 47–48.

31. "Barikht," *ICOR* 3.1 (January–February 1930): 8–15, 25.

32. "Rezolutsyes ongenumen oyfn fertn ikor-tsuzamenfor," *ICOR* 3.1 (January–Feb-ruary 1930): 32–34; L[eon] Talmy, "Barikht fun der natsyonaler ekzekutive tsum fertn tsuzamenfar fun 'Ikor,'" typed minutes, December 1929, 1–8 and appendices, USTC/YIVO.

33. Epstein, "Akhtsn yor ikor," 46–49 [Yiddish section]. On May 7, 1934, in an effort to make the project more attractive to Soviet Jews, Moscow had declared Birobidzhan a Jewish Autonomous Region (*Oblast*) of the Russian Soviet Federated Socialist Republic.

34. Prof. Charles Kuntz, "Birobidjan—1928–1943," in Rontch, *Ikor Almanakh*, 14 [English section].

35. "Barikht far der natsyonaler ekzekutive fun dem 'ikor' tsu der spetsyeler konvenshon fun dem 'ikor' un tsu der natsyonaler konferents fur birobidzhan, dem 9–10tn marts, 1946," mss. in the Abraham Jenofsky Papers, RG 734, Box 1, folder 6, YIVO Institute for Jewish Research, New York; Abraham Jenofsky, "Rapid Strides of Birobidjan," *Ambijan Bulletin* 5.3 (September 1946): 5–6.

36. For details on this period, see Bernard Wasserstein, *The British in Palestine: The Mandatory Government and the Arab-Jewish Conflict, 1917–1929* (Oxford, UK: Blackwell, 1991); Martin Kolinsky, *Law, Order and Riots in Mandatory Palestine, 1928–35* (London: St. Martin's, 1993); and Naomi W. Cohen, *The Year after the Riots: American Responses to the Palestine Crisis of 1929–30* (Detroit: Wayne State University Press, 1988).

37. The *Frayhayt* initially called the Arab attacks "pogroms." But the Communist Party leadership considered this to be a sign of "bourgeois-nationalist and social-democratic influence" in "our own ranks." "Red Party Here, Torn by 'Heresies,' Unable to Function," *New York Times*, September 8, 1929, 1, 14.

38. See Melech Epstein, *The Jew and Communism: The Story of Early Communist Victories and Ultimate Defeats in the Jewish Community, U.S.A., 1919–1941* (New York: Trade Union Sponsoring Committee, 1959), 223–33.

PART II

Local Stories

8

From Universal Values to Cultural Representations

AVNER BEN-ZAKEN

1929 was a crucial year in the history of the Marxist movement in Eretz-Israel/Palestine. After a decade of stimulating circulation of Marxist ideology and the establishment of local Communist parties that were declared official branches of the world communist movement—the Comintern—by 1929, the Middle Eastern Marxist movement abruptly changed. The Comintern came to see eastern European Jewish Marxists, who engendered and stirred these processes, as a cultural impediment responsible for the scarce reception of Marxism beyond the elite intelligentsia. Realizing that Marxism had not trickled down to the Arab masses, the Executive Committee of the Comintern dictated a personal transformation: it ejected European Jews from the leadership of the parties and installed local Arab and Jewish activists. The Arabization of the parties had profound ideological ramifications. The universal working class in the Middle East, which included European immigrants, had to follow a leadership that was no longer devoted to the universal struggle of the working class but that accommodated Marxist ideology to national and cultural differences. Marxism transformed from a free-floating universal ideology into a national discourse affected by practices of local "monadic" cultures.

When Marxism circulated outside Europe, cultural tension was the prism through which it was introduced and received. The presentation of Marxist discourse not as an artifact of European culture and history but as a "scientific," "objective" program to analyze history and to transform society further intensified this cultural tension. Marxists needed intermediaries fluent in both European and Middle Eastern cultures and languages who could effectively disseminate Marxist ideology in the Middle East. The Comintern assigned eastern European Jewish Marxists, who arrived at the turn of the century with the buds of Zionist immigration, to circulate Marxism in the region. Marxism's "objective scientific truth" installed in eastern European Jews a sense of conviction that they could easily bridge cultural differences and transform the cultures and consciousnesses of local Middle Eastern workers.

The October Revolution further stirred various radical socialist circles already active in Eretz-Israel. Members of these circles came to the region as part of Zionist immigration with a utopian international vision, leaving their original socialist organizations, which unexpectedly took part in the October Revolution in Russia. Disenchanted with the Jewish national vision and increasingly excited by the possibility of world communist revolution, in which they could take part, they looked for ways to contact the Executive Committee of the Comintern, to win its favor, and to become official representatives of the organization in the Middle East. Sometime in 1919, they composed a document to the Comintern titled "Manifesto: The Palestinian Communist Party, the Company of Resurrection" (*Hevrat tehiyyat ha-metim*). Calling for the recognition of the crucial role of the Jewish proletariat in Palestine in intensifying the process of world revolution, they named their organization "the Company of redemption from the old world." The purpose of the Company, the manifesto stressed, was "to establish a center for the Jewish proletariat that will be a role-model to the whole world." Already in Soviet Russia they trained devoted activists, sending them to Palestine to organize the workers in unions. The cultural vocation of the Company in Palestine was "to promote cultural and intellectual activities such as opening clubs, organizing lectures and issuing newspapers and pamphlets . . . so to educate the next generation according to the socialist worldview."[1]

The romantic vision, however, paid no heed to cultural barriers. Minutes of the meeting of the Executive Committee of the Comintern from September 21, 1920, provide the first indication of the inarticulate dialogue Jewish radicals had in their encounter with the Arab workers. The meeting was chaired by the executive secretary of the Comintern, Gregory Zinoviev, who hosted a representative of these Palestinian circles, named in the minutes as Meirson. In Meirson's briefing of the committee on their activity among the Arab workers, he stressed the efforts in organizing the Arab workers in unions and educating them in political and social matters. The cultural encounter between Marxism and the Arabs, however, did not go smoothly. The eastern European Jewish Marxists "stumbled on a great impediment," since the Arabs did not have enough "intelligent workers" who could propagate Marxist ideology among the locals. "We are still convinced," Meirson optimistically concluded, "that the prospects of having a revolution in Palestine are quite high."[2]

At this early stage, the committee did not have doubts about the sincere intentions of and the practical prospects of using eastern European Jews as agents of the world communist movement in the Middle East. Nikolai Bukharin, who participated in this meeting, further urged the Jewish Communists in Palestine to detach themselves from any Zionist affiliation and to devote major parts of their activity to recruiting Arabs, an activity that was an "enormously important vocation."[3] By May 10, 1923, the Comintern officially approved the admission of the Palestinian Communist Party (PCP), whose role the Comintern had clearly defined: "to educate supporters from the Arab masses; to look for constructive connections with Arab national groups and with peasants; and to help in establishing a Communist party in Lebanon and Syria."[4]

The PCP enthusiastically followed the Comintern's assignments, primarily in pursuing activists in Lebanon and Syria with whom they could initiate the circulation of Communist ideology. In 1924, Joseph Berger-Barzilay came to the Oriental Department of the Comintern in Moscow, which was responsible for supplying political and social assessments of the conditions and possibilities of promoting the anti-imperialist struggle and the establishment of Communist parties. Berger-Barzilay found there "various Orientalists deeply engaged with research work on the orient, and maps of the Middle East decorated the walls."[5] Beyond briefings on the general conditions in Syria, Lebanon, and Egypt, the officials in the Oriental Department particularly instructed him to travel to Beirut and to seek among the growing socialist circles potential activists who could establish a local Communist party. Berger-Barzilay met local radicals such as Yusūf Yazbak and Fu'ād Shamālī,[6] as well as Artin Madoyan, a representative of a small Armenian Marxist organization called Spartacus, informing them that the Comintern had empowered him to establish a local Communist party. A few weeks later, Berger-Barzilay orchestrated the negotiations between the various groups, finally bringing them together, on October 24, to a convention in Beirut's Kristal cinema hall, where they announced the establishment of the Syrian Communist party (*al-hizb al-shuyū'ī al-sūrī al-lubnānī*) as a branch of the PCP.[7] After leaving Beirut and arriving at Haifa, Berger-Barzilay promptly recruited Nahman List and his wife and sent them to Beirut, where they were installed in the Central Committee to coach, inspect, and train the Communist party according to the policies of the Comintern.[8]

In 1925, the PCP also had a crucial involvement with the Egyptian Communist party. The Egyptian party faced a fatal crisis as the English police persecuted its members, most of whom were Europeans who lived in Alexandria. These persecutions completely paralyzed the party, which had not yet been able to develop grassroots support from local Egyptians. In Tel-Aviv and Jerusalem, the representatives of the Comintern in the Middle East followed the events in Egypt with great concern. By 1924, they sent to Alexandria several messengers, highly skilled in political tactics, to help reignite the party and to recruit new members who could replace the many who were imprisoned.[9] Most of the messengers, however, were either arrested and deported or failed to make a significant change in the recruitment of local Egyptians to the party.

The failure in Egypt did not stop the PCP from further manifesting its sense of entitlement for regional leadership. In 1925, when a revolt against the French occupation sparked in Syria in the Druze Mountains, party members looked for ways to contact its leaders and to instigate an anti-imperialist struggle. They first sent messengers from Beirut's newborn party, but Sultan al-Atrash, the leader of the revolt, refused to speak to any Arab Communist "who upholds atheist ideology."[10] The refusal, ironically, created a situation in which only eastern European Jews could contact the Druze in the name of the Comintern. Two messengers from Tel-Aviv promptly arrived in Syria and infiltrated the French forces, pledging Sultan al-Atrash Soviet weapon to maintain the revolt in the name of the Comintern.[11] The pledge, however, was taken independently of Soviet international considerations. The Soviets were interested in maintaining the improving relations with France, one of the first Western powers to recognize the Soviet government, and they instructed the Comintern to tame its Middle Eastern representatives and to keep them away from the insurgency against the French forces.

Hopes for regional anti-imperialist struggles were let down, and soon the French suppressed the revolt.

The PCP's regional aspiration for leadership suffered a series of failures. By the second half of the 1920s, the party retreated to its home base and focused on creating grassroots support from the Arab workers in Palestine. The cultural nature of Sephardic Jews, however, complicated the simplistic dichotomy between Arabs and Jews. In rejecting the national Zionist implications of the revival of Hebrew, the party printed most of its pamphlets in Yiddish. As late as 1923, it published the first Hebrew pamphlet which targeted Sephardic Jewish workers, "the bridge between Arabs and European Jewish population," who were designated "to remove the cultural curtain between eastern European and Arab workers, and to fully apply equality between all workers without a distinction of nation and culture."[12] The efforts in the Sephardic sphere were partially successful when some activists who were not part of the Zionist immigration joined the party, and in the late 1920s, the party sent two Palestine-born activists, Meir Slonim and Simhah Tsabari, to Moscow to study in the Comintern's University of the Oriental Workers.

In the Arab cultural sphere, the party started publishing pamphlets and newsletters in Arabic through a local press in Haifa. Ilya Zakā and a Russian woman who was his press worker printed the newsletter, named *al-Nafīr* (Mouthpiece).[13] The party also sent a few Arab workers, such as Mahmūd al-Mughrabī, to the University of the Oriental Workers, where they were trained in the ideology and practice of the communist movement, in the hopes that they would become future leaders of the Arab workers.

By the late 1920s, it became clear that the complex cultural space made things worse. The party's various efforts to recruit Arabs, to transform local political culture, and to maintain the international universal vision had reached a dead end. The belief that cultural differences disappeared as everyone embarked on Marxism's universal platform transformed into a more nuanced approach that explained the lack of circulation of Marxism among Arabs. This was the Comintern's postmodern twist. Instead of searching for the social and economic conditions that might support the circulation of Marxism, the Comintern turned to identity politics. The eastern European Jewish leadership was blamed for its lack of understanding of the "Arab Street," for its strong affiliation with Zionist immigration, and moreover, for being educated in Marxism before the October Revolution, when anarchists played a central role in the communist movement. The Comintern argued that such "anarchists," who led the PCP, believed that world revolution should occur in other countries and, therefore, accused them of aligning with Leon Trotsky in his struggle against the secretary of the Soviet Communist Party, Joseph Stalin.

As the first graduates of the University of the Oriental Workers started returning to the Middle East, the Comintern slowly promoted them to the party's leadership at the expense of the "Trotskyite" Jews. The return of the graduates from Moscow and the manifold insinuations of dissatisfaction from the current leadership were insufficient to convince the eastern European Jews to step down. The Arab riots of 1929 supplied the Executive Committee of the Comintern the pretext for a complete, radical transformation of the leadership, shifting it into the hands of native Arabs and Jews.

On Friday, August 23, 1929, a tension of months, involving the rights of Jewish worship at the Western Wall, came to a cataclysmic eruption. Incited by preachers, who claimed that Jews were conspiring to take over the Temple Mount, an Arab mob, mostly peasants from the villages around Jerusalem, stormed the Jewish communities of Jerusalem and Hebron, massacring dozens, wounding hundreds, and expelling the entire Jewish community of Hebron from the city. The riots repelled the Jewish leadership of the PCP, who judged that reactionary nationalist elements of the Palestinian leadership had incited the mob. Joseph Berger-Barzilay closely observed the riots from his home in Jerusalem and was responsible for the party's interpretation of the events. At the end of August 1929, the party published a pamphlet in Hebrew and Arabic that called to "avoid making the Western Wall a wall of hatred between the two peoples."[14] A month later, the party published a short essay which described the riots as resulting from the rise of the reactionary forces among the Arabs, who used "false religious slogans and disinformation" in accusing the Jews of planning to attack Muslim holy sites. Instead of condemning the rioting peasants, the PCP stressed that they were victims of a false consciousness, offering to prevent such events in the future by applying labor laws and creating an agrarian revolution.[15]

The Executive Committee of the Comintern was outraged. For the Comintern, the riots were not "an anti-Jewish pogrom" but an "anti-imperialist rapture" that could shake the British Empire's hold and enable the world communist movement to break through and take hold among the Arab workers and peasants. The misinterpretation of the riots confirmed the Comintern's suspicions that the PCP's failure among the Arabs was generated by the cultural alienation of its leadership, which preferred to uphold universal values at the expense of local interests. In October 1929, in a crucial meeting of the Oriental Department, the PCP was described as completely detached from the political reality in the Middle East. The meeting's minutes include the statement that "whoever does not understand that thousand of Arab peasants and Bedouins rebelled against imperialism is an opportunist and gone astray from the communist movement." The Oriental Department unequivocally demanded the Arabization of the party's leadership.[16]

In November 1929, the Executive Committee of the Comintern adopted the report of the Oriental Department and issued a formal report, insinuating that anyone who claimed that Jewish workers, rather than Arab peasants, constituted the revolutionary focal point was a Trotskyite. "Whoever thinks this way," the report admonished, "is not reflecting the idea about the eternal revolution, but in the concrete conditions of Palestine, is actually calling for the establishment of a dictatorship of minority of Jewish workers on the Arab population." The report also criticized the PCP's failure to recruit Arab members as resulting from "the unenthusiastic efforts of the Jewish leadership to give way to Arabs in the leadership." In order to be ready to cope with similar anti-imperialist raptures in the Middle East, the report concluded that the Comintern should establish a federation of the parties in the region—a federation that could be effective only if the PCP and the Syrian-Lebanese parties would turn completely Arab.[17]

The Comintern reacted promptly and explicitly requested a shift in the party's leadership to Arab hands. The leading candidates for leadership were Ṣidqī Najātī and Mahmūd al-Mughrabī, who returned from the University of the Oriental Workers in Moscow and whose training could liberate the Arabs from the ideological, linguistic, and organizational dependence on eastern European Jews. The Comintern called on the Jewish members to understand that their role in Palestine was "to assist Arab Communists and not to educate or to lead them."[18]

Applying the Arabization, however, turned difficult. A lack of substantial numbers of Arabs, and unenthusiastic Jews who refused to follow the orders, sabotaged the whole process. A year later, the leadership of the party was still in the hands of eastern European Jews, and in October 1930, the Comintern, in an act of despair and distrust, sent a letter over the PCP leadership's heads, directly to all members of the PCP, calling for members to pressure the leadership and to allow the party to function under a non-European leadership.[19]

When it became clear that members of the party were not willing to assist the new Arab leaders al-Mughrabī and Najātī, the Comintern tried to institutionalize the Arabization and in December 1930 organized the seventh party convention, which was called the Arabization Convention. The convention's resolutions mentioned that the purpose of the Arabization was "to form a party that in its content and form is international, that has the ability to penetrate to the Arab masses, to lead them to national independence." This new Communist party would be "the axis of a federation of Arab Communist parties; a federation that will struggle for Republics of Peasants and Workers in the Arab countries." The resolution also condemned those who opposed the process and accused them of being in "explicit alliance with Trotskyism."[20] The convention, in an exceptional act, sent a letter to the party's students in the University of Oriental Workers in Moscow, stating its hopes that after they graduated with a Leninist-Marxist education, they would "lead the party in its struggle and . . . apply the resolutions of [the] convention to the Arabization of the party."[21]

The first students to return from Moscow were al-Mughrabī and Najātī. Before they could apply their newly acquired revolutionary skills to a coherent cultural transformation of the party, the British high commissioner deported them from the country. The second wave of graduates, including Raduan al-Hilū and two native Palestinian Jews, Simhah Tzabari and Meir Slonim, returned in 1931. Beginning in 1933, with the Comintern's assistance, this triumvirate took over the PCP and shifted its cultural direction. The Comintern's Executive Committee appointed a representative who scrutinized, on its behalf, the PCP's activity. The inspector, named Avigdor, wrote a report in 1934 in which he described the radical transformation that the triumvirate brought about. "The party," the inspector reported back to Moscow, "strengthened its hold in the villages among the peasants. . . . All these indications show that the party is on the right path to reversing the isolation from the Arab masses." For Avigdor, the process of Arabization faced many obstacles not only because the Jewish leadership was reluctant to give up its place or its Trotskyite inclinations. He named a major cultural flaw of Jewish leadership—the inclination of the Jews "to argue endlessly about questions that the Comintern had already resolved. The Talmudism of the semi-bourgeoisie Jews was well felt."[22]

Shortly after the removal of the Jewish leadership, Arab members of the new Central Committee expressed their national antagonism toward their Jewish members. In March 1935, Comrade Amin 'Arif sent a letter to the Comintern which concluded,

> All the people the Communist International sent to lead the PCP showed clear incompetence to lead the Arabs and were made rotten by Zionism. . . . Some of them said that the Arab masses have not reached yet to a sufficient cultural level that would allow them to receive and understand the Marxist revolutionary ideas. . . . At the same time, the Arab masses perceived the PCP as a Jewish party in which the Arab members were not more than just "tails."[23]

The displaced Jewish leadership resented the triumvirate's sense of ideological and cultural entitlement to leadership. Nahman List, a member in the Central Committee of the Syrian-Lebanese party, was also ejected when the party's leadership shifted to Syrians and Lebanese who returned from training in Moscow. List, many years afterward, testified,

> I did not like the national criteria that guided the division of positions in the party. After all, Russian Jews generated the glorified October Revolution. If some of them are still in the leadership of the Soviet Union, why then will Russian Jews in the Middle East be discriminated against? Is it possible that in a communist movement there will be two ranks of

comrades: on the one hand assistants, who according to their skills and revolutionary spirit should be leaders; and on the other hand, leaders, not by their merits, but only for their national origins?[24]

The PCP slowly but surely got closer to the Arab National Movement, until it supported and partially participated in the Arab revolt during 1936–39. The rise of fascism in Europe further intensified the polarizing process that separated Jewish and Arab Marxists. While Arab leaders of the Communist parties were slowly marginalized for not voicing clear and decisive arguments against Arab leaders who collaborated with Germany, Jewish Marxists returned to the leading positions in the communist movement, playing a central role in the antifascist movement. By 1943, the PCP divided into the Jewish Movement, called the Communist Party of Eretz-Israel, and an Arab party, called the League for National Liberation. The Jews emphasized the particular local identity of Marxists in Israel, and the Arabs strengthened their affinity to the Arab National Movement. Middle Eastern internationalism revived in 1949 when the two reunited under the Israeli Communist Party.

The ambition to create a "common proletariat culture" of cooperatives and unions united in an anti-imperialist struggle was a messianic vocation of eastern European Jewish Marxists in the Middle East. The discourse they used in their activities in the region embodied their belief that one can apply the values of internationalism in any country without taking into consideration local and cultural conditions. This universal vision, however, failed to recruit the local native population to the party's ranks. The forced process of Arabization indicated that even the Comintern recognized both the limits of the internationalist vision and the strength of local and cultural identities. Internationalism was not completely defeated, however. Instead, eastern European Jews in the Comintern installed local leaders, not all of whom were Arabs. Raduan al-Hilū was appointed as secretary; next to him were Simhah Tzabari and Meir Slonim, both Jewish natives of the country. The new party was based on local cultural forces that, according to the Comintern, provided a more secure basis for Jewish-Arab coexistence. The struggle within the party was therefore not a nationalist struggle between Jews and Arabs. Instead, the circulation of Marxism in the Middle East represented a fight between two forces: on the one hand, eastern European

Jews who claimed a universal application of Marxist values and, on the other hand, local Marxists who perceived the universal values as super-imposed European artifacts and upheld the belief in shaping Marxism from below according to particular cultural conditions. Thus, the history of Communism in the Middle East in many ways represents the history of the struggle for cultural hegemony. The contours of this struggle were marked by the various attempts of the Comintern, eastern European Jewish Communists, and Arab Communists to introduce, accommodate, and sometimes even reject an alienated culture.

NOTES

1. The documents of the Comintern related to Palestine were collected from the Comintern archives and published recently by Leon Zehavi in *Lehud o beyahad: Yehudim ve Aravim'al pi mismachi ha-Comintern* [*In Separation or Together: Jews and 'Arabs according to the Documents of the Comintern*] (Tel-Aviv, 2005), 21–22.

2. Ibid.

3. "Protocol of the Executive Committee of the Comintern 21.09.1920," in ibid., 26–30.

4. "A Resolution of Admission of the PCP as Section of the Comintern," in ibid., 42.

5. Joseph Berger Barzilay, *The Tragedy of the Soviet Revolution* (Hebrew) (Tel-Aviv, 1968), 15.

6. Shamālī later wrote one of the introductory books of Marxism in Arabic. See Fu'ād Shamālī, *al-Ishtirākīyah* (Beirut, 1936).

7. Avner Ben-Zaken, *Communism as Cultural Imperialism* (Hebrew) (Tel-Aviv, 2006), 76–80.

8. Nahman List, "The Comintern Was Right (7)," *Keshet*, 1968, 128.

9. "A Letter to the Executive Committee of the Comintern, November 1924," in Zehavi, *Lehud o beyahad*, 57.

10. Nahman List, "The Circulation of Communism in the Arab Lands" (Hebrew), *Mulad* 4 (1979): 302.

11. According to the testimony of Berger-Barzily, Hagana Archive, Department 80, file 238.

12. National Library, Department of Manuscripts and Letters, Archival Material, 1272v/1923 file 1.

13. See Bulus Farah, *From an Ottoman to a Jewish State* (Arabic) (Nazerth, 1985), 35–46.

14. National Library, Department of Manuscripts and Archives, PCP, v1272/1929, file 7, document 196.

15. "Workers Unite: A Bloody War in Palestine," in Zehavi, *Lehud o beyahad*, 180.

16. The protocol was published as "Proposals of the Oriental Department to the Executive Committee of the Comintern," in Zehavi, *Lehud o beyahad*, 189–194.

17. "A Decision of the Executive Committee Regarding the Revolt in Arabistan," in Zehavi, *Lehud o beyahad*, 198.

18. Nahman List, "The Comintern Was Right (5)," *Keshet* 3 (1965): 89.

19. "A Letter to the PCP, from the Executive Committee of the Comintern, 23rd October 1930," in Zehavi, *Lehud o beyahad*, 238.

20. Zehavi, *Lehud o beyahad*, 254–255.

21. Ibid., 276.

22. "A Letter Report from 'Avigdor' to the Executive Committee of the Comintern," in Zehavi, *Lehud o beyahad*, 307, 310–313.

23. "A Letter of Comrade 'Arif,'" in Zehavi, *Lehud o beyahad*, 343.

24. List, "The Comintern Was Right," 91.

9

The Struggle over Yiddish in Postimmigrant America

ERIC L. GOLDSTEIN

In 1930, the first convention of the recently formed *Yidishe kultur-gezelshaft* (Yiddish Cultural Society) in New York provided the Yiddish journalist Bentsien Goldberg—the son-in-law of Sholem Aleichem—an opportunity to reflect on the differences between Yiddish culture in the United States and in eastern Europe. As Yiddish-speaking intellectuals discussed the future agenda of the society, which aimed to promote the growth of schools, publishing houses, periodicals, and other forms of Yiddish cultural activity in the United States, Goldberg mused that such an effort would not have even been plausible on the other side of the ocean. "In Vilna," he wrote, referring to one of the largest centers of Yiddish cultural efflorescence in the old country, "such a society would not *have* to sit down and think about what to do. There [all these activities] would have been a [natural] part of life. Here, however, the entire Yiddish culture movement . . . is [nothing but] a supplement to life, and it is not always easy to find a place for a supplement."[1]

As true as Goldberg's unfavorable assessment of Yiddish culture in America may have been in 1930, this had not always been the case. Just three decades earlier, Yiddish cultural institutions in the United States were growing at a rapid pace and were capturing the imagination of a growing audience. In fact, during the late nineteenth and early twentieth centuries, Yiddish newspapers, journals, and theaters blossomed in America, while they remained stymied in much of eastern Europe, where government censorship and the conservative tone of Jewish society combined to prevent the growth of a mass culture in the people's tongue. Even after the lifting of the Russian ban against press and theater in Yiddish in years between 1903 and 1905, the institutions of

Yiddish mass culture in the United States continued to enjoy an edge over their eastern European counterparts, which often modeled themselves on American enterprises.

As time went on, however, this trend began to reverse itself, with a growing eastern European market for Yiddish eventually eclipsing a declining American consumer base. The collapse of the Russian and Austrian empires during World War I and the emergence of several successor states that recognized Jews as a national minority group gave to Yiddish an officially recognized and government-supported status in many parts of eastern Europe. True, during the interwar period there was a degree of cultural assimilation among eastern European Jews, who began using Polish and other local languages to a greater extent than before. Yet regardless of such pressures, Yiddish clearly retained its position as the dominant language of Jewish life and institutions among eastern European Jews in the decades before the Holocaust.[2]

Meanwhile, with the cutting off of immigration to the United States and the continual acculturation of Jewish immigrants and their children to an English-speaking milieu, Yiddish institutions in America quickly became only a pale reflection of their former selves. Because there was almost no question as to whether English would become the dominant cultural factor in the lives of American Jews, there was virtually no serious intellectual or political wrangling over Yiddish at all. To the extent that one can speak of a struggle over Yiddish in America during the 1920s and 1930s, it was a much more emotional and personal struggle over what it meant to live in a world where Jews were quickly losing their distinctive linguistic identity.

American Jewish historians have often described the Jews of the 1920s and 1930s as a generation able to successfully reconcile their desire for Americanization with their strong commitment to group solidarity. According to Deborah Dash Moore, a leading scholar of this period, the markers of this successful "second-generation ethnic synthesis" included an emphasis on education, the construction of modern places of worship, the emergence of an Americanized Jewish politics, and perhaps most importantly, the growth of strong ethnic neighborhoods that simultaneously bound Jews together and proclaimed their desire to emulate American middle-class norms.[3] Viewed through the lens of Yiddish culture, however, the period emerges in quite a different light, reminding us that the 1920s and 1930s were not a period in which it was very easy for American ethnics to live in a hyphenated world. By casting attention on a cherished aspect of Jewish life that grew increasingly difficult to square with American identity during the 1920s and 1930s, this chapter demonstrates how American Jews of the period sometimes found themselves torn between conflicting imperatives, suffering a great sense of cultural loss even as they shed the unwanted encumbrances of their immigrant past.

During the late 1920s and early 1930s, Jewish and non-Jewish newspapers and journals in America were abuzz with discussions of the "fate" of Yiddish culture in the United States. Exposés appeared in periodicals as wide ranging as the *Nation*, the *American Mercury*, the *Menorah Journal*, and the *Yidishe Gazetn* on whether Yiddish had any future in the United States.[4] Writers debated the circulation figures of the daily Yiddish press and calculated how many Yiddish books were being checked out of the public libraries. While commentators differed somewhat on how healthy Yiddish cultural institutions remained and how long they might continue to flourish, the general consensus was that Yiddish was experiencing a downward trend. "Yiddish is dying," argued a writer for the *Nation*. "In twenty years there will be no readers for its great metropolitan dailies, no audience for its numerous and now crowded theaters; and its contemporary literature—already readerless, and printed by the authors for mutual presentation—will be a closed set, a completed classic, like the four-and-twenty books of the Old Testament."[5]

Predictions of the death of Yiddish in America were not a totally new phenomenon in the 1920s. Harvard's professor of Slavic languages and literatures, Leo Wiener, had argued that the disappearance of Yiddish print culture was close at hand as early as 1899, the year he published his landmark *History of Yiddish Literature in the Nineteenth Century*. "The younger generation never looks inside a paper now," he wrote, "and the next . . . generation will no longer speak the dialect, unless something unforeseen happens."[6] Of course, Wiener did not anticipate the pogroms of 1903 and 1905 and the further waves of immigration that carried another million and a half eastern European Jews to the United States before the outbreak of World War I, roughly three times as many as had immigrated in the years between 1881 and the publication of his book.[7]

Occasional mention of Yiddish's fate in the United States was made over the next two decades, but not until the 1920s did the question emerge as a significant one on the American Jewish scene. With the lull in new arrivals during World War I and the eventual closing of the gates to unrestricted immigration in 1924, it seemed beyond doubt that the disappearance of Yiddish culture was imminent. Not only were an increasing number of Jews American born and English speaking, but the demand among native-born white Protestants for a culture of "100% Americanism" hastened the move among Jews toward a thoroughgoing linguistic acculturation. To the extent that Americanizing Jews continued to celebrate the linguistic aspect of their heritage, most looked increasingly to Hebrew and not Yiddish. Although a network of Yiddish schools existed in the United States well into the twentieth century, by 1929 the education of young American Jews was overwhelmingly focused on Hebrew as the language of Jewish identity and culture. A study of that year revealed that 110,000 students were enrolled in Hebrew weekday schools, while only 7,500 attended similar Yiddish institutions.[8] "We cannot pride ourselves," wrote Yiddish educator Leibush Lehrer in 1932, "on the fact that we have made great progress in the last twenty years. There were too many obstacles to be overcome, not the least of which was, and is, the traditional negative attitude toward Yiddish."[9]

In the public schools, Hebrew also won out over Yiddish. In 1930, at the request of several Jewish educators affiliated with Columbia University Teachers College and the Jewish Theological Seminary's Teachers Institute, the New York City school board allowed Hebrew instruction in two of its high schools on an experimental basis, and the following year approved it as an elective subject citywide. A request the same year from the *Yidishe kultur-gezelshaft* to introduce Yiddish instruction in public schools was turned down, due in no small part to the lack of support among New York Jews.[10] These trends reflected not only the growing centrality of Zionism to American Jewish identity but also Hebrew's greater recognition among non-Jews as a language of universal moral and cultural significance. Given both the push toward English and the growing cultural cachet of Hebrew, wrote the editor of a leading Anglo-Jewish weekly, "Yiddish has no chance."[11]

The concrete indicators of Yiddish's declining fortunes were visible even to the casual observer. Beginning in 1921, plummeting book sales heralded what commentators termed a "crisis in the Yiddish book market," which swept away almost all of the dozen or so literary publishing houses that had blossomed during the war years.[12] As a list of new Yiddish books published between 1927 and 1931 indicates, many of the leading American Yiddish authors were now forced to turn to publishers in Warsaw and Vilna to issue their works.[13] The declining interest in Yiddish books was also felt by public libraries in the largest urban centers. These institutions had long stocked large inventories of Yiddish books for their enthusiastic audience of immigrant readers, but they now registered a sharp decline in Yiddish book circulation.[14] The Yiddish press fared better than the book market, but there, too, appeared statistical evidence that circulations were falling. In 1928, the *Yidishes Tageblat* (Jewish Daily News), the oldest Yiddish daily not only in New York but in the world, went out of business, and its assets were sold to the owners of one of its competitors, the *Morgen Zhurnal* (Jewish Morning Journal). The following year, the circulation figures for the surviving daily papers began to decline, first by a few thousand each year and after 1931 by the tens of thousands.[15]

Yiddish publishers, trying to ensure their own survival, adapted as best they could to the new realities of American Jewish culture. The Hebrew Publishing Company, which had been the largest and most profitable Yiddish publishing house in the United States and one of the few to survive what was called the crisis of the Yiddish book, began to add English-language works—mostly books on Jewish holidays, Bible stories, and legendary heroes for younger readers—to its offerings beginning in the late 1920s.[16] Newspapers, too, increasingly embraced the trend toward English. English pages had been a familiar feature of the Yiddish press since the *Yidishes Tageblat* first experimented with this genre in 1897. By the 1920s, however, English pages took on greater importance, becoming an indispensable feature of almost every major Yiddish daily. *Der Tog* (The Day), for example, now began to run English editorials on the front page, and the *Forverts* (Jewish Daily Forward), which began an English supplement in 1923, doubled the number of English pages in 1926 from two to four.[17] Critic Alter Brody predicted that soon English papers would be publishing "a Yiddish Page for the Old, occupying the supplementary position at present held by an English Page for the Young."[18]

Contrary to Brody's prediction, however, there was a conspicuous lack of interest in the English pages, not because readers were uninterested in English but because most readers of the Yiddish press had already moved beyond the need for a specially designed English page and were able to read full-fledged English publications on their own. Survey research conducted on the Yiddish press in 1923 by Jewish educator Mordecai Soltes revealed that 66 percent of Yiddish newspaper readers also regularly read the English newspapers.[19] This trend was apparently broadening quickly, since a few years later, the Yiddish writer Joseph Opatoshu estimated that 90 percent of the readers of the Yiddish press knew English.[20] Thus, by the mid-1920s, the Yiddish press, like Yiddish culture in general, had retreated significantly from its earlier, more all-embracing role in the lives of Jewish immigrants. Instead, Yiddish had become a supplement to American Jews' growing participation in English-language media.

Given the fact that the increasing shift from Yiddish to English affected a diverse group—old and young, newer immigrants and those who had been in America for decades—it inspired a range of responses from eastern European Jewish immigrants and their children. Those with the most to lose from the decline of Yiddish were the Yiddish writers, journalists, and cultural activists themselves. Some of these figures responded by simply avoiding the question as long as they could. "Why worry about the future?" asked an unnamed Yiddish poet when being interviewed for the *Nation* in an East Side café. "Is not Yiddish here today?"[21] The most ideological among the Yiddish-speaking intellectuals, however, felt the need to mobilize and began around 1928 to hoist the banner of Yiddishism, the romantic nationalist language movement that had first crystallized two decades earlier in eastern Europe. To address what they saw as the dire situation of Yiddish in America, they founded the *Yidishe kultur-gezelshaft*, mentioned earlier, which embarked on a vigorous public campaign to promote Yiddish culture of all kinds. The society, which aimed to "oppose the assimilatory tendencies in Jewish society," imposed a strict discipline on its members, who had to pledge to speak Yiddish in their homes and in Jewish circles, to educate their children in the language, and to buy several Yiddish books each year.[22]

The Yiddishists who founded the *kultur-gezelshaft* drew much of their inspiration from the philosophies of Khaim Zhitlovsky, a writer and language activist who had lived on and off in both eastern Europe and America and in 1908 had been one of the conveners of the Yiddish Language Conference in Czernowitz, Bukovina (today Chernivtsi, Ukraine), where Yiddish was declared to be a national language of the Jewish people.[23] Zhitlovsky envisioned Yiddish as a language that could give Jews access to all the treasures of modern secular culture but allow them to remain distinct from the peoples among whom they lived. Despite some rather long stints in the United States, Zhitlovski never came to terms with the attraction most Yiddish-speaking Jews here felt for English-language American culture. As late as 1925, he implored American Jews to be less like the Jews of France, who saw French as the "language of their hearts," and more like the Jews of Poland, many of whom spoke the language of the land only for business reasons.[24]

Zhitlovsky also reviled the tendency of American Yiddish speakers to incorporate Anglicisms into their Yiddish. He denounced this "wild-growing Yiddish-English jargon" as "potato-chicken-kitchen language," which he contrasted to "the cultivated language of Yiddish culture all over the world."[25] Following Zhitlovsky's lead, many of the activists of the *kultur-gezelshaft* went to what many American Jews considered ridiculous lengths to banish English words from their speech. In 1934, reporter George Wolfe attended a meeting of the society and was struck at how several speakers, despite their ideological devotion to the "purity" of Yiddish, could not keep themselves from using Anglicisms in their speeches, a habit for which they were sometimes booed by the audience. The well-regarded poet B. J. Bialistotsky, for example, announced to the crowd that the society had succeeded in organizing many *brentshes* (branches), only to apologize and quickly explain that he had, of course, meant *tsvaygn*.[26]

The humor with which such stories were told in the press indicates that the doctrinaire Yiddishists were very far in their attitudes from the bulk of Yiddish-speaking Jews in America, who used English words with relish and had little desire to seclude themselves from the larger cultural milieu. Even within the ranks of the Yiddishist movement, there were a few individuals—such as Bentsien Goldberg, quoted at the beginning of this chapter—who realized that the shift to English was inevitable and that Yiddishists could never hope to change the outlook of the Jewish masses on these shores. Goldberg, along with two other well-known members of the *kultur-gezelshaft*—Leibush Lehrer, who headed the Sholem Aleichem *folks-shules* (people's schools), and Shmuel Niger, the renowned literary critic—argued that the organization ought not to pursue the unrealistic goal of attracting a mass following but instead ought to concentrate on addressing the emotional and spiritual needs of the faithful few who found comfort and solace in Yiddish activism.[27]

If few American Jews imbibed the ideology of the Yiddishist movement, however, many did demonstrate significant ambivalence about the loss of their mother tongue, which had been the central vehicle for Jewish self-expression not only in the years before immigration but also in the transitional years of immigrant adaptation. While the social pressures and anti-Semitism of the 1920s and 1930s resulted in a high degree of cultural conformity among American Jews, it also produced a heightened consciousness of the costs of assimilation. As a result, Jews of the period often demonstrated a dualistic, contradictory approach to the issue of Yiddish.

On the one hand, Jews of the period often came to see Yiddish as a mark of foreignness. Memoirs of second-generation Jews abound with recollections of "pained embarrassment" over their parents' accented English and their own occasional tendency to use a Yiddish term or intonation in mixed company. "A 'refined,' 'correct,' 'nice' English was required of us at school," recalled writer Alfred Kazin, an English "that we did not naturally speak and one that our teachers could never be quite sure that we would keep." This English, Kazin explained, was "the language of advancement" and "every future young lawyer was known by it. . . . We were expected to show it off like a new pair of shoes."[28] Despite such pressures, most young Jews greeted the transition to English enthusiastically, viewing mastery of the language as a ticket to success and inclusion.

The push toward English and away from Yiddish also found reinforcement at home. "The pull of the environment toward English," explained Uriah Zevi Engelman, "is in most cases strengthened rather than weakened by the parents, who remember their own halting English as a handicap which they are anxious that their children escape. The importance of flawlessly correct English, in grammar and accent, is sometimes almost obsessively insisted on by Jewish parents," who "strive to speak English with their children with as few Yiddishisms as possible."[29] As Kazin's memoir suggests, the linguistic issue was closely tied to the attainment of financial success, an issue that became particularly pressing amid the economic depression and the employment discrimination that was rampant in the late 1920s and early 1930s. Even Yiddish cultural figures such as Abraham Cahan, the veteran editor of the daily *Forverts,* warned during these years that "young college-educated men and women are being disqualified as teachers because they speak and conduct themselves like 'foreigners.'" Given such trends, Cahan spoke of the "absolute necessity" of bringing up Jewish children with "thoroughly American pronunciation, intonation and gestures."[30]

Despite widespread agreement that Yiddish needed to be downplayed and English emphasized, however, the loss of Yiddish as a cultural system resulted in emotional misgivings on the part of many Jews, including those of the American-born second generation. Yiddishist activism may have meant little to them, but Shmuel Niger's assertion that the death of Yiddish would leave Jews "without a language for their Jewish thoughts and emotions" seems to have struck a responsive chord.[31] Evidence of such feelings may be found in the growing assertion among English-speaking Jews during these years that Yiddish was a particularly expressive language and that certain Jewish concepts and feelings could not be conveyed as effectively or powerfully in English. According to several contemporary sources, even as American Jews were trying to banish Yiddish words and phrases from their English vocabulary, there was a simultaneous effort to cast this hybrid pattern of speech as a "picturesque and useful" dialect known variably as "Yinglish," "Judeo-English," and "Yiddish-Americanese."[32] In 1926, for example, Leo Robbins, a writer for the English section of the *Forverts,* argued for the utility of such Yiddish words as *nebakh, schlemiel, kibitser, shnorer,* and *khutspe* for English-speaking Jews, describing them as capable of expressing ideas and sentiments that "have no parallel in the English language." To bolster his case, Robbins argued that even non-Jewish cultural figures such as *American Mercury* editor H. L. Mencken and journalist Heywood Broun had recognized the expressiveness of such words and had mentioned them in their columns and books.[33]

The attractiveness of "Yinglish" as a cultural phenomenon was confirmed by the appearance in the late 1920s of Milt Gross's popular Yiddish dialect stories—*Nize Baby* (1926), *Hiawatta, Wit no Odder Poems* (1926), and *Dunt Esk!!* (1927)—and in 1930 of Abe Gross's *Kibitzer's Dictionary*, an English-Yiddish glossary that initiated a genre later exploited successfully by Leo Rosten (*The Joys of Yiddish*) and in audio form by Sam Levenson (*Basic Yiddish*).[34] The success of all these works depended on the widespread agreement of cultural consumers with the argument Robbins made in 1926—that Yiddish words and phrasings (Milt Gross, for example, did not use Yiddish words as much as Yiddish pronunciation and word order) contained a richness and offered a directness of expression that could not be communicated in standard English. Significantly, however, these claims were always made in a rather nonaggressive way, conveyed through the use of a self-deprecating humor that preempted nativist fears of non-English languages and cultures by making them seem quaint and harmless. By reinventing Yiddish as a "funny language," Jewish writers and artists hoped to soothe their own sense of emotional loss without inviting the opprobrium of those who would demonize them as foreigners.[35]

Ambivalence about whether Yiddish embodied a Jewish expressiveness that could not be translated into English was also visible in the efforts to create a new Jewish literary culture aimed at native-born American Jews. The late 1920s and early 1930s saw a swirl of activity to promote a Jewish culture of reading in English, including the establishment of book review departments in most of the leading Anglo-Jewish journals, the launching of National Jewish Book Week, and the founding of a Jewish Book of the Month Club.[36] While much of this activism was aimed at encouraging the production of original Jewish literary works in English, there was also significant effort devoted to issuing English translations of the works of prominent Yiddish authors. Both efforts were intended not only to serve as the basis for the growth of an indigenous Jewish culture but also to demonstrate to a non-Jewish reading public the cultural sophistication and contributions of Jews. Attempts to issue Yiddish works in English, however, raised persistent questions about the extent to which something essential in this literature might be lost in translation.

Part of this dilemma stemmed from the great selectivity with which Yiddish works were chosen for translation into English. Works of classic authors such as Sholem Aleichem and Sholem Yankev Abramovitsh

(Mendele Moykher Sforim), which had a strong emotional appeal for Jewish readers, were largely left untranslated during this period because they evoked the folksy world of the shtetl, from which American Jews were trying hard to disassociate themselves. By contrast, the authors who were translated with the greatest success—figures such as Sholem Asch, David Pinski, Solomon Bloomgarden (know as Yehoash), Leon Kobrin, and Peretz Hirschbein—relied on realism, naturalism, and in some cases eroticism to engage with universal themes and questions that might be appreciated beyond the Jewish sphere.

It was this universal quality that promoters of translated works emphasized in arguing for their value in the American literary market. Alfred Kazin, the same writer who was pushed by his teachers to rid himself of Yiddish intonation as a child, wrote of Yiddish literature in a 1936 *New York Times* review as a "rich contemporary regional fiction" which "deserves to be better known in English." It was, according to Kazin, "perhaps the only regional fiction ever written with so many cosmopolitan insights."[37] In 1923, another writer, Lewis Browne, similarly cast Yiddish writers as worldly and cosmopolitan. "There is a universal note in much of their work, a note struck so truly in the heart of the Jews that it finds echo in the heart of the world," he argued. "Asch's *America, Uncle Moses* and *Mottke the Vagabond*, Pinski's *Temptation*, and Kobrin's *Lithuanian Village*—to mention only certain of the classics already translated from Yiddish to English—belong with those precious writings that reveal through men the soul of man and discover in a hamlet the spirit of the wide earth."[38] Sholem Asch, perhaps the most famous of the group, was hailed by *New York Times* reviewer Louis Kronenberger in 1933 as "a great deal more than the finest of living Yiddish writers." Asch, he explained, was "a genuinely significant novelist for the whole world—a magnificent story teller, a vivid and large-scale historian, an able interpreter."[39]

Translated works such as these were successful because they filled the need of acculturating Jews to highlight the universal tendencies within Jewish culture and to demonstrate the artistic abilities of Yiddish (and therefore Jewish) writers to the non-Jewish world. At the same time, however, there were frequent suggestions that these translations failed to convey the perceived authenticity and "genius" of Yiddish culture that many Jews paradoxically felt compelled to emphasize as they moved increasingly into an English-language milieu. Very often, reviewers expressed this frustration by complaining that the translations were of poor quality. According to one reviewer, "the stark reality of Asch has evidently troubled the translators," whose renderings "could never be more at variance with the spirit of the original."[40] Another reviewer criticized the translation of Asch's *Uncle Moses* by Isaac Goldberg, stating that it was not "quite up to the high standard [Goldberg] has set for himself in his other numerous translations from other languages."[41] Such complaints seem strange in light of the fact that Goldberg, the most important translator of Yiddish works to English during this period, seems to have had the emphatic approval of the Yiddish authors themselves, many of whom knew English well. Since Kobrin, Bloomgarden, and Pinski all expressed complete confidence in his translations, we are left to conclude that these criticisms had more to do with a general anxiety about the limits of translation rather than with any actual deficiency in Goldberg's work.[42]

As all of these contradictory feelings and frustrations show, the increasing loss of Yiddish left a noticeable emotional gap for American Jews of the 1920s and 1930s, many of whom were the children of eastern European immigrants. Anxious for inclusion within American culture, they distanced themselves from the language of the immigrant generation. Yet as they entered the English-speaking world, nostalgia for what they imagined as the expressiveness of Yiddish only seemed to grow. Efforts to craft an English-Yiddish dialect and to develop a Yiddish literature in translation expressed a hope that in some way, Yiddish might be preserved in the new linguistic setting. After all, reasoned writer Alter Brody, "If the Jew . . . nationalized German, why can't he nationalize English?"[43] Brody's vision, however, proved utopian given the limitations of the era. In a climate hostile to cultural diversity, Jews were only able to hold on to Yiddish in piecemeal ways, either as a vehicle for ethnic humor or as a universalized literary genre that did little to soothe their craving for authenticity. As a result, American Jews would continue to struggle with the loss of Yiddish until the rise of a generation that had never known it.

NOTES

The research for this article was undertaken with the generous support of a Franklin Research Grant from the American Philosophical Society and a Dina Abramowicz Emerging Scholar Fellowship from the YIVO Institute for Jewish Research.

1. B. Z. Goldberg, "Far yidishe kultur," *Der Tog*, Mar. 31, 1930, 4.
2. For a discussion of linguistic assimilation and its limits among eastern European Jews of the interwar years, see Yankev Leshtshinski, "Di shprakhn bay yidn in umophengikn Poyln," *Yivo-bleter* 22 (1943): 147–62; Lucy Dawidowicz, *From That Time and Place: A Memoir, 1928–1947* (New York: Bantam Books, 1989), 106–7.
3. See Deborah Dash Moore, *At Home in America: Second Generation New York Jews* (New York: Columbia University Press, 1981).
4. Uriah Zevi Engelman, "The Fate of Yiddish in America," *Menorah Journal* 15 (July 1928): 22–32; Lewis Browne, "Is Yiddish Literature Dying?," *Nation*, May 2, 1923, 513–14; Alter Brody, "Yiddish: A Childless Language," *Nation*, June 9, 1926, 631–33; "A Moribund Language?," *American Hebrew*, June 18, 1926, 177, 196; I. Brill, "Can Yiddish Live?," *Yidishe Gazetn*, May 25, 1923, 16.
5. Brody, "Yiddish," 631.
6. Leo Wiener, *The History of Yiddish Literature in the Nineteenth Century* (New York: Scribner, 1899), 229.
7. For statistics on Jewish immigration to the United States, see Jonathan D. Sarna, *The American Jewish Experience*, 2nd ed. (New York: Holmes and Meier, 1997), 360.
8. Alexander M. Dushkin, "Two Decades of Progress in Jewish Education—A Survey," *Jewish Education* 4 (Jan.–Mar. 1932): 5.
9. Leibush Lehrer, "The Yiddish Secular School," *Jewish Education* 4 (Apr.–June 1932): 104.
10. For a fuller discussion, see Moore, *At Home in America*, 110–15.
11. "A Moribund Language?," 177. See also Engelman, "The Fate of Yiddish," 32.
12. On the "crisis of the Yiddish book," see Moshe Shmuel Shklarsky, *Dos yidishe bukh in Amerike* (New York: privately published, 1924); Shklarsky, *Vegn yidishe bikher* (New York: privately published, 1928); Sh. Niger, "Der yidisher lezer in Amerike," *Tsukunft* 35 (Jan. 1930): 55–59.
13. Jennie Meyerowitz, "Yiddish Books from 1927–1931," *Library Journal* 56 (Dec. 15, 1931): 1041–47. Even books on American themes, such as Borukh Glassman's *Oyf di felder fun Dzshordzshya* (On the fields of Georgia; 1927), Joseph Opotashu's *Lintsheray* (Lynchings; 1927), and Isidore Kopeloff's *Amol in Amerike* (Yesterday in America; 1928), were published in Vilna and Warsaw. The focus of Yiddish publishing also shifted to eastern Europe during these years for economic reasons, as it was much cheaper to publish there. The rising costs of Yiddish publishing in the United States, however, were ultimately the result of the shrinking reading audience, and therefore a less profitable market, for Yiddish publications.

14. See Shklarsky, *Vegn yidishe bikher*, 17.

15. "Jewish Daily News Sold," *New York Times*, Apr. 30, 1928, 11; Nathan Goldberg, "Decline of the Yiddish Press," *Chicago Jewish Forum*, Fall 1944, 15–21; Goldberg, "Di yidishe prese in di fareynikte shtatn, 1900–1940," *Yivo-bleter* 18 (Nov.–Dec. 1941): 129–57 (see especially the chart following p. 136).

16. See *Catalogue of Publications* (New York: Hebrew Publishing Company, 1930); *Folshtendiger ferlags katalog* (New York: Hebrew Publishing Company, 1932–1933).

17. Mordecai Soltes, *The Yiddish Press: An Americanizing Agency* (New York: Teachers College, Columbia University, 1925), 178–79; *Forverts*, Apr. 4, 1926, 3; *Forverts*, Apr. 11, 1926, 3.

18. Brody, "Yiddish," 631.

19. Soltes, *The Yiddish Press*, 44.

20. "Y. Opatoshu vegn yidish un yidishe literatur in Amerike," *Literarishe bleter*, May 8, 1925, 2. In addition to the 66 percent of those who read in both languages, Soltes also identified an additional 20 percent of readers who had more limited English capability. It seems reasonable that these readers improved their English over the next few years and joined the ranks of those who could read both Yiddish and English papers. See Soltes, *The Yiddish Press*, 44.

21. Browne, "Is Yiddish Literature Dying?," 514.

22. *Vos vil di yidishe kultur-gezelshaft?* (New York: Farlag kultur-gezelshaft, 1930), in box 1, folder 3, Yiddish Culture Society Papers (RG 258), YIVO Institute for Jewish Research, Center for Jewish History, New York.

23. On Zhitlovsky's activity in the United States, see Sh. Elsberg, "Dr. Zshitlovskis tetikayt in Amerike," in *Zhitkovski-zamlbukh* (Varshe: Farlag Kh. Bzshoza, 1929), 172–89; and his speech to the first convention of the Yiddish Culture Society, box 1, folder 7, Yiddish Culture Society Papers. On Zhitlovsky more generally, see Emanuel Goldsmith, *Modern Yiddish Culture: The Story of the Yiddish Language Movement* (New York: Fordham University Press, 1997); David H. Weinberg, *Between Tradition and Modernity: Haim Zhitlowski, Simon Dubnow, Ahad Ha-Am, and the Shaping of Modern Jewish Identity* (New York: Holmes and Meier, 1996).

24. Khayim Zhitlovsky, "Di 'englishizirung' fun di yidishe masn," *Literarishe bleter*, May 28, 1926, 344–47.

25. Zhitlovsky, quoted in George Wolfe, "Notes on American Yiddish," *American Mercury* 29 (Aug. 1933): 478.

26. Ibid.

27. Goldberg, "Far yidishe kultur," 4. Similarly, some of the more doctrinaire Yiddishist intellectuals such as Zhitlovsky ultimately realized the counterproductive nature of their attacks on the use of Anglicisms by Yiddish-speaking American Jews. In 1928, Zhitlovsky expressed a more conciliatory attitude, describing the use of English words by Yiddish speakers as a natural phenomenon, but still maintained his objections to localisms in Yiddish because, in his words, the "struggle" toward vital "national and cultural objectives" required the forging of

a "common Yiddish language." See Gennady Estraikh, "Khayim Zhitlovsky on Localism in Yiddish," *Yiddish* 15 (2008): 74–78 (quotation on 78).

28. Quoted in Moore, *At Home in America*, 104–5.

29. Engelman, "The Fate of Yiddish," 24.

30. *Forverts*, Apr. 25, 1931, quoted in Isaiah Trunk, "The Cultural Dimension of the American Jewish Labor Movement," *YIVO Annual of Jewish Social Science* 16 (1976): 366.

31. Niger, quoted in Alter Brody, "Yiddish: Our Literary Domain," *Nation*, Apr. 20, 1927, 435.

32. Leo Robbins, "How Many Yiddish Words Do *You* Know?," *Forverts* [English section], May 16, 1926, C; H. B. Wells, "Notes on Yiddish," *American Speech* 4 (Oct. 1928): 66.

33. Robbins, "How Many Yiddish Words Do *You* Know?," C.

34. Milt Gross, *Nize Baby* (New York: George H. Doran, 1926); Gross, *Hiawatta, Wit no Odder Poems* (New York: George H. Doran, 1926); Gross, *Dunt Esk!!* (New York: George H. Doran, 1927); Abe Gross, *Kibitzer's Dictionary* (New York: Melvita, 1930); Leo Rosten, *The Joys of Yiddish: A Relaxed Lexicon of Yiddish, Hebrew and Yinglish Words Often Encountered in English* (New York: McGraw-Hill, 1968); Sam Levenson, *Basic Yiddish*, sound recording (New York: Apollo, [194?]). Milt Gross's books have been republished in *Is Diss a System? A Milt Gross Comic Reader*, ed. Ari Y. Kelman (New York: NYU Press, 2010), which includes an excellent introduction by Kelman. For period press reviews of these works, see *New York Times Book Review*, Apr. 11, 1926, 7; Jan. 16, 1927, BR7; and Nov. 27, 1927, BR8.

35. On the link between Yiddish and humor, see Esther Romeyn and Jack Kugelmass, "Yiddish as a Funny Language: Talking Jewish," in *Let There Be Laughter! Jewish Humor in America* (Chicago: Spertus Museum, 1997), 78–80.

36. Jewish Book Week, which later paved the way for the founding of the Jewish Book Council, was the brainchild of Boston librarian Fanny Goldstein. See Margaret Kanof Norden, "Necrology: Fanny Goldstein (1888–1961)," *American Jewish Historical Quarterly* 52 (Sept. 1962): 69–73. See also the literature on the Jewish Book of the Month Club in box 4, folder 38, Yiddish Culture Society Papers.

37. Alfred Kazin, "A Yiddish Novel," *New York Times Book Review*, Aug. 16, 1936, 22, 24.

38. Browne, "Is Yiddish Literature Dying?," 514.

39. Louis Kronenberger, "Sholom Asch's Great Trilogy," *New York Times Book Review*, Oct. 22, 1933, 1.

40. Johan J. Smertenko, "Sholom Asch," *Nation*, Feb. 14, 1923, 181–82.

41. *New York Times Book Review and Magazine*, Feb. 20, 1921, 24.

42. All indications given in the correspondence between Goldberg and Bloomgarden, Kobrin, and Pinski are that these three authors thought highly of Goldberg's translations. They made few corrections to his work, and they

compared him favorably to other translators, with whom they were dissatisfied. See Kobrin to Goldberg, July 9, 1919; Bloomgarden to Goldberg, May 9, 1920; and Pinski to Goldberg, Feb. 13, 1919, all in the Isaac Goldberg Papers, manuscript collection 1167, Manuscripts and Archives Division, New York Public Library.

43. Brody to Isaac Goldberg, Jan. 4, [1927?], in ibid.

10

When the Local Trumps the Global

The Jewish World of São Paulo, Brazil, 1924–1940

JEFFREY LESSER

I am not sure if 1929 was a particularly significant year for Jews in Brazil. 1930—perhaps? That year a *golpe de estado* brought Getúlio Vargas to power, eventually leading to a protofascist dictatorship that had a profound impact on both Jewish immigration and images of Jews, both positive and negative. 1934 was also an important year for Jewish-Brazilians—Brazil instituted a quota system modeled along the U.S. National Origins Act of the previous decade. 1938 might also seem a year of great import—Brazil began an official ethnic homogenization campaign. And in 1942 Brazil joined the Allies and repressed Yiddish and Zionism as part of its oddly democratic turn.

So why 1929? Perhaps we might use that year as the final one in a decade when Ashkenazi Jewish leaders had built enough institutions that they were able to set the parameters for an intraethnic debate that was to have a profound impact on Brazilian Jewry during the World War II era. While the two poles represented in the conflict are expected, central European versus eastern European, Brazil provides a counterpoint to many other American republics where the status quo was set primarily by German Jews. In Brazil, however, the eastern European Jews who had arrived first made issues such as the Yiddish language and Zionism part of a "community standard" that seemed foreign to many central European Jews.

Between 1920 and 1950, Brazil had one of the most rapidly developing economies in the Southern Hemisphere. Into this setting came a large population of immigrants, some fleeing persecution but most hoping to find economic and social mobility in Brazil's expanding industrialization process. Jewish-Brazilians from a variety of backgrounds created what today is the second-largest collectivity of Jews in Latin America but with a markedly different pattern of development than the large Jewish populations in the United States, Argentina, or Canada.[1] Jewish-Brazilian communal life thus provides insights into the processes of immigration and ethnic identification as a national, rather than diasporic, phenomenon.[2]

With World War I and its aftermath, Brazil became an important haven for people leaving economically and politically devastated Europe. Between 1914 and 1923, more than 500,000 people made the voyage to Brazil, the majority coming from Portugal, Spain, Italy, and Germany.[3] For many, North, not South, America was the preferred destination, and the United States received more than five million newcomers between 1914 and 1924.[4] Restrictive legislation, however, culminating in the 1924 National Origins Act, effectively ended non-northern-European movement to U.S. shores.[5] Furthermore, Argentina also began to restrict Jewish immigration in the second half of the 1920s.[6] Not surprisingly, immigration to Brazil jumped by 50 percent, to 737,000, in the ten-year period after 1924.[7] Among those groups migrating in significantly larger numbers were the Japanese (500 percent) and the Germans (200 percent).[8] Additionally, those fleeing dislocations caused by political and economic upheavals in eastern Europe, especially in Poland, Romania, and Lithuania, began journeying in substantial groups to Brazil. Combined immigration from those nations grew from 9,400 in the decade before 1924 to ten times that number in the decade after.[9]

Jews made up a significant portion of the increased eastern European migration to Brazil in the years after World War I, and it was during this period that the first national Jewish-Brazilian communal organizations were formed.[10] Although religion was not a category in the Brazilian census of 1920, the international organizations that acted as sponsoring groups for most Jewish immigrants did keep track of the numbers.[11] The Hebrew Sheltering and Immigrant Aid Society (HIAS), for example, reported that 22,894 Jews migrated to Brazil between 1925 and 1930, and demographers U. O. Schmelz and Sergio DellaPergola note that "the period of most intensive migration to Brazil was in the late 1920s."[12] The *American Jewish Year Book* reported that the Jewish population of

Brazil jumped from 6,000 in 1920 to 30,000 in 1930.[13] Jews, then, appear to have constituted approximately 25 percent of the eastern European migrants to Brazil after 1924. Subject to many of the same economic and political factors encouraging general eastern European emigration, Jewish relief organizations began seeing Brazil as a viable option for relocation because of its open-door policies and opportunity for occupational and social ascension.[14] An increase in popular anti-Jewish movements in eastern Europe and the closure of U.S. and Argentinean gates further served to encourage Jewish migration to what had been previously believed an unpromising destination.[15]

Jewish-Brazilian life in 1929 had only modest internal conflict. Rapid economic ascent left many of the eastern-Europe-based Jewish political groups, especially on the left, with marginalized institutional significance. In São Paulo, anti-Semitism was minimal (indeed, virtually nonexistent) when compared to the European situation prior to immigration.[16] Furthermore, wide opportunities for economic and social advancement left most Jews with few reasons for discord. Most important for our discussion, Brazil had not experienced a nineteenth-century German-Jewish immigration such as had occurred in the United States and Argentina. Thus, it was not until the entrance of central European, mainly German, Jewish refugees in the mid-1930s that a struggle began for leadership of the Jewish-Brazilian community. This conflict was fought on the ground of myths transferred from the European milieu and transmuted within the Brazilian setting.[17] Nowhere was this clash more vibrant than in São Paulo, Brazil's largest city and the one with the most immigrants (including Jews).[18]

By the end of the decade that began with 1929, two very different groups of Ashkenazi Jews populated São Paulo. The pre-1935 migration was of religiously traditional, mainly working-class origin, encouraged by international organizations to seek better economic and social opportunities outside eastern Europe. German refugees, on the other hand, eventually constituting about 25 percent of the Ashkenazi population in São Paulo, tended to be more urbanized, more socially assimilated with non-Jewish populations, and of mainly professional and managerial class background. In addition, most German Jews were members of the Liberal (Reform) movement, which emphasized religion as less a matter of daily appearance than internal thought. As elsewhere, even matters of ritual practice constituted a point of difference among European Jews in Brazil.

It should not be unexpected that Ashkenazi Jewry, united in name but differing in most other regards, clashed upon encounter in Brazil. This certainly was the case throughout the Americas. Yet conflicts in São Paulo appear notably divisive, especially when compared with Porto Alegre and Rio de Janeiro, cities with virtually the same ratio of eastern European to German Jews. Simple transmission of former European enmity, then, does not adequately explain the lack of harmony within São Paulo's community. Rather, Brazilian national political events must be examined in conjunction with economic changes taking place in São Paulo in order to comprehend the factors that encouraged turbulence among Jews in the city.

As early as 1938, just three years after significant numbers of German Jews had begun to settle in São Paulo, the various sectors of the Jewish community began showing signs of tension, in part because the Germans had neither the desire nor the opportunity to enter Jewish communal organizations run by eastern Europeans. The Jewish Telegraphic Agency reported,

> [A refugee] relief committee, in which the so-called "East-European Jews" who have been residing in Brazil for many years are not given any representation, has stimulated antagonistic feeling within the Jewish community. In fact, it has split the Jewish community in Brazil into two separate camps, one representing the "Ost-Juden" who are the bulk of the population, and the other representing the newcomers from Germany.[19]

Thus, almost immediately upon arriving in São Paulo, the German-Jewish community formed an organization which would ostensibly represent the interests of the German refugee. It was the *Congregação Israelita Paulista* (CIP; Jewish Congregation of São Paulo), a religiously Liberal *einheitzgemeinde* (unified community), which acted to encourage social integration through the teaching of Portuguese and "especially [helped] provide for immigrants."[20]

Under the leadership of the stridently anti-Zionist Dr. Ludwig Lorch, the *Congregação Israelita Paulista* became the focal point of German-Jewish life in São Paulo.[21] It is clear German-Jewish leaders believed from the start that eastern European Jewish organizations could not, or would not, provide relief and support for new German refugees. The creation of the CIP, however, was taken by eastern Europeans as a challenge for community leadership. The establishment of the CIP thus provided a German-Jewish forum for expressing intragroup hostilities.

The gauntlet of challenge presented by the *Congregação Israelita Paulista* quickly divided Jews in São Paulo. The conflicts between the *Centro Hebreu Brasileiro* (Brazilian Jewish Center), a loose confederation of eastern European organizations, and the CIP diverted energy away from refugee relief, probably the most critical issue of the moment. In June 1939, Friedrich Borchardt and David Glick issued a report for the American Joint Distribution Committee (JDC) which expressed concern over the formation of CIP since "forming a religious congregation . . . conducted in a very beautiful manner by an ordained rabbi . . . may segregate the German Jewish group from the . . . East-European Jews," thus preventing the maximization of community efforts towards refugee relief.[22] Implied is that the "beautiful" services of the CIP would be viewed by many in the eastern European community as assimilationist and therefore anti-Jewish.

Members of many nonlocal Jewish organizations were by the late 1930s primarily concerned with the peaceful relocation of Jewish refugees. Having little time to oversee actual resettlement, they were not hesitant about showing dissatisfaction with local groups on whom this burden fell. Alfred Jaretzki, Jr., Chairman of the JDC's Subcommittee on Refugee Aid in Central and South America, wrote a pointed letter to Ludwig Lorch and Salo Wissman of the CIP expressing annoyance over national/religious divisions. "The Subcommittee . . . reiterated its opinion that a program of aid conducted and centered about a German Jewish religious body is disadvantageous from the point of view of Jewry in that it emphasizes differences between Jewish groups which, in their result, must inevitably lead to disharmony and defeat coordinated action."[23] Given the need to maximize donations for refugee support, communal unification was encouraged by the JDC.[24]

By 1940, Jews in São Paulo were witnessing an internal crisis. The policies of Getúlio Vargas's *Estado Novo* further exaggerated tensions with the antiforeigner *brasilidade* campaign. Legislation that restricted refugee immigration and limited economic opportunities for non-Brazilians was particularly divisive for São Paulo's Jews since German Jews usually entered Brazil financially dependent on international and local relief organizations, a problem compounded in 1938 when Brazilian legislation made it illegal for aliens without permanent resident status to find jobs.[25] Psychological and financial pressures were especially high for the many Jewish refugees who had entered Brazil with tourist or transit visas, often purchased from Paraguayan consulates in Europe.[26] Such visas gave the holder no employment rights and little guarantee of a permanent visa.[27] Regulations on tourist visas decreed that foreigners might enter Brazil only "if they can prove that they are able to return to the country whose national they are . . . and that they are in possession of means" to do so.[28] Refugee Jews with tourist visas were thus caught in a bind. In 1940, there were "2600 persons who are not permitted to remain in Brazil and who at the same time are unable to leave the country" to return to Nazi-occupied Europe.[29]

The need rapidly and efficiently to raise money for the relief of thousands of Jews with expired tourist visas brought out the divisions among São Paulo's Ashkenazi Jews in a highly developed form. Bruno and Lena Castelnuove, writing to Rachelle S. Yarden, director of the Latin American Division of the Jewish Agency for Palestine, complained,

> There exists . . . two powerful factions: the centro hebreu brasileiro [eastern European Jews] . . . and the congregação israelita paulista [German- and Italian-speaking refugees]. When these ten thousand refugees, many of them without any means and without the right to engage in remunerative occupations, descended upon the São Paulo community of some twenty-five thousand east European Jews, they presented a grave problem. The centro hebreu brasileiro protested against [the *Congregação's*] "squandering of Jewish money to build a stronghold of assimilationism in Brazil.[30]

The numbers of refugees in São Paulo, the high costs of relief, and the magnification of tension between the CIP and eastern European organizations led many eastern European Jews to stop contributing financially to causes that were connected to the *Congregação Israelita Paulista*. These Jews not only rejected what they saw as the "assimilationist" nature of the CIP; they also assumed, incorrectly, that organizations with central European members were rich and antireligious.[31] In other words, many eastern European Jews were afraid that contributions funneled through the CIP might be used to support Liberal Judaism rather than refugee relief. A fundraising drive begun in April 1940 managed to collect only three-quarters of its goal, and Lorch pointedly informed the JDC, "You overestimate our possibilities [for raising money]. . . . This result has only been obtained under greatest efforts, owing to the reserved attitudes of older resident [eastern European] Jews towards the German Jews."[32]

Further difficulties stemmed from the CIP's alliance with the JDC. The JDC was believed by many eastern European Jews to be anti-Zionist, in part because of its well-publicized fights with the World Jewish Congress, the leading Zionist organization in the pre-1948 period and an affiliate of the *Centro Hebreu Brasileiro*. Attempts by the JDC to act as the primary and exclusive refugee organization for European Jewry were seen by other groups as "imperialistic."[33] Competition by Jewish groups at the international level therefore became mirrored by a similar situation locally.[34]

The *Estado Novo* promulgated numerous laws aimed against legal resident aliens and those citizens still tied culturally to their places of birth, which further deepened cleavages among Ashkenazi Jews.[35] The targets of most antiforeign legislation were Germans, Italians, and Japanese, who nativist elites wrongly believed would form a "fifth column" in Brazil, but these laws also affected Jews. Foreign-language schools and cultural activities were restricted, all foreign organizations were banned, and foreign press outlets were censored. In August 1941, all foreign-language newspapers in Brazil were required to print in Portuguese, and the CIP newspaper, the *Crônica Israelita*, was forced to change its advertising, the only portion of the weekly still in German.[36] In another instance, a Jewish radio program with commentary in Portuguese and music in Yiddish was forced to stop playing the "foreign" records. The producer of the radio program *Hora Israelita* (Jewish Hour; launched in 1940), Francisco Gotthilf, after being told that there was no distinction between German and Yiddish because both were subversive, went as far as to give members of the local police a lecture on the differences, but to no avail.[37]

Antiforeigner laws were easily used by nativists against refugee
Jews since many government officials were uninterested in making a
distinction between Jews fleeing from Nazism and fascism and those
Brazilian citizens and immigrants potentially tied to right-wing ideologies. In 1936 and 1937, legal Jewish immigration to Brazil dropped
over 40 percent, to 2,003. In 1938, when general immigration to Brazil
showed a decrease of 44 percent, only 530 Jews were allowed to enter.[38]
The high hopes that Brazil would provide safe haven for refugees were
dashed when Jewish immigration was officially curtailed between 1937
and 1939 as the *Estado Novo*'s anti-Semitism became "most evident
in the area of refugee policy."[39] By 1940, the Vargas government had
eased its regulations somewhat but, by placing nonnative Jews in the
legal category of "foreigner," effectively controlled all Jewish entrance.[40]
Simultaneously, intracommunal tensions were increased as Brazilian
Jews were forced to choose between support of the government and
support of refugee Jews.

Into the morass of antiforeigner legislation fell Zionism, banned in
1937 as a movement based on allegiance to another state. Jews were
left with two options, to reject Zionism or to support it clandestinely.
One simple means by which Jewish organizations skirted the law was
to reorganize themselves along the nationalist lines set out by the Vargas regime while still participating secretly in Zionist activity.[41] These
paper reorganizations led a small but growing Zionist faction in the
CIP to attack the *Centro Hebreu*'s new non-Zionist charter. Vittorio
Camerini, the ardently Zionist, Italian-born first secretary of the Executive Committee of the CIP, claimed that the changes showed that
central European Jews "in spite of all pre-Hitler assimilative tendencies never lost their Jewish consciousness . . . and only a very few
lost their feeling of *Kol Israel haverim* [All Israel is one]."[42] Camerini's
analysis of the situation was far from accurate. The *Centro Hebreu*,
although publicly operating along the guidelines set out by the Vargas regime, did clandestinely support Zionist organizations such as
the *Keren Hayesod* (Palestine Foundation Fund).[43] Camerini, once
known affectionately as "Kamerinsky" because of his early attempts to
form an alliance with eastern European Zionists, allowed antagonism
against eastern Jewry to inform his pro-Zionist activity after becoming
a leader in the CIP.[44]

Although the antiforeigner laws caused immense intracommunal tension, Jewish community elites were understandably hesitant about taking the Vargas government to task for its policies. Furthermore, the *Estado Novo* showed little mercy to its enemies, at one point expelling the Jewish wife of Brazilian Communist leader Luís Prestes to her native Germany, where she was thrown in a concentration camp and murdered. In this tense atmosphere, even former European language differences became a point of conflict between Brazil's eastern and central European Jews.

Rejected by German Jewry as *zhargon*, Yiddish had remained the language of eastern European Jewry. As early as 1924, Jacob Schneider, the German-born president of the Brazilian Zionist Organization, expressed a widely held belief that the far-reaching changes brought on by the *haskalah*, the artistic and cultural Jewish enlightenment of eastern Europe, had led to a dismissal of political Zionism by eastern European Jewry on the grounds that a Jewish homeland was unneeded by those living Jewish lives in segregated areas. "Among the new [eastern European] arrivals in Brazil there are few Zionists and many anti-Zionists of whom *the most active are the Yiddishists* . . . coming from the Ukraine."[45] During the crisis caused by the *Estado Novo's brasilidade* policies, however, eastern European Jews appropriated Yiddish as a sign of pro-Zionistic thought. A major point of contention between the *Congregação Israelita Paulista* and the *Centro Hebreu* was that the leaders of the CIP "resented their being classed as assimilationists 'for the sole reason we cannot speak Yiddish.'"[46] In Brazil, Yiddish, not Hebrew, represented a continued tie to a national Judaism as power laid with eastern Europeans who had migrated earlier, who were numerically stronger, and who set the agenda for conflict.

Zionists in the CIP actively responded to the charges of assimilationism. As late as 1945, central European Jewish leaders in Brazil were contending, as Schneider had more than twenty years earlier, that eastern European Jews had "changed the sky but not their souls" and were

concerned . . . more with problems of Diaspora policy than with those of Palestine and the policy of the Jewish Agency [because] . . . having been in Eastern Europe part of a visible Jewish Nation, protected by minority rights with a language and cultural life of their own, very often higher than that of their surroundings and, therefore, rather proud of Judaism, but with some of their old mentality, Zionism was never a problem to them.[47]

The study of Jewish-Brazilians in the decade starting in 1929 provides a series of important correctives to the traditional view of Jewish immigration to the Americas. In São Paulo, we find a large Jewish population in which eastern, not central, Europeans insisted that all Jews follow their models. The national Jewish experience was closer to the national experiences of Brazilians of Japanese, Syrian, and Lebanese descent than it was to a diasporic Jewish one. In Brazil, we are reminded of the importance of the local, and we see how intracommunal conflicts were reinforced and promoted by national policies.

Prior to migration, eastern and central European Jews were divided on the basis of national origin, class, and language, all the while bound by a common religion practiced in different ways. In Brazil, where acculturative pressure was high, conflict rarely took place between Jews as a group and non-Jewish society. Rather, as strains within the Jewish community increased during the World War II era, old conflicts between Jews were re-created in São Paulo.

Jews are often examined as a single community both nationally and transnationally, but such assumptions about homogeneity are problematic.[48] Scholars should move away from the a priori assumption of "community" to develop a more sophisticated framework of the evolution of how ethnic communities, often developing within societally imposed assumptions of uniformity, can be constructed.

NOTES

1. U. O. Schmelz and Sergio DellaPergola, "World Jewish Population, 1984," *American Jewish Yearbook—1986* [hereafter *AJYB*] (New York: American Jewish Committee, 1986), 357.

2. Jeffrey Lesser and Raanan Rein, "New Approaches to Ethnicity and Diaspora in Twentieth-Century Latin America," in Jeffrey Lesser and Raanan Rein, eds., *Rethinking Jewish-Latin Americans* (Albuquerque: University of New Mexico Press, 2008).

3. *Revista de Imigração e Colonização* [hereafter *RIC*] (Rio de Janeiro: Conselho de Imigração e Colonização) 1.4 (October 1940): 641–42. An overview of immigration patterns may be found in Maria Stella Ferreira Levy, "O Papel da Migração Internacional na Evolução da População Brasileira (1872 a 1972)," *Revista de Saúde Pública* (supplement) 8 (1974): 49–90.

4. U.S. Immigration and Naturalization Service. *Annual Report* (Washington, DC: U.S. Government Printing Office, 1973), 25.

5. The passage of this immigration bill "left a conviction in various quarters that the chief purpose . . . was to keep out Jews." John Higham, *Strangers in the Land: Patterns of American Nativism, 1860–1925* (New Brunswick: Rutgers University Press, 1955), 310.

6. Haim Avni, "Argentine Jewry: Its Socio-Political Status and Organizational Patterns," *Dispersion and Unity* 12 (1971): 141.

7. *RIC* 1.4 (October 1940): 641–42. This does not include Russian immigration to Brazil. Immigration and its effect on economic growth are discussed in Thomas W. Merrick and Douglas H. Graham, *Population and Economic Development in Brazil: 1800 to Present* (Baltimore: Johns Hopkins University Press, 1979).

8. *RIC* 1.4 (October 1940): 641–42.

9. Ibid. Between 1924 and 1933, more than 13 percent of Brazil's immigrants came from eastern Europe; between 1914 and 1923, eastern European immigration totaled less than 2 percent.

10. On the earliest Jewish communal groups in Brazil, see Nachman Falbel, "Early Zionism in Brazil: The Founding Years, 1913–1922," *American Jewish Archives* 38.2 (1986): 123–36.

11. Only in 1941 was the category *israelita* added, under the nationality heading, to official immigration statistics. *Boletim do Departamento de Imigração e Colonização* 5 (December 1950): 16–59.

12. "Rapport d'activité pendant la période 1933–43," YIVO Institute for Jewish Research Archives, New York [hereafter YIVO-NY], Records of HIAS Main Office/New York, Series 13–Brazil, Folder 1; and U. O. Schmelz and Sergio DellaPergola, "The Demography of Latin American Jewry," *AJYB-1985* (New York: American Jewish Committee, 1985), 68.

13. *AJYB-5683* (Philadelphia: Jewish Publication Society of America, 1922), 301; and *AJYB-5691* (Philadelphia: Jewish Publication Society of America, 1930), 242.

14. Salo Wittmayer Baron, Arcadius Kahan, and Nachum Gross, *Economic History of the Jews* (Jerusalem: Keter, 1975), 104.

15. Brazil was not seen as having a high potential for Jewish life prior to World War I. This is amply demonstrated through a comparison with South Africa, whose Jewish population swelled from 4,000 in 1880 to 49,926 in 1911. Stephen Cohen, "Historical Background," in Marcus Arkin, ed., *South African Jewry: A Contemporary Survey* (Cape Town, South Africa: Oxford University Press, 1984), 3.

16. Roney Cytrynowicz, "Beyond the State and Ideology: Immigration of the Jewish Community to Brazil, 1937–1945," in Lesser and Rein, *Rethinking Jewish-Latin Americans*.

17. On conflicts between eastern and central European Jews, see Stephen Aschheim, *Brothers and Strangers: The East European Jew in German and German-Jewish Consciousness, 1800–1928* (Madison: University of Wisconsin Press, 1982).

18. Jeffrey Lesser, "How the Jews Became Japanese and Other Stories of Nation and Ethnicity," *Jewish History* 18.1 (2004): 7–17.
19. Memorandum of unnamed Brazilian correspondent of the Jewish Telegraphic Agency (JTA) to Jacob Landau, sent by Landau to Joseph C. Hyman of the Joint Distribution Committee, 22 April 1938, Archives of the American Joint Distribution Committee (New York City) [hereafter AAJDC-NY], File 1092.
20. Rabbi Fritz Pinkus, first rabbi of the Congregação Israelita Paulista, interview with the author, 1 September 1986, São Paulo, Brazil.
21. According to Alfred Hirschberg, "two thirds of [the German Jews in São Paulo] are registered with the . . . Congregação Israelita Paulista." Alfred Hischberg, "The Economic Adjustment of Jewish Refugees in São Paulo," *Jewish Social Studies* 7 (January 1945): 31.
22. "Report of Friedrich Borchardt and David Glick," 27 June 1939, American Jewish Archives, Cincinnati [hereafter AJA-C], Rhodes Collection, Box 2249.
23. Alfred Jaretzki, Jr., to Dr. Ludwig Lorch and Mr. Salo Wissman (CIP), 27 September 1939, AAJDC-NY, File 1092, 2.
24. The JDC also supported a German/Liberal congregation, the *Associação Religiosa Israelita* (ARI) in Rio de Janeiro.
25. Decree Law of May 4, 1938, Art. 12, and Decree Law of August 20, 1938, Art, 1(b), in Karl Loewenstein, *Brazil under Vargas* (New York: Russell and Russell, 1942), 172.
26. Nathan Eck, "The Rescue of Jews with the Aid of Passport and Citizenship Papers of Latin American States," *Yad Vashem Studies* 1 (1957): 125–52.
27. "Report of Friedrich Borchardt and David Glick on São Paulo, Brazil Dated New York City, June 28, 1939," AAJDC-NY, File 1093.
28. Quoted in Loewenstein, *Brazil under Vargas*, 181.
29. "Situation of Refugees without Permanent Status in Brazil," 14 October 1940, AAJDC-NY, File 1093.
30. Bruno and Lena Castelnuove to Rachelle S. Yarden, 14 June 1945, Central Zionist Archives, Jerusalem [hereafter CZA-J], s5/779 no. 244.
31. Jaretzki to Lorch and Wissman.
32. Ludwig Lorch, Salo Wissman, and Martin Friedlaender to American Joint Distribution Committee, 8 June 1940, AAJDC-NY, File 1093.
33. Henry Shoskes (HIAS Delegate for Latin America) to Marc Leitchik (Jewish Colonization Association), 4 October 1946, YIVO-NY, Records of HIAS Main Office/ New York, Series 13–Brazil, Folder 48.
34. In 1940, the JDC attempted to discredit the World Jewish Congress among Rio de Janeiro's Jewish leadership: "Claims [were] made by the World Jewish Congress that it was providing relief to Jews in Poland and in Germany. . . . Our investigations satisfy us that the World Jewish Congress has not and is not doing any relief work in these areas." Moses A. Leavitt to Dr. Paulo Zander, president of the *"União" Associação Beneficente Israelita* (Allied Jewish Benevolent Association), 6 November 1940, AAJDC-NY, File 1099, 1.

35. Robert Levine, *The Vargas Regime: The Critical Years, 1934–1938* (New York: Columbia University Press, 1970), 167.

36. The *Crônica Israelita* ran large stories on Vargas at least twice a year. Beginning with the edition of 15 August 1941 (no. 70), the *Crônica* was printed entirely in Portuguese.

37. Francisco Gotthilf, interview with the author, 5 June 1986, São Paulo, Brazil.

38. YIVO-NY, Records of HIAS Main Office/NY, Series 13–Brazil, Folder 1. In 1938, 19,388 immigrants entered Brazil. *RIC* 5.3 (September 1944): 590, table 4.

39. Levine, *The Vargas Regime*, 54. Vargas himself claimed that laws passed against foreigners were not anti-Semitic in origin. Alfred Houston to the Refugee Economic Commission, reporting on a personal interview with President Vargas, 27 January 1938, AAJDC-NY, File 1092, 5.

40. In 1940, 1,230 permanent visas were given to *"Hebraicas."* *RIC* 2.2–3 (July–April 1941): 435.

41. In Europe, as in Brazil, groups were divided over what the proper conception of Zionism should be. See David Vital, *The Origins of Zionism* (Oxford: Oxford University Press, 1975).

42. Henrique Veit and Vittorio Camerini to President of Zionist Organization (London), 24 December 1945, CZA-J, ZU/10229, 2.

43. The *Keren Hayesod* was founded in 1920 as the financial arm of the World Zionist Organization.

44. Helena Mortiz, daughter of Vittorio Camerini, interview with the author, 29 June 1986, São Paulo, Brazil.

45. Minutes of report on interview with Jacob Schneider, 2 November 1924, CZA-J, ZU/2350, 2; emphasis in original.

46. Bruno and Lena Castelnuove to Rachelle S. Yarden, 14 June 1945, CZA-J, s5/779, no. 244.

47. Veit and Camerini to President of Zionist Organization, 2.

48. Jeffrey Lesser and Raanan Rein, "Challenging Particularity: Jews as a Lens on Latin American Ethnicity," *Latin American and Caribbean Ethnic Studies* 1.2 (September 2006): 249–63.

PART III

Literature

11

Patterning a New Life

American Jewish Literature in 1929

GABRIELLA SAFRAN

The notion of delimiting the object of literary analysis to texts produced in a specific year—in this case, American Jewish texts produced in 1929—might make a critic conceive a project in two ways. One might tackle the project historically (or diachronically) in an attempt to determine how the American Jewish literature of 1929 arose, its causes, and its most historically significant aspects. One might also address it experientially (or synchronically), focusing not on change over time but rather on the depth of a single moment, attempting to reconstruct the literary culture, the intellectual or emotional texture of the reflection of the Jewish experience available to the American reader, and working to define the larger aesthetic categories that were most relevant to these readers. Rather than choosing one of these approaches or the other, this chapter addresses them sequentially by analyzing the material first diachronically, then synchronically, and at the end bringing the two approaches together.

I focus on three texts written in 1929: Michael Gold's famous "proletarian novel" *Jews without Money* (he worked on it throughout the 1920s and published it in February 1930; thus, one can assume that he finished the bulk of the writing in 1929),[1] Charles Reznikoff's *By the Waters of Manhattan* (a miscellany that he published in 1929; he went on to revise and repackage some of that material and publish it under the same title the next year—an issue to which I will return at the end of this chapter), and the English translation of Isaac Babel's revolutionary Russian story sequence *Red Cavalry Stories*, as well the American criticism surrounding it.[2] These texts are dramatically different in their tone, style, ideology, popularity, and brow level. Gold's novel was meant to (and did) appeal to a broad, left-wing, possibly working-class American audience; Reznikoff's self-published works were a success with high-brow critics but did not sell; and Babel's violent modernist depictions of the Russian Revolution fascinated audiences throughout the world, for whom they signified the possibility of a new kind of art under socialism.[3]

Nonetheless, these texts are similar in that they are all semiautobiographical and they all feature a male Jewish protagonist in difficult, often violent confrontation with the non-Jewish world and with modernity. Gold's hero, Mike, is the child of immigrants from Hungary and Romania, growing up on the Lower East Side; over the course of the novel, he becomes deadened and hopeless under the pressure of poverty, crime, and tragedy, before he is awakened at the end to the revolutionary cause. Reznikoff's miscellany contains some Biblical poetry and two long stories: the autobiography of his mother, Sarah Yetta, a girl who grows up in southern Russia but, frustrated by poverty and the lack of educational opportunities for girls, emigrates to America; and a novella about a young man, Joel, who grows up on the East Side, founds a bookshop, and has an affair with a blonde but, in spite of seemingly having attained what he desired, is not happy. Babel's stories follow the movements of Liutov, a Jew who has been attached to a unit of pro-Bolshevik Cossacks in 1920 on the Russo-Polish front: much of the drama centers on Liutov's attempts to fit in among the Cossacks. Although these authors are disparate geographically, stylistically, and ideologically, they are united, I argue, by the ways in which they all fundamentally challenge the generic limitations of the Bildungsroman, or novel of education; that is, they set themselves against the notion that in spite of difficulties and regrets, a person's life can and does move along a comprehensive path from one self to another.

Let us start with the diachronic approach. Outside the literary sphere, the year 1929 was a watershed for Jews as for non-Jews: it saw the founding of the Jewish Agency and the Hebron riots in Palestine in August, and of course the American stock-market crash on October 24. For the texts at issue, another event seems yet more significant: on July 1, 1929, the Immigration Act of 1924 went into effect, instituting a quota system for immigrants to the United States that severely limited the number of eastern European Jews. At the same time that it became more difficult for Jewish immigrants to enter the United States, it had become more difficult for them to leave a part of eastern Europe where many of them were living, the Soviet Union. Thus, 1929 was not only the beginning of a time of increasing poverty and the shifting of the ideological boundaries around Zionism but also a moment when the international borders that had been permeable for decades became more solid, almost impassable. For the Jews already in the United States, this was the beginning of a shift in population patterns that led to linguistic and cultural shifts. As the population of Yiddish-speaking immigrants failed to be replenished, the Jews of the United States grew more English speaking: the potential audience for and supply of producers of Jewish American literature or culture in English increased.

The books I have selected both shed light on and enact some of these large changes that are connected with the ways in which the past and the present are related. One might theorize that for Gold and Reznikoff, as for Babel's American interpreters, the writers' distance from the Old World, the fact that they grew up in the United States, made possible the introduction of a nostalgia about Europe that was not available to earlier generations of American Jewish writers. As Svetlana Boym asserts, nostalgia is a historically constructed phenomenon that arose among some groups of writers in Europe in the late eighteenth and early nineteenth centuries in response to literary Romanticism, the beginnings of mass culture, and the sense that a certain unmediated relationship to the past and the natural world was no longer available.[4] In the Jewish context, of course, nostalgia has its own genealogy, connected to the vision of a return to Zion that lies at the heart of religious practice. It seems, though, that it is precisely in the late nineteenth and twentieth centuries that a kind of secular and diasporic Jewish nostalgia (one focused on a location other than Zion) becomes possible.

This shift is exemplified by the differences between two of the depictions of "bad fathers" in classic works of American Jewish fiction that were *not* written in 1929: Anzia Yezierska's *The Bread Givers*, from 1925, and Henry Roth's *Call It Sleep*, from 1934. Yezierska's hostility to the ways of life and the ideals of the traditional Jews of eastern Europe is embodied in the horrific father figure in that novel, who unashamedly exploits his daughters and ruins their lives. It is clear throughout the novel that if the father only had been brought up differently, everyone's lives would be better. For Roth, in contrast, the father of his hero is psychologically troubled, and Jewish traditions are in no way to blame for his destructive behavior. Indeed, the New World and the urban environment of New York seem to have exacerbated his problems: he only seems calm when he remembers how he used to work on a farm, tending the cows. In Yezierska's novel, the depiction of the father fits into a neat set of binaries in which most of what is associated with the Old World is dangerous, ugly, and bad, whereas much of what is associated with the New World—at least that part of the New World that lies beyond the borders of the Jewish East Side—is attractive and healthy: the task of the hero (or heroine) is to traverse the space from Old to New successfully. Even when that journey does not lead to perfect happiness, the necessity of the journey itself remains unquestioned. Roth's novel offers no such efficient dichotomies: the Old World figures as confused but often beautiful memories, the New as dangerous, ugly reality; and the father, like his son, has difficulty understanding how to negotiate the differences.

As Hana Wirth-Nesher observes in a recent study, Jewish American writers, from the earliest generations until the most recent ones, have thematized language and multilinguality in their fiction and produced a fantastic variety of meditations on accent, dialect, and English style.[5] In keeping with her findings, the transition from the father figure in Yezierska in the mid 1920s to the father figure in Roth in the mid 1930s is mirrored in the ways in which the immigrant parents that these two writers depict use language. When Yezierska's parent characters speak Yiddish, it is represented as slightly incorrect English ("And the landlady is tearing from me my flesh, hollering for the rent") with a few admixtures of actual Yiddish words ("'Gazlin! Bandit!' her cry broke through the house" [7]). When Roth's parent characters speak Yiddish, their language is slightly archaic ("'And no kiss?' She caught him by the shoulders, kissed him. 'There! Savory, thrifty lips! Don't be late!'" [173]), whereas the children's English is represented as a distorted dialect ("But mine fodder made it" [21]). This linguistic shift, which reflects the tastes of the reading public,[6] also suggests that by the mid 1930s, it had become possible for an American Jewish writer to advertise linguistic nostalgia by representing the Yiddish language of the Jewish immigrants from eastern Europe as beautifully archaic, far more attractive than the American dialect of their children (though one must also note that Roth's novel, unlike Yezierska's works, was not a commercial success when first published). Whereas the heroes of Yezierska (like those of Abraham Cahan in another landmark American Jewish novel, *The Rise of David Levinsky*, 1917) have moments of regret about the ways in which their lives have turned out in America, they are fundamentally not nostalgic; they do not venture into the kind of dramatic revaluation of values that would allow them to see Europe's oldness as pregnant with the possibility of Romantic newness, as a potential Eden.

Given this picture of change over time, our 1929 texts are situated interestingly in the middle. Gold focuses on the horrors of life on the Lower East Side, to the exclusion of almost anything else. His characters know they could never go home to the Europe of persecution and pogroms: "The East Side never forgot Europe. We children heard endless tales of the pogroms. . . . We were obsessed by wild stories of how the Christians loved to kidnap Jewish children, to burn a cross on each cheek with a red-hot poker" (164).[7] At the same time, Gold's adult characters long for the pastoral ideal of their European memories, and his narrator even asserts nostalgically that there were no Jewish criminals in Europe—America, it seems, had perverted an innocent people. Gold's positive assessment of Europe is reflected in the representation of the Yiddish speech of the parent characters, which is closer to standard English than in Yezierska, though not as elegant as the language of the parents in Roth. Gold's mother announces, "Let others be proud! I am a work horse" (157); "'Your food is *Dreck*, it is fit only for pigs,' she told the manager bluntly" (247). The case of Reznikoff is a bit more complex. In the 1929 edition of *By the Waters of Manhattan*, the experiences of Sarah Yetta in Europe and emigration and the experiences of her son Joel are divided into separate texts. Neither conforms to the model of *The Bread Givers*: rather, the European and American experiences of Sarah Yetta are in many ways similar, and Joel's American life does not take on meaning through its difference from a European life.

The shift from condemning the horrors of Jewish life in Europe to reevaluating Europe as a place of fresh potential emerges most obviously in the American Jewish reception of Babel. In 1921, soon after the 1917 Russian Revolution, Gold had hailed Soviet art as "the resurrection" and as an art that grows out of "the deep need of the masses for the old primitive group life," out of "tranquility and humane strength," and "out of the soil of life, freely and without thought."[8] His language is Romantic, more precisely Rousseauian, figuring the Soviet Union as a new Eden, an ideal state of nature, as perceived by the artistic genius. He made no mention in that essay of the specifically Jewish experience in the Soviet Union or of any Soviet Jewish writers. Eventually, Isaac Babel in particular came to be seen as an exemplar of the new possibilities for Jews in the Soviet Union: writing in *Menorah* in 1928, Alexander Kaun asked, "Is not the present-day relative prominence of Jewish writers in Russian letters due to the acquisition on their part, since the fall of the monarchy, of a sense of serenity and equality in the land that had previously treated them as hateful stepchildren? In the writings of Isaak Babel are to be observed some of the important changes that have taken place in Russian literature" (400). Whereas the pogroms of 1919–1920 at the time inspired American Yiddish writers to produce threnodies and angry screeds (such as Moyshe-Leyb Halpern's "A nakht" (Night, 1916–1919) and Lamed Shapiro's "Vayse khale" (White Challah, 1919), by 1928 Kaun could find in Babel's representation of the massacres of Jews that accompanied the Russian civil war evidence of improvement in the lives of Russian Jews. Kaun's review of Babel uses language similar to that in Gold's 1921 essay, insisting that Soviet art is above all "youthful," "heroic," with life moving at an "intensified tempo" (400–401). He concludes his essay on *Red Cavalry* with a description of the "overwhelming innocence hovering over these valleys of tears and blood, the innocence of children of chaos, harnessed to elemental forces and performing their terrible work with the ease of a sinless conscience" (410). The accumulation of evidence from Gold, Reznikoff, and the review of Babel indicates that these works of 1929 represent shifts in the understandings of the United States and Russia that were available to the US public. Now that the borders were closed, it had become more possible to be nostalgic about Russia and enthusiastic about the Soviet experiment and to imagine Europe as not only a place one left behind but potentially a place to which one might want to return. (In some cases, of course, American Jews did return from the United States to now-Soviet Russia.)[9]

* * *

The second part of this chapter moves from the diachronic to the synchronic, looking at aspects of the texts that are harder to analyze as historical phenomena in order to fill in and fill out the picture of American Jewish culture of this era and in that context and to inquire what made these works successful. Again, stylistics offers an entry point for analysis, specifically the use of markedly Jewish terminology and the use of metaphor. With Gold, Jewish (Hebrew or Yiddish) words are simply treated like any other English word. On a snowman, he writes, "This Golem with his amazed eyes and idiotic grin amused us all for an afternoon" (242). The "Golem"—a Frankenstein-type figure from eastern European Jewish folklore—has been transposed seamlessly into the New York landscape. With Reznikoff, in contrast, Jewish words all appear in English: "Besides, now we are in exile" (27); "'Do you want her to marry an ignorant fellow,' said Grandfather Benjamin Hirsh, 'a man a century behind the times? I had a talk with him: he knows nothing of the Talmud. He is just a religious fanatic" (61). An informed reader can hear the Yiddish or Hebrew originals of these words (*golus* for "exile," *am-ha-orets* for "ignorant fellow") behind the English, but the only exotic term here is the relatively mainstream "Talmud."

With Isaac Babel, the situation is made more complex by the fact of translation. In the original Russian of *Red Cavalry*, a few Jewish words do appear—terms such as "Talmud" and "Ibn Ezra," both with a scholarly ring—and a few characters, such as Gedali, speak with a somewhat Jewish intonation.[10] (This is quite different from his "Odessa Stories," in which the narrator and the characters all speak a Jewish-Odessan dialect.) In the English translation of 1929, not only has the Jewish intonation been edited out, but mistakes have been introduced that make this version less Jewish. In the oddly transliterated "Crossing the Zbrouch," the narrator is billeted to the house of some Jews who had been attacked by Poles. The 1929 translation reads, "I discover turned-out wardrobes in the room I am given, and bits of women's winter coats on the floor, human filth and fragments of the precious crockery the Jews use only once a year, at Easter" (9). The phrasing is jarring because this speaker—the Jewish Liutov—seems not to realize the difference between Passover and Easter. In fact, Babel had described the holiday with the Russian word *Paskha*, which could be translated as "Passover" or "Easter" (and he clearly meant "Passover"). The translator's mistake suggests not just ignorance but also the urge to make it clear that this narrator—or even this author—did not identify with the despoiled Jews. (Another translation of this period, though [of 1928, not 1929], avoids this problem.)[11]

With these varied approaches to the use of Jewish terms in an English context, each of these authors and translators attempted to naturalize Jewish language and thereby, perhaps, to assert the legitimacy of themselves and their subject matter on the American literary scene. Unlike Babel's 1929 translator in "Crossing the Zbrouch," Gold and Reznikoff do not edit out marks of Jewishness. Neither Gold nor Reznikoff created separate dialects to distinguish Jewish characters from non-Jews; neither resorted to lengthy explanations of Jewish terms in the texts themselves or in footnotes. They both seemed dedicated to creating and writing in a version of English that would have room for Jewish subjects.

Another stylistic area in which these works bear comparison is that of metaphor. Yezierska's novel has few striking metaphors (nor does an arguably much better American Jewish novel written before 1929, Cahan's *Rise of David Levinsky*). Babel is famous for his metaphoric language, particularly for the shocking, jarring quality of his juxtapositions.[12] For example, the 1929 English translation of "Crossing the Zbroutch" includes, "The orange sun rolls down the sky like a decapitated head" (8). (This is bad English, since a body, rather than a head, can be decapitated, but it conveys the original metaphor.) The story "Gedali," better translated in 1928 in *Menorah*, offers, "I behold the marketplace, and the death of the marketplace. The fat soul of abundance is slain. Dumb locks hang on the shop doors, the granite of the pavement is clean like the bald head of a corpse. The timid star winks and splutters" (411). "The sky changes colors. Up above tender blood flows from an overturned bottle, and I am enveloped by a light odor of decay" (412). Babel's grotesque metaphors make everything bloody: they turn all phenomena, natural and man-made, Jewish and Russian, into amputated or decaying body parts, reflections of the bodies of the victims of the war. In "Crossing the

Zbroutch," which ends with the revelation that Liutov has been sleeping next to the corpse of a good Jewish father, the introductory metaphor (the setting sun like a cut-off head) makes the entire landscape part of the tragedy of the Galician Jews—judaizes it, in a sense.

Reznikoff may have read Babel, but Gold certainly did so with admiration.[13] And like Babel, Gold used a style that was rich in metaphor, often startling metaphor. Gold's Babelian influence emerges in the metaphors that he uses to highlight physicality, disgust, and the lack of freedom. "From the glimmering sky the pigeons descended like a heavenly chain gang, and returned meekly to their prison" (129). "She chased us, flopping again and again, like a bird with broken wings" (179). "Winter. Bums sleep in rows like dead fish on the sawdust floors of the saloons" (259). Gold uses metaphor to draw together humans and animals, the dead or disfigured and the living, the free and the imprisoned. At every step, he debases the world he describes and forces the reader to notice its horror. Reznikoff's metaphors, though equally abundant (at least in the narrative about Joel; the Sarah Yetta narrative has almost no metaphor), are far less physiological. Joel thinks metaphorically, almost always with metaphors drown from literature. "Surely a necktie, he thought, is Jeremiah's halter that a man ties about his neck each day as a symbol of his life" (183). "If only those ponderous sentences he had forged in his heart would now clothe him in wrought gold, that his wit and imagery would cover him with garments smelling of myrrh and aloes and cassia, that his arrows were sharp in the hearts of his enemies, that his tongue were the pen of a ready writer, as the psalmist boasted" (208). Over and over, this secular character uses Biblical language to describe the world of New York and his bookstore: often, as in the sentences cited, the ornate quality of the vehicle contrasts sharply with the mundane quality of the tenor. I would argue that while superficially it would seem that Gold succeeds better than Reznikoff at imitating Babel, with his startling, bodily metaphors, in fact Reznikoff accomplishes better the goal of judaizing the world he describes—but while Babel colors his Galician landscape with the red of Jewish blood, Reznikoff associates his New York with the myrrh of the Hebrew Bible. In both cases, though, the result might be read as a sort of literary manifesto, a proclamation of the at-homeness of the Jewish writer in a non-Jewish literature, the legitimacy of that writer and his subject matter.

Not only do these three writers use metaphors in marked fashion, but they all demonstrate their fascination with perception in their depictions of eyesight, especially compromised eyesight. One of the older boys that Gold's Mike knows is Louis One-Eye, who defended his mother when his father beat her, was sent to a reformatory, and was beaten there by a guard with a belt whose buckle gouged out his eye. The narrator explains bitterly, "The State 'reformed' him by carefully teaching him to be a criminal, and by robbing him of his eye" (128). This loss of an eye in a minor character is a central event: it prefigures the culminating body-part loss in the novel, when Mike's sister is run over by a street car and decapitated (280), and it also makes Louis One-Eye a more perfect representative of this world, who sees it in its true horror (as Gold wanted the reader to see it as well): "His remaining eye had become fierce and large. It was black, and from it poured hate, lust, scorn and suspicion, as from a deadly headlight to shrivel the world" (129). The cynicism associated with Louis One-Eye's perspective resembles that of the narrator, who decides to work instead of going to high school and, even though he loves to read, does not read for five years (305). Reznikoff appears even more interested than Gold in eyes and eyesight. Sarah Yetta has poor vision because of a childhood illness, but she wants to spend all her time reading (16, 34–35). Her conservative older relatives tell her that girls do not need to read (47), which spurs her dreams of going to the United States and makes her particularly relish her children's educational opportunities there. Babel's Liutov, like Reznikoff's Sarah Yetta, likes to read and ends up wearing glasses. The story "My First Goose" begins when Liutov is warned that his glasses will make the Cossacks know that he is not one of them, and if he wants them to accept him, he will have to perform some act of brutality. Once he kills an old woman's goose, the Cossacks accept him and happily listen as, through his glasses, he reads them Lenin's speeches from the newspapers.

It is not surprising that all these writers are concerned with seeing and reading. For each of them, images of compromised vision are connected to both modernization and Jewish identity. The phantom behind each of these texts is the traditional Jewish love for reading. This can be the reading of rabbinic texts (manifested in another of Babel's stories as Gedali in his smoky glasses, reading Rashi [411]) or (especially for Gold and Reznikoff) the maskilic faith in reading not Rashi but the texts that signify a secular education. For each of these writers, it seems that the rabbinic or maskilic past has to be challenged and overcome, in order to make reading truly relevant. Babel's hero can read Lenin only after he proves himself by killing the goose; Joel can at least hope for happiness in his bookstore only after his mother no longer hopes herself to become an educated American (as she and a cousin see their children leaving school and realize that only the younger generation has the hope of becoming educated, "his eyes filled with tears" [146]); Gold's hero can be inspired (at the end) by a Communist soapbox orator who forced him "to think" only after his five years without reading. Whereas the use of metaphor in these texts is tied to the writers' urge to situate themselves as legitimate denizens of the literary tradition whose language they use, their shared focus on compromised eyesight may indicate the difficulties attendant on becoming a legitimate writer as a Jew writing in a non-Jewish language (whether English or Russian). For each of these writers, there is something compelling about the idea of a person who cannot see well enough to read, an image that remains in the background even as reading and writing do take place.

* * *

The first part of this chapter argues that the American Jewish literature of 1929—or at least those particular, representative examples that I have chosen—represents a watershed in that it spoke for a nostalgia about Europe and a skepticism about America that were becoming possible just at that moment. The second part, focusing on a few aspects of the 1929 texts—Jewish terminology, metaphor, and images of compromised eyesight—argues that these literary devices suggest that these Jewish writers were concerned with defining a place for themselves in the national literary tradition, in English or Russian letters, even while they recognized that task as difficult. This conclusion combines the diachronic and the synchronic, close textual analysis with the analysis of change over time. It requires a return to Reznikoff. We know he published a miscellany called *By the Waters of Manhattan* in 1929; he then revised the materials, which were published by Charles Boni under the same title in 1930. The changes that he made are telling, for they suggest that some of the attitudes that seemed implicit in the 1929 book—in all these 1929 books—could emerge much more explicitly a mere year later. In the 1930 version, he combined the two long narratives of the 1929 version, the autobiography of Sarah Yetta and the story of Joel the bookstore owner, into a single novel, and he made it clear that Joel (now given Reznikoff's own Hebrew name, Ezekiel) is Sarah Yetta's son. He made very few other changes, but he did add a few paragraphs at the very end of the novel, in which some of the devices I have examined appear in a new form. Sarah Yetta is standing at the stove, thinking about the distance between herself and her son:

> It seemed to her that if she only had had time to read when she was young, she would have patterned her life on the wisdom in books and lived wisely and happily. So, time and again, she had spread a pattern carefully on cloth and cut others a garment that fit and was becoming. And yet her son with all the education so cheap in America, this blessed land—Sarah Yetta took up her long fork to turn the meat in the pot. As she lifted the cover the steam rose and gathered in a mist on her eyeglasses. (253)

Ezekiel leaves her and walks home, thinking of Jane—the woman he is not sure he loves—and of his life. These are the last lines of the novel: "Jane would be in her blue kimona, her feet in little blue slippers. These had an ornament in felt and gold thread. The design had probably been modeled on a leaf or a flower, but the copyist had obscured its meaning so that Ezekiel saw only patches of colored felt stitched with tinsel" (255).

This chapter argues that the American Jewish fiction of 1929 reflects the changes of that year, when eastern European Jews stopped being able to come to the United States in large numbers. From around 1929, American Jewish writers began to abandon the plot that had governed earlier American Jewish fiction, the plot of a Bildungsroman, or novel of education, a journey from the Old World to the New that represented— or was supposed to represent—a journey from ignorance to enlightenment, sickness to health, and poverty to wealth. The American Jewish writers of 1929 looked for new plots, whether in nostalgia for the old country, in yearning for the revolution, or in the "elemental forces" and "overwhelming innocence" of the Russian Cossacks that Kaun found in Babel's stories (410). At the same time, these writers were tremendously conscious of their own still tenuous position within American English literature and the ways in which they needed to claim legitimacy, whether by appealing to a broad or a narrow audience. The changes that Reznikoff made to his book in 1930 speak to both of these concerns. In the few paragraphs that he added, the mother's poor vision is connected to the simple plot for which she yearns—the plot connected to the notion of making a plan, cutting out a pattern, coming to America, and finding a result that "fit" and was "becoming." All American Jewish novels of this period touch on the garment industry, so it is logical for the cutter's son to think about the work that has gone into creating his girlfriend's clothes. The design on the slippers has been obscured, so that "Ezekiel saw only patches of colored felt stitched with tinsel." This last line speaks of obscured vision, of the failure of old plots, and of the artist's self-consciousness about his creative work. Nevertheless, even more clearly with this 1930 version than the 1929 one, the Jewish writer had found his way into American literature.

NOTES

1. Barry Gross, "Michael Gold (1893–1967)," Cengage Learning Online Study Center, http://college.hmco.com/english/lauter/heath/4e/students/author_pages/modern/gold_mi.html.

2. Charles Reznikoff, *By the Waters of Manhattan: An Annual* (New York: n.p., 1929); Charles Reznikoff, *By the Waters of Manhattan* (New York: Charles Boni, 1930); Michael Gold, *Jews without Money* (1930; repr., New York: Carroll and Graf, 1996); I. Babel, *Red Cavalry*, trans. Nadia Helstein (New York: Knopf, 1929); Alexander Kaun, "Babel: Voice of New Russia," and Isaak Babel, "Gedali," trans. Alexander Kaun, both in *Menorah Journal*, November 1928. Subsequent references to these sources are to these editions and are cited parenthetically in the text.

3. On Reznikoff's attitude toward the literary marketplace, see Milton Hindus's introductory essay in *Charles Reznikoff: Man and Poet*, ed. Hindus (Orono: National Poetry Foundation, University of Maine at Orono, 1984).

4. Svetlana Boym, *The Future of Nostalgia* (New York: Basic Books, 2001).

5. Hana Wirth-Nesher, *Call It English: The Languages of Jewish American Literature* (Princeton: Princeton University Press, 2006). Cf. another study that places Jewish American literature in a broader immigrant literature context and that notes the ways in which various immigrant authors engage with and question paradigms of assimilation: Thomas J. Ferraro, *Ethnic Passages: Literary Immigrants in Twentieth-Century America* (Chicago: University of Chicago Press, 1993).

6. Yezierska herself first cultivated a very literary "high English" style, but her readers preferred this dialect-like style. "The Great Tide: 1881–1924," in *Jewish*

American Literature: A Norton Anthology, ed. Jules Chametsky, John Felstiner, Hilene Flanzbaum, and Kathryn Hellerstein (New York: Norton, 2001), 121.

7. The image of Christians marking Jews with cross-shaped scars appears most famously in Lamed Shapiro's American-Yiddish story "Der tseylem" (The Cross, 1908).

8. Gold, "Towards Proletarian Art," in *Mike Gold: A Literary Anthology*, ed. Michael Folsom (New York: International, 1972), 66, 69, 70.

9. On the attitude of American Jewish socialists to the Russian revolutions and the Soviet Union, see Tony Michels, *A Fire in Their Hearts: Yiddish Socialists in New York* (Cambridge: Harvard University Press, 2005), esp. chap. 5. For a filmic representation of Russian Jewish back-migration (from the United States to the Soviet Union), see the 1932 Soviet Yiddish talkie *Nosn Beker fort aheym* (The Return of Nathan Becker).

10. "There's enough of a pinch of a Jewish intonation to spice up the stew, plus a pinch of Polish-accented Russian ('laskowy pan'). How does he do it? There is a stiffness in the syntax making it sound a bit like a translation or just stiff Russian spoken by one who is improvising the language a bit. How did Babel 'hear' it, what did he want us to imagine as the language here? I think he 'heard' Gedali straining to speak Russian through his Yiddish and Polish, and Liutov trying to fall into step with him and using—in order to be understood—the same simple vocabulary and plain, or stiff, syntax. The story is almost all dialogue, marked by strong interrogative intonations—whether the phrases are really interrogative or affirmative." Gregory Freidin, personal communication.

11. The problem was rectified in another translation in *Menorah*, November 1928: "shards of sacred dishes which the Jews use once a year, during their Passover" (409).

12. As Viktor Shklovsky famously said, "Babel's principal device is to speak in the same tone of voice of the stars above and of gonorrhea." Victor Shklovsky, "Isaac Babel: A Critical Romance," trans. John Pearson, in *Modern Critical Views: Isaac Babel*, ed. Harold Bloom (Philadelphia: Chelsea House, 1987), 12.

13. In 1935, Gold wrote about an encounter with Babel in Paris. "If you will read his work, you will find that his is an intensely romantic nature, which sometimes distorts reality because he is vainly trying, like Arthur Rimbaud, to pierce beyond all its veils." "A Love Letter for France," in *Mike Gold: A Literary Anthology*, 234. "He was surprised and glad to hear about the militant Jewish workers of New York. 'In the Soviet Union one forgets one is a Jew. The whole race question has already become dim, like ancient history. But here in Paris it comes back to me'" (ibid., 235).

12

David Vogel

Married Life 1929

GLENDA ABRAMSON

During the period of transition from *Haskalah* literature to the literature of the so-called revival (1880 to 1920), Jewish intellectuals, many of
them writers, debated the future and nature of Hebrew literature, drawing up prescriptive lists of what the literature should or should not do.
Questions of national ideology and Jewish tradition constituted central
evaluative criteria in the process of literary canonization. Despite the
fidelity to these criteria of poets, including Avraham Shlonsky and U. Z.
Greenberg, by 1929 they were bringing about something of a modernist upheaval within Hebrew letters, in answer to H. N. Bialik's colossal,
but by that time reactionary, influence. In that year, some of the most
significant figures in Hebrew literature were composing their poetry,
fiction, and literary scholarship. For example, Saul Tchernichowsky
published "Al harei gilboa" (On the Mountains of Gilboa), his response
to the Arab riots in Hebron. These riots, which galvanized Greenberg
into political activism, were also responsible for S. Y. Agnon's suffering
the second of his great traumas when his library, reconstituted after a
disastrous conflagration in Berlin in 1924, was again burned down in
Jerusalem.

In 1929, another writer—neglected, scorned, and actively disliked by
most of these exalted figures and excluded from the canon—produced
one of the finest, if deeply flawed, novels in the Hebrew language: *Haye
nisuim* (*Married Life*),[1] published in Palestine. Its author, David Vogel
(1891–1944), was an enigmatic figure who was forgotten for many years
until his rediscovery by the Israeli poet and scholar Dan Pagis in the

1960s. Since then, he has become one of the most canonical of the modern Hebrew writers, more suited to the aesthetics of our time than those of the original literary arbiters.

Vogel was born in Satanow, Podolia, in 1891. Little is known about his education or his family. He appears to have been orphaned at a young age and to have begun his life of wandering at thirteen. The facts of his adult life are dismal. He arrived in Vilna in 1909 or 1910 and left there in 1912 after having been arrested for avoiding the army. On his release, he moved to Lemberg and, in 1912, to Vienna. In 1914, he was imprisoned as an enemy alien. On his release, he returned to Vienna, married, and in 1926 moved to Paris, where he remained for three years until a brief attempt to live in Palestine (1929–1930). After that, he wandered for two years, earning his keep as a Hebrew teacher while suffering from tuberculosis. He eventually settled in Paris. With the advent of the Second World War, Vogel was again imprisoned, this time by the French, as an enemy alien and deported by the Nazis in 1944. These events are not recounted in his poetry or fiction; the only aesthetic mark they have left is a sense of ominousness and personal loss.

Despite the origin of this sense of loss in Vogel's life events, it was not unique to him but constituted part of the aesthetic equipment of his contemporary European artists during the interwar period. Whether he was influenced by specific contemporary trends is uncertain, but there is no doubt that his poetry and fiction conformed in mood, theme, and style with much of the experimental writing of the time. Yet his almost total disregard of the apocalyptic events of his time and of his own life in all but a few of his poems and his lack of references to Judaism, Jewish history, Jewish nationalism, or Zionism throughout his work make him difficult to place within Jewish literary history.

If Vogel is considered in the context of modernist rather than Hebrew literature, of European mood and style rather than Jewish culture, he finds a secure, if rather strange, place as a European writer who wrote in Hebrew, exemplified by *Married Life*, about which the literary scholar Gershon Shaked dismissively ruled, "[It] is an Austrian-Viennese novel that happened to be written in Hebrew."[2] At the same time, many factors in Vogel's life are typical of the life of a Jewish writer at that time: his traditional education, his rootlessness, detachment, and poverty. At the end of the 1920s, the emphasis on cultural disintegration and social breakdown was as much the province of the deracinated European Jewish intellectuals as of modernism, as was the desire to replace the ruined structures of the past with new aesthetic constructions. Even in Vogel's later poetry and in *Married Life*, when he concentrates increasingly on wandering and uprootedness, he is reflecting the Jewish experience in addition to the modernist aesthetic. As Ruth HaCohen argues, "Discontinuities were essential to the artistic process, and they were acutely pertinent to modern Jewish artists, however differently the latter interpreted their Jewishness."[3]

Yet the charting of the movement away from Jewishness and traditional Jewish culture, the *kera* (split), which became the motivation for so much Jewish literature of the time and, in fact, for the development of the modernist impulse in this literature, is totally lacking in Vogel. Why, then, did this most estranged Jew write in Hebrew, so much associated at that time with nationalist ideology? He certainly spoke Yiddish, and he became proficient in German and probably knew Russian. Shortly after his unhappy year in Palestine (May 1929–Spring 1930), he published his acid criticism of contemporary Hebrew writers.[4] Perhaps he intended to show them that he should be counted among the ones he praised: Brenner, Gnessin, and Dvora Baron. A less romantic reason is that *Married Life* was published in Palestine, written, perhaps, for the Hebrew readership there. We know from his diary that before the war he read German texts to the exclusion of any others, but he also expressed his desire to become proficient in Hebrew and by intense application learned the language to perfection. "The first of my endeavors was to learn Hebrew fully—I wanted to learn Hebrew completely" (diary, 5 February 1913).[5] He gives a strange reason for this endeavor: he wanted a job as a *shamash* at the synagogue.

None of these possibilities is entirely convincing on its own, particularly in relation to the essentially European *Married Life*. Perhaps the most persuasive reason for his writing in Hebrew is his realization that he would not achieve acceptance into the German-language mainstream represented by Schnitzler, Musil, and their circles, whereas writing in Hebrew, he would be a unique partner to them.[6] In an echo of Maurice Ravel's famous advice to George Gershwin, Vogel might not have wanted to be a second-rate Schnitzler but, rather, a first-rate Vogel.[7]

Vogel's Hebrew in *Married Life* was a transmutation of the classical Hebrew he had studied into a language that suited the complexities of interwar Vienna. With its "phono-semantic transposition," that is, the concealed presence of German in his Hebrew,[8] it became a fittingly innovative instrument for a narrative that ignores the other Hebrew writers' teleological concerns to echo only the prevailing preoccupations of modernist Vienna. Also, as Ruth HaCohen has pointed out, his characters do not "speak" Hebrew.[9] Vogel's linguistic style was unique, drawing here and there from Gnessin and Brenner and perhaps from Schnitzler's German, but ultimately an instrument identified as his own and, according to some scholars, possessing modern overtones, almost as if his prose were written today.[10] However, in Vogel's own time, Bialik accused him of creating a disproportionate number of unnecessary neologisms, particularly adjectives and adverbs,[11] and contemptuously dismissed his style.[12] In fact, the editor of *Married Life*, Asher Barash, altered some of Vogel's unusual formulations in order to accord with more conventional linguistic usage. With Vogel's idiosyncratic use of Hebrew, the authentic expression of a verbal *gedanke*, he attempted to transform Hebrew into a vehicle to serve his own vision, almost akin to the experiments in musical morphology and structure taking place in Vienna at the time.

Vogel himself recognized his identity as a child of Europe. In 1914, he writes, "Again I'm facing a new period in my life whose focal point is German culture" (diary, 5 February 1913). After his abortive experiment in Palestine, he returned to Paris with many excuses and, after being reprimanded by Leo Motzkin, retorted to a friend, "Let him bear the *hamsins*. Me—my home is here. This is the only air I can breathe."[13] In a short tribute to Y. H. Brenner, Vogel admits to identifying with Brenner's characters and hence with "the Jewish tragedy" but concludes, "We have already given ourselves in the great world to a new moulding, to European garb."[14]

It was this European garb that contributed to Vogel's alienness within the mainstream of modern Hebrew literature. At twenty-one, he was already thinking about himself as a European, offering a modern psychological observation of the processes of his life rather than "filtering his experience through the Bible and Talmud and hassidic homily."[15] There seemed to be something offensive to the Hebrew literary canonizers of the day about a Jewish writer creating European literature in Hebrew. Early in Vogel's career, he noted in his diary, "In my deepest heart I feel something in me that others don't have, that it's impossible that my talents should achieve no more than the level of a teacher—and then at the same time I feel, it seems to me, that there is no greatness in me—and then—I have a terrible pang in my heart. I can't accept the idea that I'm one of the mass" (17 March 1913). "I would like to develop and perfect my literary talent, because I will not surrender and doubt my talent. I haven't been discovered [*hitgaleti*] as much as I could be; I haven't yet found *me* and it isn't yet clear to me what I am, but that I have something in me—that is not in doubt" (24 May 1913). Later, Vogel confirmed his youthful instinct and summarized his own achievement: "I haven't written much, but I'm thankful that there has never been any writing in Hebrew such as mine. I have something different in me. Is this not so?"[16] This "difference" that constituted Vogel's poetic sensibility was alien to the developing Hebrew literature both in Europe and in Palestine during the first two decades of the twentieth century.

Vogel and Vienna

The exact period of the composition of *Married Life* is not known. Pagis suggests that Vogel was already writing it in 1926 while living in Paris, and he might have completed it in Tel Aviv. The novel exemplifies Vogel's "incorrigible Europeanness"[17] while offering rare instances of a Jewish sensibility in his assimilated Jewish protagonist, a writer named Rudolf Gurdweill who dines on pork and reads the New Testament. Gurdweill once mentions anti-Semitism and describes his own childhood fear of the Christians in his town. He becomes engaged to an Austrian baroness, Thea von Takow, and inexplicably insists that they marry in a synagogue in Vienna's Jewish quarter, to which she, equally inexplicably, agrees. Elsewhere in the novel, Gurdweill sits in a café and imagines a speech given by the president of the Aryan Nature Lovers Meeting which reflects every anti-Semitic staple of the day: love of nature and pure fresh air in the spirit of Christ's teaching and the importance of preserving this teaching from undesirable foreign elements penetrating from the East. Gurdweill finds this imagined diatribe

"highly agreeable and soothing" (*ML* 178), as if he were one of the Jew-
hating nature lovers.

The bipolar marriage of Thea and Gurdweill is disastrous, a sado-
masochistic union from which Gurdweill is unable or unwilling to
escape. Vogel portrays in mimetic detail Thea's savage contempt for
her husband and her willful abuse of him. They have a child who dies
in infancy. Generally Gurdweill soothes his agitated psyche by roam-
ing the city's streets, meeting friend in cafés, and attempting to work.
Schnitzlerian in scope, the novel is nothing like Schnitzler's anato-
mization of Viennese society or of the Jewish dilemma, his moralism
or political musing, but it is rather an introspective expression of pas-
sive helplessness and "transcendental homelessness"[18] exemplified by
Gurdweill's ceaseless peregrinations through Vienna's streets. It is this,
perhaps, that lends some conceptual justification to the teasing out of
a Jewish sensibility. Of course, if one wants to read the novel as an allegory, the German baroness Thea serves as the brutal and unrelenting
germanism that first woos and then oppresses the innocent Jew.

During the times of Vogel's sojourn in Vienna, the city was already
emerging from its fin-de-siècle ferment, the "joyful apocalypse," as
characterized by Herman Broch in an oxymoron that embodied all the
city's paradoxes and contradictions. *Married Life* communicates Vogel's
perception of the city's role in social and psychological breakdown. In
the late 1920s, it was still suffering the scars of the war, "burdened by
daily cares, boredom or simply fear. . . . The rootlessness grew even
worse after the war until it seems that all these people are actually sorry
they survived" (*ML* 75). Perhaps as a consequence of the war, the city
bred "suicide, madness, masochism, prostitution, death, like an urban
nightmare. Perversion of the norm inside and outside" (*ML* 159–160).
The journalist Ferdinand Kürnberger formed his own assessment: "lazi-
ness, frivolity, vulgarity, moral degradation, unmanly childishness,
wicked lust after pleasure, panting after smut, worship of filth, hatred of
culture, callous, dissolute, self-glorifying, absolute shabbiness."[19] Gurdweill meditates on Vienna's

> sense of desolation, in the air, of a dreary, futile, hopeless poverty, of a
> profound and permanent misery, which was hidden by day and now
> crawled out of its holes and exposed itself boldly in all its nakedness,

breaking out of the silent houses and the wretched creatures left in the street, welling up from the very paving stones. The other side of life revealed itself, like the shabby lining of a garment which looked well enough on the outside. (*ML* 403)

Yet this wholly negative Vienna attracts Gurdweill, as it did Vogel on his arrival there in the winter of 1912. On December 13, 1912, the twenty-two-year-old Vogel exults in his diary, "Ha-ha-ha, at last I'm in Vienna." Almost immediately he begins to complain about hunger, homelessness, and exhaustion after having traversed the city for many days looking for work and lodgings. At this time, poverty and the housing crisis in Vienna were so acute that even the local people were forced to live in caves dug in railway embankments, in boats, and in hiding places under the bridges and to sleep in rented bed space. Vogel confesses to his diary that he is weary of life and ready to die (within ten days of his arrival!). The diary's leitmotif from that point is constant hunger, homelessness, exhaustion, a kind of *ennui*, and loneliness. He considers suicide but notes, despite his earlier entry, that he wants to live, emphasized by two exclamation points. He has no friends, no money, and no lodgings. For a short while, during the Zionist congress, he finds work as a porter; he eats in public soup kitchens and sleeps in homeless shelters with "a thousand gentiles": "I live the life of a *shnorrer*—will it always be like this?" (diary, 20 February 1913). He considers escaping to America, Argentina, Brazil, Palestine, "no difference whither, only to escape, not to be here."[20] Despite his frequent decisions to move away and despite his appalling living conditions, Vogel remained in Vienna until after the war. He notes, "I have no friends, nothing. All my friends have stopped writing: See, I'm cut off" (diary, 18 July 1913). With unintended irony, he uses the word *talush*, a common designation for the deracinated European Jewish writers of his generation. He is placated only by walking in Vienna's streets and smoking in his room. When he is unable to sleep—sometime for entire nights—he walks. "I walk until boredom and sadness overtake me" (diary, 10 August 1913). Yet nowhere in the diary, despite his searching for jobs and places to eat, "shnorrering" from his acquaintances, giving the occasional Hebrew lesson, is there any mention of a place name. He moved from lodging to lodging, sat in public parks and gardens, walked the streets to the point of exhaustion, yet the city topos is unspecific, simply a location for the urban wanderer, pounding any city's pavements with the impermanence of the *flâneur*.

In many works of modern urban description, psychological and textual landscapes overshadow the mimetically presented city.[21] In Vogel's diary, the landscape is exclusively internal, that of his body, hungry and suffering from consumption (an ironic English term indicating the body's devouring itself), and of his mind, striving to realize his instinctive conviction of his own poetic genius. Ironically, it is in the *fictional* narrative that the anonymous, internalized "Vienna" of the diary takes shape as both the real Vienna of the 1920s and the modernist projection of discontinuity and fracture.

One of the most extraordinary features of the novel is Vogel's intricate mapping of Vienna's postwar landscape. If, indeed, the city possessed the negative characteristics ascribed to it by Vogel, Kürnberger, Schnitzler, and others, it was a chaotic urban space. *Married Life* is a chronicle of Gurdweill's incessant and increasingly disordered movement through the city and concurrently his mind, straining to clarify the enigma of his marriage. The mapping of the real city reflects the restless movements of Gurdweill's imagination, the streets his synapses, as he seeks an escape from the thing he most desires. He walks the length and breadth of the city, enjoying it at times of emotional surcease, when "feeling quite content" (*ML* 99), and tormented by it when he is alone and penniless: "He turned his back unconsciously on the well-lit, busy street because there was a heavy darkness in his soul, and he could not bear the light" (*ML* 355). Almost inevitably, following the unpleasant scenes between Gurdweill and Thea, Gurdweill is to be found walking, riding the trams, or sitting in the cafés or parks, walking "to soothe his pain and loneliness" (*ML* 355).

Mapping the city furthers his control of his world, for his Viennese topos is an extension of Gurdweill (and Vogel) himself, a metaphor, or personification, viewed through actual locations. Also, the city as inner narrative parallels a narrative about the city. Gurdweill is a central subject within the city's text, and as the novel progresses into a portrayal of his insupportable grief, he and the city become inseparable. "There was nothing but the muffled, distant roar of the city itself, which was perceived by the abstract imagination rather than the senses as if it rose intangibly from his very soul" (*ML*127). He wanders through named streets, squares, and parks and visits a few urban interiors, his former workplace, his friends' dwellings, the Café Herrenhof, a homeless shelter, and a hospital. In fact, he feels relief out of doors, for inside is Thea's domain. The urban landscape placates him and becomes the template for his mediation of his inner space.

Streets and alleys are also the city's nerves, conducting emotions, pain, and sexual desire, a perfect metaphor for Gurdweill's state of mind. Urban profligacy is not new to modern Hebrew fiction, suggesting religious, social, and personal alienation through the city as an image of licentiousness. Vienna itself is a convincing symbol of the erotic in the novel's heightened sexuality, which, as in many works of the time, indicates the disintegration of traditional values in postwar Europe. Perversion, infidelity, sexual jealousy, and despair are the novel's inner lining. The Gurdweills' relationship is almost violently sexual; Thea walks on the city's streets with her lover; young Lotte desires Gurdweill to the point of suicide and is in turn desired by his friend Dr. Astel; Gurdweill is seduced by the wife of an acquaintance whose "lips and body had left him with a disagreeable taste" (*ML* 65–66); he recounts to the unpleasantly excited Thea the story of his adolescent seduction by the family maid. It may be this, as well as the novel's structural and linguistic difficulties, that antagonized Vogel's critics, for while sex and sexuality were not unknown in the Hebrew literature of the time, the graphic decadence of Vienna's denizens, described in detail in a Hebrew narrative, would certainly have repelled them.[22]

From the beginning of *Married Life*, when Gurdweill watches a young suicide being dragged out of the river, we follow him from street to street and from house to house, their names and numbers inscribed in the most minute detail. His friends have specific addresses. Thea lives in the Währing; she proposes to Gurdweill on Sechsschimmelgasse; after their marriage they live in Gurdweill's room on Klein Stadtgutgasse; a young woman, Franzi, faints on Karlsplatz; Lotte walks into Lerchenfelder Strasse; the shoemaker Vrubiczek lives at 17 Liechtensteinstrasse; Lotte lives at 15 Myrtengasse; they turn left and right into and out of the streets and alleys. Gurdweill spends much time in cafés, mainly the Café Herrenhof, the most prominent literary café of postwar Vienna.[23]

Two deaths in the novel increase Gurdweill's pace and distance. His baby son, Martin, becomes ill and is hospitalized near the Augarten. Thea is indifferent to her child's condition, commensurate with her hostility to him since his birth, and Gurdweill, already hysterical with worry, becomes severely ill when the baby dies. Martin's death is both a narrative element to indicate Thea's far too literary evil and also a trope signifying Gurdweill's inability to write. Earlier in the novel, Thea had torn up the manuscript of his stories, and that, together with the child's death, recalls Hedda Gabler's burning of her former lover's manuscript, which both she and his new love, coincidentally called Thea, had characterized as his "child."[24] For Gurdweill, the baby's death signifies the end of any significant creative endeavor. He responds by taking to the streets and cafés, scuttling among the anonymous crowds that loom out of the darkness, as a means of avoiding his wife and her fatal attraction. As he is crossing Mariahilferstrasse after having left the hospital and his dead son, "a street opened up in front of him" (ML 380), reflecting his creation of the city in the image of his emotional upheaval. For once the street is not named: both his internal order and the city's order have been breached. Yet in one sense alone Gurdweill begins to heal: his determination that Thea's dominance is ended.

After the second death, that of Lotte—the only positive element, apart from the child, in the novel, the young woman whose love Gurdweill has ignored—his manic restlessness and confusion increase, and the novel's pages bristle with directions and place names. His mind in chaos, Gurdweill compulsively spreads himself across the city, covering vast distances from northeast to south: Rathaus Park, the Landstrasse District, Radetzskyplatz, Praterstern, Schrank Cemetery, back to Praterstern and Schwartzenbergplatz, all traceable on a contemporary map of Vienna. Some time later, the malevolent Thea casts Gurdweill out of their lodging, and again he wanders the streets during two nightmarish, expressionist nights, the novel's descriptive and emotional peak.

During the first night of wandering, Gurdweill muses that "he . . . now lived not at this or that address, but in the city of Vienna as a whole; in the literal sense of the words, he lived in Vienna" (ML 412). Soon after Vogel's arrival in Vienna from Komerna in 1912, he was dogged by poverty. As we have seen, entry after entry in his diary dwells on his hunger, his homelessness, the lack of work, the potential for starvation.

He refers to this in his novel, blurring the fictional boundaries: "[Gurdweill] remembered several nights a number of years before, when he had been obliged to wander the streets of this very Vienna for lack of lodgings or money, some of them when the autumn was quite well advanced, like now—" (*ML* 392).

The city, Gurdweill, and Vogel himself coalesce into one entity. Devoid of an address, living on benches in the park, riding the trams, and drinking unwanted cups of coffee, paid for by a few borrowed schillings, in the cafés for a temporary refuge from the rain, Gurdweill's homelessness robs him of the status of citizen when he is transformed into an element of the city itself. Not only that: it also awakens his compassion; he notices an urban panorama that transcends himself and Thea and allows the transmission of sentiments unknown in Vogel's diary, in which there are no characters other than himself. Vogel's diary entries suggested that, after a few nights spent in a synagogue courtyard for want of lodgings, he alone was reserved for the miserable fate of homelessness and poverty. The novel, written only a decade later, is his more mediated response to Viennese society as a whole. "Ah, the poor woman," Gurdweill muses, "how cold she must be! Without a hat, poor thing" (*ML* 404).

> And pity welled up in him for those unfortunates in Vienna and in the great cities of the world who were still outside forced to spend their nights on a bench under the open sky, or under a bridge or in the sewers. Society should see to it that every human being had somewhere to live and a bit of bread to eat—that at least!" . . . [He] reflected that the theatres, cinemas and so on could easily be converted into shelters for the homeless at night when they were empty anyway and no use to anyone. . . . It was shocking that people were forced to wander the streets all night long while these buildings stood empty! (392, 401)

Gurdweill's transformative experience during one long, cold night is akin to Lear's empathetic awakening on the heath. In fact, Gurdweill's physical and emotional odyssey takes place on a stormy night. Yet his recognition, no more than sentiment, leads nowhere, certainly not to the breaching of his egocentric isolation.

The two homeless nights begin with Gurdweill's importuning a friend, Perczik, for money. Perversely, Perczik obliges only after

Gurdweill has unburdened himself of all his secrets, in the duplicitous
city where "there really was no point in creating an open scandal" (*ML*
395) and secrets are kept well hidden. The confession is a therapeutic
unburdening of his life's travails, which contributes to his new determination to draw Thea's sting. Thereafter the activities of the night are
drawn in temporal and spatial detail, the time given from hour to hour
and every street, train station, and district visited by Gurdweill named,
as if his new resolve has been concretized in the city's space. Again he
seems to walk in a circle: to the Währinger District, the Volksoper, the
Kai, Praterstrasse (near his home), the Tegethoff monument, Heines-
trasse, Praterstern, Hauptalee, a ride on a tram for warmth, then back
to Praterstern. Throughout this long *Winterreise*, he reflects, his mind
as disordered as the layout of the streets, on his past, his relationship
with Thea, the capriciousness of his friends, his unrealistic plans for his
future, and his growing compassion for others, "the wretched creatures
who were obliged to be out on the street at such an hour" (*ML* 403).
Gurdweill, now exhausted and cold, shares a bench with other homeless
people; he has a midnight conversation with a waiter; he encounters a
woman with a red scar cutting across her face; he quarrels with another
woman over a few groschen and a newspaper. "He no longer thought of
the reason for his wanderings—he only knew that he was sentenced to
go on walking and walking, despite his terrible weariness. . . . 'There's
no rest for the wandering Jew!' he said to himself" (*ML* 401), a wry
aside, rather than a comment on Jewish history. At one point, Gurdweill fancies that he is split in two, one half in his bed, the other outside
his room, staring in at the window. Vogel frequently addressed himself
in his diary as a kind of twin, one living in the real world, the other a
viewer of beauty and nature.

While generally the streets have provided Gurdweill with liberation
from the agonies of the domestic interior, on his two homeless nights
they become a prison. His friends have disappeared, he has no money,
his home is barred to him. He finds shelter in a public facility with other
"benighted souls" (*ML* 414). The narrative moves between naturalism,
expressionism, and fantasy, when Gurdweill spends the night listening
to an extraordinary tale told by one of the men in the shelter. Finally,
demented by his isolation, hunger, and grief over Lotte's death, he goes
home, finds Thea in bed with her lover, and kills her. After the many

pages of detail about Gurdweill's descent into hell over two nights, Thea is dispatched in one sentence: "There was a brief groan, a shudder in the bed. A distant clock struck two" (*ML* 485). Throughout both nights, Gurdweill had noted the time, hour by hour, sometimes minute by minute, as if time were leading inevitably and deterministically to this hour of two, the hour of his ironic liberation.

Married Life is not cathartic; it ends with an inevitable tragedy and without any emotional purification or redemption, as is fitting in a work of naturalism. On the contrary, the novel's characters function within the inevitability of moral failure. Vogel is suggesting that the Viennese poison, like the mist that often dogs his protagonist's footsteps, seeps into every character, into Gurdweill, who collects razors, an intimation of the novel's subtextual violence and dismemberment; into Gurdweill's friends, who seem to do nothing but sit in the cafés; into his seductress, Gustl; into her husband, who joins a long line of Thea's lovers; into his brother-in-law Freddy, who tortures animals; and into the child, who is unable to survive the malevolent atmosphere despite his father's love. The consequence of all this is the "absolute nothingness" which is Gurdweill's judgment on life in the city, echoing Vogel's judgment in his diary entries of 1913. In a typically perverted moment of self-awareness, "Healthy people!—thought Gurdweill—He did not have the least desire to be of those healthy people. Besides they too were sick, sick without knowing it" (*ML* 176).Vogel claimed in his diary that suffering and illness contributed to his art. "I need suffering, insecurity, a life of abandon [or abandonment, *hefker*]" (6 October 1914). Gurdweill offers as an example of Vienna's sickness the strange behavior of the populace: "A crowd of curiosity seekers clustered round a huge furniture van which had lost one of its wheels" (*ML* 176). This mixture of horror and the banal, which characterizes the novel, completes the hallucinatory urban picture. The crowd is the collective voyeur, watching a drowned woman being pulled from the river, gawking at another fainting in the street, listening to yet another screaming in an asylum, a crowd always on the periphery of Gurdweill's vision.

Apparently Vogel wrote the majority of the novel while living in Paris. The story of Gurdweill and Thea could have taken place there, where there is no dearth of unhealthy sexual relationships. I believe, however, that *Married Life* is set in Vienna due to the author's own experience there, because Vogel had, like Gurdweill, lived "in Vienna" as a whole. Yet it seems he could write about the city he knew so well only when he was away from it. The novel charts the outer landscape perhaps as a memory, perhaps an exorcism of those years of unsettlement, at a time in Vogel's life when Vienna, the city and the image, could be relegated to the past. More likely, however, is that Vogel resolves his Viennese alienation by his elaborate mapping, despite the fact that the narrative of *Married Life* is not redemptive. Ultimately the proliferation of German place names increases the novel's *verfremdungseffekt*, reinforcing the strangeness of its language and setting. This essentially European story was published while Vogel was once again attempting to become ensconced, this time in a new world, far away from the preoccupations of Europe eternally tainted by the war. 1929 should have been a year of promise for him, but even the Palestinian sun could not outshine Europe's lure.

NOTES

1. Jerusalem/Tel Aviv: Mitzpeh, 1929–1930 (dates of publication are given as 1929 or 1929–1930, indicating that it was published in two parts). English translation by Dalya Bilu, *Married Life*, published by Peter Halban, London, 1988. Subsequent references are to the translated edition and appear parenthetically (as *ML*) in the text.

2. Gershon Shaked, *Modern Hebrew Fiction* (Bloomington: Indiana University Press, 2000), 127.

3. Ruth HaCohen, "Sounds of Revelation: Aesthetic-Political Theology in Schoenberg's *Moses und Aron*," *Modernist Cultures* 1.2 (Winter 2005): 111.

4. David Vogel, "Lashon vesignon basifrutenu hatze'ira" (Language and Style in Our Young Literature), *Siman Kri'ah* 3–4 (1973): 367–372. In an early entry in his diary, Vogel mocks a Zionist official for trying to persuade him to go to Palestine, with promises of all subsistence found. According to the entry, this person—"the principled man," as Vogel mockingly terms him—informs him that it is against his principles that he, Vogel, should remain in Vienna but that he should leave without delay for Palestine. "Ha-ha. To go to Palestine to work on the land—this does not suit my physical strength or my desire . . . the devil take them all!" (23 August 1913). During the Zionist congress, which Vogel scarcely mentions, he notes that he had managed to see the "greatest of our writers and poets . . . ha-ha-ha-ha!" (28 August 1913). 5. *Tahanot kavot*, ed. and with an afterword by Menahem Peri (Tel Aviv: Hasifriya Hahadasha/Hakibbutz Hameuhad, 1990), 271–326.

5. *Tahanot kavot*, 271–326. Subsequent references are cited parenthetically in the text.

6. I would like to thank Adriana X. Tatum (Jacobs) for her insights on this point.

7. See Howard Pollack, *George Gershwin: His Life and Work* (Berkeley: University of California Press, 2006), 728n. 5.

8. See HaCohen, "Sounds of Revelation," 133n. 23.

9. Ibid., 112.

10. Galila Mor, *Tsurah umashma'ut: 'Iyun bi-leshon ha-prozah shel David Fogel* (Be'er Sheva, Israel: Ben-Gurion University of the Negev, 1994), 8–9.

11. Ibid., 6–7.

12. He might have taken exception to Vogel's lines, "Now my forefathers have also said [*nishu*] / I am first," which seemed to suggest that Vogel saw himself replacing the traditional poets. See Yitzhak Bakon, *David Vogel: Hameshorer ke'oman "nistar"* (Jerusalem: Carmel, 2005), 18–19.

13. Dan Pagis, "Vogel: Ha'ish veshirato," *Molad* (June–July 1964): 196.

14. Vogel, "Lashon vesignon basifrutenu hatze'ira."

15. Robert Alter, "Fogel and the Forging of Hebrew Self," *Prooftexts* 13.1 (January 1993): 8.

16. Hillel Bavli, *Hadoar* 29 (1949): 33.

17. Alter, "Fogel and the Forging of Hebrew Self," 5.

18. Lukács's formulation, quoted in HaCohen, "Sounds of Revelation," 112.

19. Quoted in Steven Beller, *Vienna and the Jews, 1967–1938* (Cambridge: Cambridge University Press, 1989), 178.

20. That Vogel drew on the minutiae of his Viennese sojourn for the novel is reinforced by Gurdweill's brother-in-law Freddy's suggestion: "You know what, Rudolf, why don't we leave all this old junk behind us and go abroad together? To France, America, Brazil—the devil knows where! I'm sick of everything" (*ML* 323).

21. William Chapman Sharpe, *Unreal Cities: Urban Figuration in Wordsworth, Baudelaire, Whitman, Eliot, and Williams* (Baltimore: Johns Hopkins University Press, 1990), 10.

22. Pagis reports that in 1931 Vogel arrived in Berlin with the intention of publishing *Married Life* in German translation but met with little success. He suggests that the German Jews were reluctant to sponsor a Hebrew work whose Jewish hero marries a German Christian noblewoman and endures a pathological sexual relationship with her. Pagis, "Vogel," 197.

23. The Café Herrenhof on the Herrengasse was a famous literary coffeehouse that replaced the Café Central after the First World War. Both cafés were largely frequented by Jews. Regular guests included (at different times) Torberg, Werfel, Freud, Musil, and Hoffmansthal. Between the wars, there were over 1,250 coffee houses in Vienna.

24. Hedda, jealous of Thea, Løvborg's new amanuensis and inspiration, destroys his manuscript, his and Thea's "child." When the distraught Løvborg (who recognizes that he has lost the "child") returns to her house, she encourages him to commit suicide. She throws the pages into the fire and whispers, "Now I am burning your child, Thea! . . . Your child and Eilert Lvborg's . . . am burning—I am burning your child." Henrik Ibsen, *Hedda Gabler*, in *Our Dramatic Heritage*, vol. 4, *Romanticism and Realism*, ed. Philip G. Hill (Madison, NJ: Fairleigh Dickinson University Press, 1989), 357.

13

Radical Conservatism

Bashevis's Dismissal of Modernism

JOSEPH SHERMAN

1.

In Warsaw in 1929, the publishing house of Boris Kletskin brought out a miscellany titled *Amol in a yoyvl*. Bearing the subtitle *zamlbukh far beletristik*, this volume contained a selection of poetry and prose by some of the leading Yiddish writers of the day, including Kadia Molodowsky, Rokhl Korn, Meylekh Ravitsh, and Yehoshue Perle. Also included was a short story titled "Shammai Vayts" by a twenty-five-year-old newcomer, Yitskhok Bashevis, whose work had already attracted some favorable comment. Though by no means the first of Bashevis's stories to be published, this one was significant not only on account of the distinguished literary company it kept but also—and chiefly—because it put into skillful practice a theoretical commitment to literary realism, and hence a dismissal of experimental modernism, which Bashevis had outlined in a critical essay two years before.

By the mid-1920s, Yiddish writers in eastern Europe had to decide what direction their continued work should take. The stimulating modernist innovations in European literature that a number of contemporary Yiddish writers were keen to follow had been initiated before World War I and continued even more vigorously in its aftermath.[1] The problem with modernist experiments in Yiddish literature, however, was that outside the limited circles of an elite minority, there were few people to read and appreciate them. The radical new prose styles that had distinguished the work of David Bergelson and fellow members of the Kiev Group in the period before 1917 had been acclaimed almost exclusively by an educated, acculturated middle class for whom Yiddish was only one of several languages they read. This bourgeois class had been dispossessed and effectively swept away by the Russian Revolution, and the majority of Yiddish readers in the newly independent states of Latvia, Lithuania, and Poland were little interested in writing that made heavy intellectual demands on them. This was clearly proved by the sustained failure of Der Nister's heavily symbolic, stylistically innovative stories to gain any kind of serious critical attention, let alone a significant readership. Modernism as a viable mode for Yiddish prose had clearly failed, nowhere more obviously than in Poland, the traditionalist Yiddish scene of which Bergelson had virulently attacked in "Dray tsentren," the notorious essay with which he had launched his pro-Soviet journal *In Shpan* in 1926:

> Because of its conservative backwardness, [the Yiddish center in Poland] will take no risks for the new Yiddish culture and will under no circumstances defend it. . . . The Yiddish words with which this Jewish majority communicates are just as unproductive as they are themselves, and serve, like worn-out straw, exclusively for the bourgeois yellow newspapers they read; they . . . embody in themselves the Yiddish writer's delusion, his false hope that if such readers swallow the Yiddish yellow press with such avidity, they will eventually also begin to read literary works of art.[2]

Bergelson himself, confronting the total loss of his best readers, had now started building his hopes for the future of modern Yiddish literature on the advancement in the Soviet Union of the newly emancipated working class. Since for the most part these "masses" were uneducated and hence unsophisticated in their literary tastes, the rarefied innovations of form and language characteristic of modernism were wholly outside their reach and could have no appeal for them. Indeed, within the Soviet Union itself, a battle had by now been joined between those writers and critics such as Yekhezkel Dobrushin, Nokhum Oyslender, and Arn Kushnirov who attempted to retain a measure of artistic autonomy and those such as Moyshe Litvakov, Peretz Markish, and Khaim Gildin who demanded that literature should serve the aims of the Revolution by promoting the dogmas of the Bolshevik Party. Outside the Soviet Union, it was increasingly clear that for Yiddish prose to retain its readership, it had to be broadly accessible, a consideration that inevitably led in the direction of realism.

Against this background, in 1927 Yitskhok Bashevis published an essay in Warsaw's preeminent Yiddish literary journal, *Literarishe Bleter*, titled "Verter oder bilder."[3] Though it does not directly engage in polemics with any opposing viewpoint, by defending realism as the mode in which fiction can best represent observed reality, this essay makes a subtle critique of the limitations of modernism by articulating an artistic credo that Bashevis practiced throughout his career. Drawing a distinction between "*dos bild, der gesheener fakt*" (the picture, the event that has taken place), which, he maintained, has always been the attribute of "*der epishe-realer dertseylung*" (the epic-realistic story), and words, which are all that are needed to express "*dos gefil un gemit*" (the feeling and mood) that dominates the lyric, he insisted that "*der liriker* reagirt *oyf gesheenishn, ober der epiker-realist shtelt avek di gesheenishn gufe un lozt reagirn dem lezer*" (the lyric poet *reacts* to events, but the epical realist lays bare the events themselves and lets the reader react; 663, col. 1). Unlike the lyric poet, who can deal in generalities, he argued, the realist is of necessity confined to particulars, because the more subtle the mood that he wishes to convey, the more he needs details and the less he can rely on impressions. For Bashevis, the writer can only convince the reader through the presentation of what he calls "facts," data that can be apprehended by the five senses. The sole reality apprehended by the writer of the realistic story is the conduct—the actions—of the characters he describes; the only access the writer-observer can have to the interiority of his characters is their dialogue. Even here, Bashevis argues, dialogue serves an extremely limited function,[4] since dialogue, like the thoughts and innermost experiences of characters, is justified only insofar as it contributes something necessary to the essential picture. When too much effort is made to explore interiority, he contends, "*m'derfilt teykef az do iz bagangen gevorn a farbrekhn kegn der form fun dertseyln*" (one immediately senses that there has been a disruption of the narrative form; 663, col. 1).

Bashevis accepts that this narrow insistence on presenting only external details is limiting and that it renders the realistic writer incapable of expressing a great deal of human conduct, thought, and experience. The realistic artist, who is always obliged to paint pictures of the external world, entirely lacks the ease of the psychologist, for example, who when discussing the human soul, *"ken zikh banutsn mit ale verter fun verterbukh un afile shafn naye"* (can use all the words in the dictionary and can even invent new ones). Of necessity, therefore, the realistic artist, confined solely to creating pictures rather than using words, *"muz hinken ideyish"* (is constrained in ideas) and is as result limited in the scope of what he is able to portray. The realist's emphasis on externals, for instance, makes it very difficult to present characters such as intellectuals who live the life of the mind, whose entire experience is bounded by reflection, who present no striking outward characteristics, achieve everything quietly, and are for the most part not obvious "types." These people must be presented as thinking and speaking, not in short snatches of dialogue but in long conversations, or not at all. Not to tell of them at all, however, *"heyst ignorirn di mentshn vos lebn amshtarkstn, amfarviklstn"* (means ignoring those very people who live most vigorously, in the most developed way; 663, col. 2). This being the case, Bashevis recognizes, those personages who are above all suited to the epic-realistic story are *"der folksmentsh mit zayne etnografishe simonim, mit zayn humor, . . . der kler, un biklal ale di vos zenen traditsyonel"* (the folk character with his ethnographic traits, with his humor, . . . the clergy, and in general all those who are traditional types; 663–64, col. 2) Consequently, whereas any intellectuals who might be presented in "epic-realistic" writing appear pale and shadowy, the folk characters are the types that appear most boldly there. In quest of variety, therefore, the realist is often compelled to seek his material either in the criminal underworld or in the pages of history.

Here Bashevis implicitly calls attention to the subject matter of the modern Yiddish fiction of his time. Writers from Mendele and Sholem Aleichem to Weissenberg and Oyzer Varshavski had all depicted *folksmentshn*, types invested with superficially different externals to give them some individuality, but all ultimately referencing readily recognizable figures in traditional Jewish life. The most obvious use to which this kind of characterization is put is social satire, which modern Yiddish literature practiced as vigorously and with the same moral purpose as did Henry Fielding in English fiction during the eighteenth century:

I declare here once for all, I describe not Men, but Manners; not an Individual, but a Species. Perhaps it will be answered, Are not the Characters then taken from Life? To which I answer in the Affirmative; nay, I believe I might aver, that I have writ little more than I have seen. The Lawyer is not only alive, but hath been so these 4,000 Years. . . . He hath not indeed confined himself to one Profession, one Religion, or one Country; but when the first mean selfish Creature appeared on the human Stage, who made Self the Centre of the whole Creation; would give himself no Pain, incur no Danger, advance no Money to assist, or preserve his Fellow-Creatures; then was our Lawyer born; and whilst such a Person as I have described, exists on Earth, so long shall he remain upon it.[5]

Opponents of this kind of typological characterization, Bashevis recognizes, condemn it because instead of presenting an individualistic human being, writers who use it give the reader merely externals: "*anshtot tsu gebn dem mentsh, git men zayn malbesh*" (instead of giving the human being, they give his garments). Without the external markers of identifying garments such as the general's uniform or the rabbi's capote, ordinary individuals are of no use to the realist, who, the critics of realism claim, has not, and cannot have, any grip on innermost experience, because the essence of realism lies in the inclination toward exteriority. It is curious to note that in Bergelson's savage denunciation of the Yiddish cultural scene in Poland, he specifically singled out the limited typology on which Polish Yiddish writers drew in order to condemn them for their lack of vivifying engagement with contemporary life:

Like a grey monochromatic mass with the uniform mentality of shopkeepers, they no longer even offer any subject matter worthy of the Yiddish writer's creative contribution to Yiddish literature. They form a grey workaday background, dotted with the flickering penny candles of outworn Sabbaths and outworn Holy Days. To begin a narrative about them means beginning yet again from, "Once there was a rabbi and his wife," returning to stale old clericalism, to spiritual and material poverty, isolating oneself from universal modern thought.[6]

By this time, of course, Bergelson professed to believe that once "stale old clericalism" had been swept away, the so-called working masses, whom the Revolution was working to liberate all over the world, would provide the contemporary Yiddish writer with abundant material and a vibrant readership for a new kind of fiction. Bashevis, from his earliest years a radical conservative, had no such illusions.

On the contrary, Bashevis insisted in his essay that the realist has no desire to present what his characters are *thinking*; he would rather tell what those characters have *done*. The actions of each individual make clear what he or she wanted to do and thought about doing. Unlike actions, however, thoughts are formless, hence, "*der tsil fun episher dertseylung iz tsu gebn di klore un faktishe*" (the goal of epic prose writing is to provide the clear and the factual). This is why epic prose writing is so close to simple chronicling, because epic, like chronicle, draws directly from life. By contrast with the lyric poet, who regards the whole of external existence from the standpoint of personal emotion, the epic prose writer is a portraitist whose creation is justified only by what he observes, not by personal solipsism: "*Farnakhlesikn mir oyf eyn vayle dos kval fun droysn, un mir operirin mit undzere ineveynikste formen, kumt aroys di toyte proze*" (If we neglect for one moment the external source, and operate [only] with our innermost forms, we produce dead prose; 664, col. 2). The opponents of realism, Bashevis admits, are correct to complain that the realist writer is a rationalist, an "intellectual," but he regards this not as a defect but as a supreme merit. The epic-realist tale stubbornly avoids everything that cannot be perceived with the five senses because every true artist will readily admit that there is no other means of access into the understanding of human nature:

> Di kunst ken zikh nisht farlozn oyf keyn nisim un "oyfblitsn." Normal kenen mir di mentshlekhe neshome adank tatn, handlungen, reyd. . . . Der epiker-realist, vos meynt es ernst, ken in normaln fal nisht gebn dem helds makhshoves, oyb er vil gebn faktn un nisht hashores. (664, col. 2; 665, col. 1)

> (Art cannot rely on any miracles or flashes of "illumination." Normally we know the human soul thanks to deeds, behavior, speech. . . .

The epic-realist, who is in earnest, cannot normally impart the hero's thoughts if he wishes to impart facts and not conjectures.)

Bashevis concedes that epic-realistic writing must perforce omit many areas of life and can thus lose much, because not everything in human experience permits itself to be presented in those pictures that are the lifeblood of the realist. The most important parts of our lives— our thoughts and feelings—remain hidden. But, as he puts it, "*dos iz ir natur, un hobn taynes, farvos di reale-epishe dertseylung git nisht iber in gantsn undzer inerlekh lebn is azoy umzinik, vi hobn taynes far vos broyt zet on dem hunger un shtilt nit dem dorsht*" (that is its nature, and to complain that the epic-realistic story does not impart *in full totality* our inner life is as futile as complaining that bread satisfies our hunger but does not quench our thirst; 665, col. 2). Because of these limitations, he concedes, artists rebel against realism and seize instead on other "isms" and forms to express themselves. He identifies the most powerful of these as Expressionism, which in his view "*vil mit shturem iberbrekhn di vant un dergeyn tsum same tamtses*" (wishes with violence to break down the wall and reach the quintessence; ibid.).[7] For those who wish to remain consistent realists, however, the primary condition is to acknowledge and work within these limitations: "*bilder kenen nisht ibergebn alts, ober alts vos vert gegebn in a realer dertseylung muz gegebn vern nor in bilder*" (pictures cannot convey everything, but everything that is conveyed in a realistic story must be given only in pictures; ibid.).

However sincere Bergelson's personal belief in the ideals of the Revolution may have been, one of the chief motives for his commitment to the Communist cause was his desire to reach a new and wider readership. In consequence, he had abandoned the experimental modernism of his earliest work in favor of a vigorous new mode of contemporary realism that would supposedly appeal to working-class readers. The ongoing problem of attracting appreciative readers beset many serious Yiddish writers, whose work was denigrated by boorish critics on one hand and ignored by the sensation-seeking general public on the other, to the extent that they began to wonder if there was any future left for belles lettres in Yiddish. In Warsaw in 1928, even a writer by this time as hostile to modernist innovation as Israel Joshua Singer categorically declared in an open letter that the Yiddish language could no longer nurture the creative literary imagination.[8] I. J. Singer, having set his face against all forms of experiment, had become an inflexible realist whose technique his brother's essay implicitly defended. Bashevis was quick to offer a practical illustration of his credo that modeled itself on the example set by his brother, two of whose earliest stories, "Perl" (1920) and "Altshtot" (1923), had carried the realistic depiction of character through externals to a high level.[9] In 1929, therefore, the appearance of Bashevis's four-part story "Shammai Vayts"[10] aimed to dismiss all claims that modernism might have hoped to exert on his own work.

2.

Aiming to present an unsparing picture of Jews drawn away from the pieties of the shtetl to the opportunities offered in the big city, Bashevis chooses for his chief character a highly competent man on the make. His eponymous hero, who comes to Warsaw from Josefov with a wife and several children, is a worldly individual, shrewd, dishonest, and manipulative enough to succeed ruthlessly. In his pursuit of worldly aggrandizement, Shammai casts aside religious practice, but his wife clings stubbornly and fearfully to her religious observances as a protective barrier against what are for her the city's terrifyingly unknown forces. Since the wife's fears are as strong as the husband's ambitions, the destruction of their relationship is assured. This counterpoint is established in the details provided in the narrative's description of their first night in Warsaw:

> In shtub arayn iz er aroyfgekumen ersht shpet bay nakht. Di kinder zenen shoyn geshlofn pornvayz, di fatsiyate iz ful geven mit shtroy, bretlekh, keylim. In der kikh hot gebrent a fayer un s'hot gezotn a tshaynik tey. S'vayb iz gezesn oyf a niderik benkl, az dos kleyd iz gelegn oyf der erd, hot tseshtreyt un stam azoy di gantse tsayt gehaltn a meshenem shoysl bay beyde oyern, nokh alts nisht gekent kumen tsu zikh. S'hot zikh ir nokh alts gedakht, az m'loyft arum oyfn dakh, in der vant roysht epes, un az fun der gas hern zikh moyredike yeloles, vos haltn zikh in eyn dernentern. Shamay hot oyf ir a pintl geton mevinish mit eyn oyg, rakhmones bakumen, un fundestvegn geredt hart un mit gebeyzer:
> —Halt im fest, biz tog! Mne, bist shoyn eynmol a toygerin, bistu! . . .

—Az kh'ver dul—hot di yidene ongeneygt an oyer, vi a toybe.—
kh'veys nisht vos s'tut zikh mit mir! (82–83)

(He only returned home late that night. In the garret, cluttered with
straw, planks, pots, and pans, the children were already asleep two by
two; in the kitchen, a fire was burning and a pot of tea was on the
boil. His wife, seated on a bench so low that her skirt spread out on
the floor beside her, was abstractedly clutching a brass mortar by both
handles, still unable to gather her wits. She still imagined that there
was something running about on the roof, that something was making
noises in the walls, that the frightful screaming in the street outside
was continually drawing closer. Regarding her narrowly with one eye,
Shammai felt a stab of compassion yet spoke to her harshly and angrily
nevertheless:

"Are you going to cling on to that mortar till daybreak? A fine house-
keeper you are!"

"I'm going mad," she replied, cupping her hand behind her ear like a
deaf person. "I don't know what's happening to me!")

The story's implied time frame is made factually significant in depicting the extent of Shammai's single-mindedness. He comes down to
Warsaw from Josefov *"mit yorn tsurik"* (years ago), clearly while Poland
was still part of the tsarist empire, since Shammai, we are told, took on
printing jobs—using his one and only old-fashioned pedal press—for
*"dem komisaryat, geyt mit zey in shenk arayn, redt rusish vi an emeser
fonye"* (the tsarist police [the commissariat], went drinking in bars with
them, spoke Russian like a native), keeps on friendly terms with the
corrupt, anti-Semitic chief of police, and gets involved in all manner of
illicit dealings (85). By the time he is a wealthy and successful big-time
printer, however, we are clearly in times contemporary with the story's
publication, which means that the Great War, the Russian Revolution,
restored Polish independence, and the war against the Bolsheviks must
all have come and gone, yet none of this is in any way reflected in the
narrative, which focuses exclusively on everything Shammai does. This
is obviously deliberate: events are viewed solely through the concerns of
the story's title character. War and revolution seem not to have affected
Shammai's self-advancement in any significant way, since, following his

arrival, "*ersht shpeter mit etlekhe yor*" (only a few years later), his rivals suddenly become aware "*az Shamay iz nisht geshlofn, gemakht an oyster mit gelt*" (that far from dozing, Shammai had made a fortune; 86).

The narrative's presentation of Shammai's ruthless exploitation of Zombak, a formerly self-employed Polish printer whom drunkenness has driven into destitution, is an object lesson in Bashevis's insistence that the realist can convey subtleties of mood only through an aggregation of specific sensory details and can indicate the way his characters think only through what they say:

Vi alemol, ven der goy hot zikh ongetrunken, flegt Shamay grod demols zikh nemen mit im rekhenen:

—Pani Zombak, mir rekhenen zikh op, gikher! Shpeter vel ikh nisht hobn keyn tsayt! . . .

Der goy flegt zikh koym haltn oyf di fis, gevaklt zikh beysn geyn, vi er zol tretn oyf a shtrik. Zayne groyse, breyte farshmirte hent sharn aroys fun di tsu kurtse arbl bloy-ongelofene, mit aroysgezetste odern, un zey hengen nokh. Dos ponem iz royt, shveysik, vi nokh a tifn, oysmatern-dikn shlof. Di glezern-farlofene oygn kukn mevueldik, farvirt. . . . Amol a gantser porets un a rekhnmayster, shemt er zikh tsu vayzn, az s'kumt im on shver tsu makhn a khezhbm, hust tsu mit a shvern, beyzn brum—a simen az r'iz maskem . . . beshas-mayse shoklt er tsu dem kop mit a min ongetsundener rugze, vi eyner zogt: kh'veys, yid, az du narst! . . . baroybt mikh un kh'vel zikh amol in dir noykem zayn! (88–89)

(As always, only when the man was dead drunk would Shammai set about calculating how much he was owed:

"*Pani* Zombak, let's work out your earnings quickly now! I won't have time later on!"

At such times, the Gentile could barely stand on his feet, swaying as though balancing on a tightrope when he walked, his huge broad ink-stained hands poking out of jacket sleeves that were too short and tinted blue by their engorged veins as they hung down at his sides. With his face red and sweaty as though he'd just been roused from a long, exhausting sleep, his glassy, watery eyes stared out in bewilderment and disorienta-tion. . . . At one time a substantial property owner and bookkeeper him-self, he was now ashamed to show that he found difficulty in making a proper accounting, so he coughed with a deep, angry growl to signal his agreement. At the same time he shook his head in a kind of smoldering rage as though to say: "I know you're cheating, Jew. . . . You're robbing me and I'll get even with you one day!")

The narrative never permits the reader to forget that Shammai is a Jew whose conduct is being evaluated according to the ethical imperatives of Judaism. The extent to which these are impotent in the materialistic world of Warsaw is bodied forth in the figure of Shammai's virtually mute wife, Sheyndl. Though her terror of the big city is presented in part 1 as the product of ignorant fear, and in part 2 her insistence on strictly following all the ritual observances she had known in the shtetl is dismissed by Shammai as *"yozefover narishkayt"* ([provincial] Josefov foolishness), the detailed precision with which Sheyndl's mental and physical decline is presented in part 3 invests the description with a dimension beyond itself, moving from the plainly literal to a metaphor for the death of traditional Jewish life in the social order created by Jewish emancipation. Ignored by her husband and her rapidly acculturating children, the increasingly sick Sheyndl

iz dervayl gevorn geshvolener fun tog tsu tog, ir hoyt iz gevorn glantsik, vi ongeshmirt mit boyml, di oygn—kleyn, fargosn, vayslekh, khaloshesdik un mutne, ful mit der shtoynendiker fremdkayt un meuyemdiker tseshmeykhltkayt, vi di farenderung vos kumt fun a tson-geshvir. (91)

(grew more bloated by the day. Her skin took on an oily sheen, while the cloudy, bilious whites of her narrowed, watery eyes filled with a startled sense of alienation and her face twisted into the kind of ghastly grin caused by a tooth abscess.)

The capacity of this meticulous presentation of physical details subtly to develop pictures into symbols had been demonstrated earlier in the work of Israel Joshua Singer, and it was a technique that Bashevis went on exploiting throughout his career; it manifested itself most tellingly in *Der sotn in Goray* (1935). In 1929, however, Bashevis was still exploring its possibilities, evident from the way he moves his narrative to a surprisingly bleak conclusion.

At first Bashevis seems to be following the conventions of pulp fiction by making Shammai, immediately after his wife's death, neglect his business affairs, dress like a dandy, and take up with Gentile whores. But the prurient remarks of Shammai's envious fellow printers—all Jewish themselves—are confounded when, for shamelessly material reasons, he quite unexpectedly starts paying court to a rich but ugly Jewish widow of fifty-odd years whose deceased husband was active in numerous communal charities. Though she herself is the subject of widespread slander—she is suspected of poisoning her husbands and of making a fortune in her youth from a partnership in a brothel (98)—it is ironically the Widow Vaysman who rebukes Shammai for his lack of any Jewish ethical sensibility: "*Ir zent den a yid, Shamay?—Zol yakh nisht oysdelebn s'yor, tsi ir hot in zikh far a groshn yaades. . . . Loyft arum nit shikses un shadkhnt zikh tsu alte vayber. . . . Aiyor volt aykh khotsh geshemt, volt aiyor*" (What kind of Jew are you, Shammai? May I never live to see out this year if you've got the slightest spark of Jewishness in you. . . . You run around with Gentile tarts and propose marriage to old women. . . . You ought to be thoroughly ashamed of yourself, so you ought!; 99). Of course, this is a case of the pot calling the kettle black, since for the widow as much as for the widower, Judaism is merely a routine of formal conventions, since their true commitment is to materialism.

The satiric edge of this story is designed to question whether, among the kind of temptations offered in the Polish capital, the survival of traditional Jewish values is even possible. As though deliberately trying to act out all the corruptions traditional shtetl Jews feared from the city, as soon as Shammai arrives in Warsaw, he abandons all pretense at religious observance, buying a synagogue ticket for Sabbaths only "*kedey tsu hern dem khazn, dem leybn-bariton*" (merely so he could listen to the cantor's fine baritone; 86), shaves off most of his beard, and starts wearing a short jacket. He ridicules the obsessive piety of his wife, assuring her "*az in vos far a shul m'kumt, aza kdushe shpringt men*" (that one found the same holiness in whatever synagogue one attended; 89). His pursuit of social status by aping Gentile mores intensifies in proportion to his increasing prosperity: he leases an apartment in a Gentile neighborhood, buys fashionable furniture (including a piano), employs a Gentile maid who "*ken kokhn aristokratishe maykholim*" (could cook aristocratic dishes), and above all

ongezogt m'zol nisht lozn far di tir di kaptsonim un shnorers, vos raysn
op di glokn, farshmirn di divanes, un m'iz keynmol nisht zikher, tsi
s'zenen nisht amol farshtelte ganovim un merder. . . . Di kinder hot er
avekgeshikt in di gimnazyes, ongezogt zoher-vezoher m'zol oyfhern
reydn yidish. . . . Nishkoshe, m'vet di toyre nisht fargesn! (88)

(gave orders not to permit paupers and beggars to congregate at the
front door, where they kept ringing the doorbell, soiled the carpets, and
left one continually exposed to the danger that they might be thieves
or murderers in disguise. . . . He sent his children to be educated in
secular high schools, instructing them to be firmly on guard against
ever speaking Yiddish. . . . It made no difference, they wouldn't forget
the Torah!)

Since his children have no *toyre* to start with, there is nothing for them
to forget. Shammai himself reduces even the rites of death to commercial and social calculation, haggling over the Jewish burial society's
charges yet wheeling and dealing to obtain "*a laytishe karke*" (a respectable burial plot) and paying for "*a nekrolog oyf Poylish*" (an obituary
notice in Polish; 95–96).

The story's movement into social satire—the natural mode of realist writing—is completed when Shammai marries the Widow Vaysman
in a ceremony devoid of all but materialistic significance. The detailed
description of this bourgeois bacchanal (101–2) demonstrates the effec-
tiveness of using clothing as signifiers of values, a device that has characterized the narrative throughout. When we first see Shammai as a
newly arrived provincial, he is wearing a "*shvartser galitsyaner farfle-
kter kapelyush, velkhn r'hot geborgt bay a kireshn korev, kedey oystsu-
zen daytshmerish*" (a stained black Galician-style cap, borrowed from
an Austrian relative in an attempt to look more like a Western European; 80); later, as a wealthy widower paying his first courting call on
the Widow Vaysman, he has "*genumen trogn vayse gvirishe kelner un
manketn, arayngeshtekt a diamantenem broshke in zaydenem royt-bloy-
vaysn kravat, opgegolt di resht bord*" (started wearing the starched white
collars and cuffs of a rich man, stuck a diamond pin in his red, white,
and blue cravat, shaved off what was left of his beard; 96). The desire
for assimilation that his clothes define for him is replicated in his son,

214 << JOSEPH SHERMAN

the Polish-named Shimek, who is clad in "*a hitl mit a ledernem dashek un in kurtse heyzlekh mit shtiker lidkes in droysn*" (a cap with a leather visor and short trousers adorned on the outside with suede patches; 91), and in his *arriviste* colleagues who arrive at his wedding reception "*in harte tsu kleyne kapelyushlekh un in gemzene shikh mit gumes*" (wearing hard hats that were too small for them and suede shoes with rubber soles; 101). Inner nature is exposed in outward appearance. His feral Polish mistress, Helena, is "*a hoykhe parshoynte, zeyer a dike, an opgepuderte, in a breyt hut mit blitshtshendike shpilkes un arum di akslen—a groysn breytn futernem kolner mit a beyz sharf-tseyndik khayele fun same forent*" (a tall, stout, heavily powdered individual wearing a broad-brimmed hat held in place with glittering hatpins and a substantial fur wrap fronted by the head of an angry, sharp-toothed little creature around her shoulders; 97). His rich but decaying bride, on the other hand, is enrobed in "*a vays zaydn kleyd, ful bahongen mit tsirung, in lange shvere brilyantene oyerring oyf di oysgetsoygene leflekh, di veynike hor—bashtekt mit blitshtshendike kem un hoykh baleygt mit fremde lokn. Fun ire kurtse finger hobn geloykhtn shteyner fun farshidene kolirn*" (a white silk dress, bedecked with a mass of jewelry, with long, heavy diamond earrings dangling in her elongated earlobes, while her scanty hair, pinned up with gleaming combs, was piled high with the aid of hairpieces. Gems of different colors sparkled on her stubby fingers; 101). Though separated by wealth different in both kind and degree, the adornments of both these women are characterized by the adjective *blitshtshendik*, which highlights their meretricious vulgarity, making them perfect partners for a man like Shammai. The final comment on the emptiness of all this comes in the description of the grossly overweight officiating rabbi with "*shvere horike hent, vi a shoykhet*" (heavy hairy hands like a ritual slaughterer): only after he has adamantly refused to reduce his fee by a single groschen is he then "*plutsling zikh farfrumt*" (suddenly overcome with an access of piety), so that his formulaic expression before leading the party to the bridal canopy—"*geloybt der oybershter*" (praise God)—becomes a mockingly ironic comment on the total effacement of Jewish values dramatized in the tale as a whole (102–3).

3.

With the appearance of "Shammai Vayts" in 1929, Bashevis made it clear that, in his view, the only direction Yiddish fiction in general, and his own work in particular, could follow if it was to retain its readership was that of the narrative presented in what he had defined two years previously as the "epic-realistic" mode. As far as Yiddish prose was concerned, modernism and its innovations were a dead end. With the readership of Yiddish prose dwindling as many Yiddish-speaking Jews hastened away from Yiddish culture as rapidly as they abandoned religious observance, it could only hold their attention through fiction that spoke in unambiguous language about sociopolitical and cultural situations with which they were thoroughly familiar and fully able to share. If Bergelson and the most gifted of his modernist followers had fostered a belief, however impossible of realization, in the possibilities of creating, through different style and subject matter, a substantial readership among the ranks of the "working masses," Bashevis was quite clear that he would continue to address what was left of the bourgeoisie. If Bergelson was determined henceforth to speak to *horepashnikes* of the bright promises that socialism held out in the Soviet Union's brave new world, Bashevis was equally resolved to cultivate his readers among those who still had sufficient love of the Yiddish language to want its fiction to evoke the world they knew, with all its imperfections. This, after all, was the point at which modern Yiddish literature had started, and—as far as Bashevis was concerned—by 1929, this was where it had stopped. The ironies of history, however, cheated them both. Bergelson's hopes for the preservation of Yiddish language and culture were steadily crushed by Stalinism, his own style and subject matter crippled in the straitjacket of a "socialist realism" that demanded "objective" presentation of images increasingly removed from the brute reality of Soviet life. Emigration, assimilation, and ultimately, Hitler's *Khurbm* ensured that Bashevis, following his strictly realist path in declining to sentimentalize or idealize the murdered Jews of eastern Europe, found his widest readership not in Yiddish but in translation and not among Jews but among Gentiles for whom not only the Yiddish language and its culture but Judaism and Jews themselves were wholly unfamiliar. Neither embracing modernism, as Bergelson did, nor dismissing it, as did Bashevis, ultimately preserved a significant body of general readers for Yiddish literature in the twentieth century.

NOTES

1. Rilke, Kafka, Mayakovsky, and D. H. Lawrence were among those who published work before the war; Proust, Joyce, and T. S. Eliot were among those who published after it, notably in the modernist *annus mirabilis* of 1922, when both *Ulysses* and "The Waste Land" appeared in print for the first time.
2. David Bergelson, "Dray tsentren," *In Shpan* 1 (1926): 84–96. English translation as "Three Centres," in Joseph Sherman and Gennady Estraikh, eds., *David Bergelson: From Modernism to Socialist Realism* (Oxford, UK: Legenda, 2007), 349.
3. Yitskhok Bashevis, "Verter oder bilder," *Literarishe Bleter* 34 (1927): 663–65. Subsequent references to the Yiddish text appear parenthetically in the text; translations are mine.
4. He admits Dostoevsky as the only exception to this rule: "*m'darf dafke hern reydn Dostoevskis a held kedey im tsu derzen*" (we need only hear one of Dostoevsky's heroes speaking in order to see him; Bashevis, "Verter oder bilder," 663, col. 1).
5. Henry Fielding, *Joseph Andrews* (1742), Book 3, Chapter 1.
6. Bergelson, "Three Centres," 350.
7. Though he does not say so, Bashevis may well have been thinking specifically of Peretz Markish, at this time Yiddish literature's leading Expressionist, who had worked in Warsaw in the years 1920–1922 as the leader of the avant-garde group known as *Di khaliastre*.
8. See Anita Norich, *The Homeless Imagination in the Fiction of Israel Joshua Singer* (Bloomington: Indiana University Press, 1991), 20–23.
9. Elsewhere I have examined these two stories in some detail. See Joseph Sherman, "Fiction from the Outside In: Two Stories by Israel Joshua Singer," *Slavic Almanac* 11.1 (2005): 61–77.
10. First published in *Amol in a yoyvl: zamlbukh far beletristik* (Warsaw: B. Kletskin, 1929), 80–103. Subsequent references appear parenthetically in the text; translations are my own.

14

Desire, Destiny, and Death

Fantasy and Reality in Soviet Yiddish Literature around 1929

MIKHAIL KRUTIKOV

1929 was the last year when texts that openly challenged the proletarian aesthetics could still appear in the Soviet Union, but this was also a year when a series of high-profile ideological campaigns against prominent writers made it clear that this kind of writing would not be tolerated any longer. In one way or the other, these ideological storms affected practically every Yiddish writer of note, including Leyb Kvitko and Der Nister, Lipe Reznik and Noah Lurye, Itsik Kipnis and Perets Markish.

Markish's two books about the revolution which appeared that year, the novel *Dor oys, dor ayn* (A Generation Goes, a Generation Comes) and the long narrative poem *Brider* (Brothers), were labeled by the leading Communist critic Moshe Litvakov as nationalist for celebrating exclusively Jewish heroes and martyrs of the revolutionary struggle. In some cases, ideological accusations served as a pretext for settling personal scores. So Kvitko, who by that time had established a solid reputation as a popular poet for both children and adults, was severely reprimanded for his trenchant poetic satire of Litvakov, in which he allegorically portrayed the powerful editor of the Moscow daily *Der emes* as "Shtingkfoygl Moyli" (Stinking Bird Moy[she] Li[tvakov]). Kvitko was accused of violating party discipline and sent to work at the Kharkov Tractor Factory.

The international situation also had its effect on Soviet Yiddish politics. In the aftermath of the outbreak of Arab violence in Palestine, a group of high-profile American Yiddish writers, including H. Leyvick, publicly resigned from the American Communist daily *Morgn-frayhayt,* which stuck to the Soviet line of supporting the Arabs against the Jews. The Soviet Yiddish writers were forced to sign a resolution declaring the rupture of all relations with the "supporters of British imperialism."[1]

The eventful year 1929 marked the watershed between the period of relative stylistic and thematic freedom and the new era of the ideological dictate in Yiddish literature, which by 1934 had solidified into the doctrine of socialist realism. Yet 1929 was also a year of remarkable literary productivity, a fact that is often allowed to be overshadowed by the bleak political situation of the 1930s. Along with the aforementioned works by Perets Markish, among the most interesting publications were collections of stories by Der Nister and Shmuel Godiner, as well as the novels *Midas hadin* (The Measure of Judgment) by David Bergelson and *Ele Faleks untergang* (The Downfall of Ele Fakek) by Meir Wiener.[2] All these works were experimental in their style and approach to the material and reflected the sense of perplexity and disorientation among the east European Jewish intelligentsia in the aftermath of a turbulent period of wars and revolutions, when things had settled down and a new order had taken clear shape.

A Bolshevik Lilith: Short Stories by Der Nister and Shmuel Godiner

For Der Nister, 1929 marked the end of his prolonged Symbolist period. To a large degree, this was enforced by ideological criticism from above, but to some extent it had come about naturally because of the exhaustion of his creative resources. Der Nister's swan song as a Symbolist was the story "Unter a ployt" (Under a Fence), which first appeared in the Kharkov-based literary monthly journal *Di Royte Velt* and was also included in the collection *Gedakht*.[3] The publication of this story caused an ideological upheaval which prevented Der Nister's fiction from being published for the next five years. The protagonist of the story, a former hermit scholar, has abandoned his vocation due to lack of students and has become a circus acrobat. The horseback act that he has to perform with a sadistic dominatrix in a lilac tricot named Lili (a name evoking Lilith, the mythological female creature responsible for seducing Adam) also includes his beloved daughter. Inevitably, his worst fear comes to pass, as the daughter falls off the horse and suffers a severe head injury. This incident triggers a series of nightmarish visions that play themselves out in the deranged scholar's mind. In one vision, he conducts a show trial in the circus of his former teacher and colleagues and sentences them all to death. In another vision, the situation is reversed. Now the protagonist stands accused by his teacher of abandoning his vocation and pursuing worthless goals; he is sentenced to death and burned to ashes. Miraculously, he survives the execution and pronounces his last words: "I spoke from the ashes and said: 'Stand up, my teacher and students. I deserved what was done to me. I brought you to shame, and you turned me to ash, and we're even, all equally brought to nothing. There won't be any grief in the circus. What kind of circus person was I really?'"[4] The story ends with the narrator waking up in his bed, apparently with a bad hangover.

This macabre and enigmatic story, inspired by the fiction of the German Romantic writer E. T. A. Hoffmann,[5] remains until today popular with scholars and critics, who offer a number of insightful interpretations. Thus, David Roskies reads it both as a premonition of the coming Stalinist terror, "the forced confession of the many writers . . . who would soon perish without a trace," and as a "universal parable on the fate and function of art in the modern world," a parable of the situation of an artist torn between the two worlds that are symbolically represented as the circus and the monastic tower. When applied to the modern Jewish situation, this story can also be read as a "statement on assimilation to European society."[6] According to Chone Shmeruk, Der Nister's tale is "nothing less than a grotesque portrayal of a Soviet writer's struggles and hardships."[7]

Yet it seems that the author himself was skeptical of any interpretation that yields a straightforward moral judgment. Indeed, the text of the story contains a statement to this effect, as if Der Nister was anticipating allegorical readings of the kind just mentioned. Like some readers of the story today, one of the protagonist's former students is also eager to grasp the meaning of the story: "What do you mean, sir? Why are you saying all this? Surely you must have something in mind," to which the protagonist replies, "but I had nothing else in mind, nothing else in the world. The only thing in my heart was the memory of how I had been insulted."[8] Accordingly, Delphine Bechtel interprets Der Nister's later Symbolist tales, including "Under a Fence," as the "collapse of allegorical symbolism": "No longer does Der Nister organize his stories around a central ideational referent, neither God, nor truth, nor any set of traditional values." In her view, this brings Der Nister's last Symbolist work close to Kafka, with both authors expressing an "irreducible opposition between a distinctively allegorical system and the obscurity of the message, between the tendency to allegorize the world and the inability to find a meaning for the allegory."[9]

It seems that Der Nister was engaged in the elaborate and hazardous endeavor of writing a parable about the situation of the time, which defied any straightforward interpretation. He constructs a fantastic situation, which anticipates, in a symbolic form, the scandal that the publication of the story would provoke in real life, that is, the show trial and forced confession of its author. This artistic provocation exposes the absurdity of the Soviet system of ideological control and affirms the sovereignty of artistic imagination over "real life." Of course, to accomplish such a remarkable feat, Der Nister had to risk his own professional and financial security, but in 1929 the punishment for an ideological transgression in literature was not as severe as in the 1930s. For some five years thereafter, Der Nister was unable to publish his original fiction and had to survive on a meager income from translations and journalism, complemented by modest support from his brother Max Kahanovich, a successful Paris art dealer.

In fact, contrary to the widespread impression, the reception of Der Nister's Symbolist works by Soviet critics was far from uniformly negative. Isaac Nusinov, a leading Soviet Marxist authority on Western, Russian, and Yiddish literature, endorsed the publication of *Gedakht* in his critical introduction to the book. Nusinov claimed that although Symbolism, as an artistic style, imposed limitations on Der Nister's ideological and artistic horizons, Soviet literature had room for writers like him: "Nister is not, and never will be, able to attain realistic creativity due to his artistic nature. His way of comprehending our reality remains that of symbolic commentary, of interpreting it through symbolic images. . . . It is Nister's responsibility to put this interpretation to the service of this revolutionary 'New Spirit' [referring to "Naygayst," the title of one of Der Nister's more optimistic earlier stories]. And this is a legitimate demand from our readership."[10]

Even Litvakov, a zealous Communist ideologist but also an admirer of modernism in literature, managed to combine his ideological criticism with praise of Der Nister's talent, drawing a clear line between Der Nister's "reactionary" ideology and his art.[11] Meir Wiener followed a similar line when he had to express his view in the form of ideological criticism of his friend's work. According to a press report from a meeting of the Kiev District Committee of the Communist Party, Wiener seemed to favor a compromise. On the one hand, he argued that "it is not right for Nister to mentor a literary group. True, he has influence because he is a strong artist and many young people learn from him." On the other hand, Wiener readily conceded that "recently Nister has tried to distance himself from his traditions, and this is a fact that must be welcomed."[12] The ambiguous position of such influential figures as Nusinov, Litvakov, and Wiener vis-à-vis Der Nister's symbolist writing left enough room for maneuver, enabling Der Nister not only to come back to Soviet literature in the late 1930s but to achieve a canonical status in it.

Shmuel Godiner, a talented young follower of Der Nister, published in 1929 a collection of stories written between 1923 and 1929. The title, *Figuren oyfn rand* (Figures on the Edge), conveyed the message that the heroes of the stories were marginal characters unable to find their place in the Soviet mainstream. They range from a Lubavich Hasid from Shklov selling cigarettes in Moscow to former revolutionary heroes unable to find their place in the peaceful life. One of them, a former Red Army commander named Tits, is now standing trial for the embezzlement of trade-union funds and a murder. Unsure whether a death sentence is justified for a revolutionary hero, the judge, a young woman named Marta, decides to pay him a visit in prison for an informal chat. Their encounter develops into an erotic attraction, and they share, in Yiddish, memories about moments in their lives, which were associated with violence and protest. Next morning Marta receives a call from a regional Party committee official, who urges her to dispose of Tits as quickly as possible and get on with the next case. This scene contains a reference to Sacher Masoch's classic *Venus in Fur*: To answer the phone call, Marta puts her naked foot on a bear skin on the floor. During the conversation, she tries to argue with the official from a legal point of view but is cut short: "you know very well what kind of law rules among revolutionaries and Communists."[13] Tits's brother, a revolutionary sailor, holds a similar view. He believes that a Communist should not be treated as an ordinary horse thief. It is better to be "dispatched in a comradely manner" than humiliated by having to clean toilets in prison like an ordinary criminal.[14]

Death in Krakow: Meir Wiener and the Galician Bildungsroman

One might say that the novel *Ele Faleks untergang* (The Downfall of Ele Falek) was written in a wrong language and published in a wrong place. Had it been written in German or Polish and come out in Berlin, Vienna, or Warsaw, it would have been likely to become part of one or another "Modern Jewish Canon," but written in Yiddish and published in Kharkov, then the capital of Soviet Ukraine, it was doomed. Its author, Meir Wiener, is known today to a small circle of Yiddish scholars for his work on Yiddish literary history, while his considerable literary legacy remains largely unknown. Born into a prosperous family in Krakow, then a multicultural city in the Habsburg Empire, Wiener attended classes at the universities of Basel and Zurich and began his literary and scholarly career in Austria and Germany. Among his early publications were German translations from medieval Hebrew poetry and essays on philosophical, political, and literary themes, as well as original poetry. Around 1921, Wiener gradually switched from German to Yiddish and began writing fiction and poetry, but he was unable to find a publisher for his works. His interest in Yiddish was probably facilitated by his friendship with émigré writers from the Soviet Union whom he met in Berlin: Kvitko, Markish, and Der Nister.

Wiener's new friends convinced him, who by that time had already been disappointed in Zionism and embraced Communist ideas, that he should come with them to the Soviet Union. They promised him a job and an opportunity to publish his Yiddish works. Both promises were kept, which enabled Wiener to launch a successful new carrier as a Soviet Yiddish writer, critic, and literary scholar. Wiener's first Yiddish publication appeared in the Soviet Union at the time of his arrival there in the autumn of 1926. A chapter from *Ele Faleks untergang* was published in 1926 in *Di Royte Velt*. The journal was founded in Kharkov in 1924 and focused initially on ideology and current affairs.

Kvitko, who returned to the Soviet Union a few months before Wiener, was appointed as one of the editors of *Di Royte Velt*. It was a period of change in that journal's editorial structure, which led to the expansion of its literary department.[15] During the first half of the 1920s, poetry was the predominant genre in Soviet Yiddish literature, and so it was not easy to find new prose works to fill the extra space allocated to literature. This might explain a certain lack of ideological vigilance in choosing Wiener's text for publication. To pay lip service to Soviet dogmas, Wiener (or one of the editors) added a short introductory note, describing the work as a "story of a Jewish intellectual who is doomed to fail because he belongs, by his origin, education, and economic position, to the so-called dwarf bourgeoisie. Ele Falek was lost in decadent bourgeois ideas and feelings that did not correspond to his real conditions. He could not rescue himself from his conflicts because he could not find the path of genuine struggle together with the only true fighter, the proletariat."[16] Interestingly, only a few months earlier Wiener had written to his Vienna friend the Hebrew writer David Vogel that he was not going to send anything to Kvitko for publication in *Di Royte Velt* because his work was not suitable for Soviet publication.[17]

Originally written in Berlin and finished in April 1923, this short novel reflects Wiener's experience of growing up in turn-of-the-century Krakow and has one of his childhood friends as its protagonist.[18] The novel opens with the boy Ele Falek visiting a Catholic hospital for the extraction of a tooth. This episode associates Catholic Christianity, an oppressive power, with pain and suffering, an association that runs through the rest of the story. Catholicism dominates the city through images, buildings, and ideas, rendering Jews impotent. Ele's father, a large, silent man in his early thirties, comes from an old Krakow family which has been declining for years. As a private Hebrew teacher for girls, he occupies the lowest step on the intellectual professional ladder. He is despised and humiliated for his traditional Jewish appearance and poor command of Polish, by both his students and their parents, assimilated Jews who live in the middle-class area of the city. As a result, all his efforts are wasted on girls who can never master the letters of the Hebrew alphabet.

Ele's mother is more active and ambitious, but she also tries to avoid contact with the outside world. "A wonderfully slender woman with a face of rare nobility" (13), she sells cigarettes in a *trafik*—a tobacco kiosk—where she spends her days reading Yiddish novels and daydreaming, barely paying attention to her customers. She never looks her husband in the eyes and rarely talks to him: "for years, the mother felt bitter resentment, not knowing against whom, not having any clear grumbles against anyone" (14). Not surprisingly, Ele grows up miserable and lonely, prone to sudden outbursts of self-destructive energy. The first premonition of his tragic end comes when he nearly falls out a window when left alone at home by his mother. As he gets older, his horizon gradually expands beyond the borders of the medieval Jewish quarter of Kazimierz. For his father, the daily routine of walking from Kazimierz to the newer Christian city is a torture he has to endure to earn his living. By contrast, Ele, eager to explore new territories, is particularly attracted by the forbidden and hostile Christian places. He instinctively tries to escape the narrow Jewish world, even at risk of getting lost in the unfamiliar streets or drowning in the river. Krakow feels both oppressive and attractive, with its majestic Wawel Cathedral, the symbol of Polish Christianity, towering over the cityscape.

Conscious of the advantages of modern education, Ele's mother persuades the father to send their son to a Polish *gymnasium* at the age of ten, after he finishes his *heder* education. Judaism remains for Ele forever associated with the oppressive atmosphere of *heder*, where he has suffered from the violent anger of the teacher's assistant, and with the absurdity of the Talmud, to which he prefers Polish adventure stories for children. Wiener portrays Kazimierz as a melancholic place full of memories guarded by people like Ele's father, for whom there is no room in the modern world. Particularly oppressive is the old, dark synagogue where his father possesses an inherited seat. Though located at the very heart of Kazimierz, this synagogue is not popular with its inhabitants because of its age and morose air: "the closer one comes to the old synagogue and to the upper market, the actual Jewish town, the older the houses, the yellower from age and the more they are weathered by the sun" (49). The synagogue is supposedly more than eight hundred years old. Built in the Gothic style, it was once used as a fortified hiding space for the entire community, and its underground passages still lead outside the town. Nearly abandoned now, its Sabbath services are attended by only a few devout poor men, among them Ele's father, who carry on the tradition of their ancestors and pray according to the old *Kroke* (Krakow) rite.

Uncomfortable and anxious in the claustrophobic world of old Judaism, Ele is eager for a change. But his encounter with the Polish *gymnasium*, with its "smell of terror, kitchen soap, and dry air" (56) and a crucifix in every classroom, does not make him any happier. He has frequent clashes with teachers and fellow students and once gets an unusually savage beating from a teacher for an offense he did not commit. This incident leaves the teacher and the other pupils with feelings of guilt and embarrassment, which aggravates Ele's situation even further and provokes him to abandon Jewish observance. One day soon after his bar mitzvah, he wakes up late and rushes to school, where he tries to catch up with his prayers in a toilet during a break. Alarmed by his long absence, other pupils suspect that he is doing something improper and start to look over the cubicle, only to observe Ele with his *tfillin* (phylacteries) around his arm and on his forehead. After this incident, which makes his situation in school even less tolerable, Ele begins to feel hatred for Judaism. Now, instead of praying, he spends his mornings walking the unfamiliar streets of the city and staring at its magnificent churches. Gradually he makes new friends among Christian Poles and assimilated Jews, among them two attractive girls who live in the city center inside the Planten, the boulevard ring which has replaced the old walls that historically separated the Christian city from its Jewish suburb.

As a child, Ele felt closer to his mother than to his father. He used to go to her little kiosk to sit and observe her daydreaming. But as he grows up and discovers a new world, the bond between them begins to weaken. He comes to believe that she is looking at him as if he himself is carrying the burden of his father's doom. Ele thinks she must be wondering to herself, "How will you end up? I *desperately* hope you don't turn out like your father. I'm so afraid you're like him, with all his ways" (67). In the meantime, the father falls ill and dies within a year in terrible suffering from what turns out to be stomach cancer. Exhausted by the physical and psychological stress, Ele looks for comfort in the quiet, clean homes of his Christian friends. Glancing during his long walks into the "clean windows of the quiet *goyish* streets, lined with trees," he often feels the desire to be "one of their own, very eager to take in and breathe in the atmosphere of this clean *goyish* home" (82). The ever-present Christian imagery fills Ele with a mixture of excitement and fear. His instincts tell him that his friends' families, despite their friendliness and liberal views, are ready at any moment to "seize a broom and sweep out 'those people' with such force that smoke will come out. But in the meantime this is not allowed" (83). This premonition is much more sinister now than when it was written.

As Ele becomes more familiar with the Christian world, he develops a taste for modernist neo-Romantic poetry in German and Polish and learns to admire medieval Christian art, which gives him a sort of masochistic pleasure. He begins to frequent the magnificent Kościół Mariacki (St. Mary's Cathedral) on Krakow's market square, famous for its fifteenth-century carved wooden altar by the sculptor Veit Stoss (known in Polish as Wit Stwosz). In the Cathedral, "the wild Gothic sculptures, the bloody Catholic images of the cross, together with the kaleidoscopic stained glass and the odor of incense, wrap Ele round about with an air of fear and strange curiosity. When occasionally Mass is said, he is overcome by a sense of extreme discomfort. Ele rushes away, paying no attention to the few worshipers on their knees who follow him with their murderously angry looks" (88). When he mentions his feelings to his Christian friends, they become suspicious that he could never really like Christians and their religion. After the graduation from the *gymnasium*, Ele begins to study mathematics and physics at the Krakow University. As a student, he is entitled to a postponement of his one-year military service in the Austro-Hungarian army until the end of his studies. But a streak of self-destructiveness in his character leads him away from the normal path, and on a sudden whim he decides to enlist in the military as a volunteer.

Sent to a small Silesian garrison town, Ele is slowly but steadily adjusting to the harsh barrack conditions and soon gets promoted to the rank of corporal in charge of drilling new recruits. This is a hard task given the fact that those soldiers come from remote Ukrainian-speaking areas in the Carpathian Mountains and understand neither Polish nor German, which is the official language of the army. The captain insists on the extensive use of physical force and orders Ele to hit the noncooperating recruits in the stomach as hard as he can. Incapable of causing pain to a human being and unable to disobey the order, Ele suffers a nervous breakdown and begins hitting himself in the face.

When others try to stop him, he runs away from his regiment and after a long journey across the country arrives home to his mother. Having immediately realized the danger of the situation, she puts him into a small rented room in a quiet neighborhood and sets off to the regiment to settle the issue. After extensive and costly efforts, she succeeds in obtaining fake papers that would protect her son from prosecution. But on the day of her return to Krakow, her son turns himself to the authorities as a result of a deep depression and disappointment in love. He falls into the hands of a military *Auditor*, a sadistic German colonel with a fixation on implementing the law in the minutest detail. After a brief investigation, he orders Ele to be taken into custody by the guards. But Ele insists that he would go by himself and vigorously resists being handcuffed. As a result, he gets beaten up so brutally that he dies the next night. To cover up the accident, the military authorities order to give him a funeral with full military honors and according to the Jewish ritual as if he had died serving the Kaiser. The funeral procession rushes to the cemetery, and the ceremony is complete before the mother and the uncle have time to get there.

A person named Ele Falek appears episodically in Wiener's memoirs about his Krakow years, which were written in the Soviet Union but not published during the author's life. He is described as a "very naïve, astonishingly helpless, and mixed-up boy" who "had a sharp and sober mind when it had to do with other people."[19] Yoyl, the autobiographical protagonist of the memoirs, and his friends are enchanted by the new eclectic vision of decadence which incorporated the recently published "Legends about the Baal Shem" by Martin Buber, the neo-Hasidic works by Yiddish and Hebrew authors Micha Yosef Berdyczewski, Shmuel-Aba Horodetski, Yehuda Shteynberg, and Y. L. Peretz, and the Polish-Catholic neo-Romantic mysticism of Wyspianski and Przybyzsewski. All these readings get eclectically mixed, producing a "wild, inappropriate brew" (*a meshunedike, umgelumperte kashe*). The young Krakow Jews spend hours meditating in front of Veit Stoss's wooden altar and discussing the parallels between the lives and teachings of St. Francis of Assisi and the founder of Hasidism, Israel Baal Shem Tov. Writing in retrospect, Wiener makes his protagonist Yoyl critical about this naïve fascination of the Jewish boys with Catholicism. He points out that the saints such as St. Francis should bear responsibility for the actions of their followers, some of whom were "the worst murderers in human history."[20]

Ele Faleks untergang is a rare Yiddish example of the phenomenon that the Polish scholar of Austrian literature Stefan Kaszyński called "Galician syndrome," which he described as a mixture of feelings of guilt, suffering, and nostalgia.[21] With a variable proportion of its ingredients, this mixture defined the ways in which the bittersweet Habsburg Galician past was re-created in Polish, German, Ukrainian, Yiddish, and Hebrew by such authors as Bruno Schulz, Joseph Roth, Ivan Franko, Melech Rawicz, and Shmuel Yosef Agnon, who came to occupy leading positions in their respective literary canons. As the Austrian scholar Zoran Konstantinović points out, "the drowned Galicia, which no longer exists in that form, has grown in the Austrian literature into the notion of the human homelessness of our time."[22] But while the German-Jewish writers from Galicia, such as Joseph Roth and Manes Sperber, remained forever enchanted by the land of their childhood utopia that was destroyed by the Great War and the collapse of the Habsburg Empire, Wiener's vision of that past was far from nostalgic. He focused on the signs of social and moral decay in the multinational fabric of the educational and military institutions, which Roth and others presented as the major bonds that kept the empire together across ethnic and social divides. Wiener also acutely discerned the dormant Polish anti-Semitism which was often downplayed in the nostalgic representation of the good old times when Poles, Germans, Jews, and Ukrainians managed to live peacefully together under the benevolent scepter of Francis-Joseph.

The Habsburg *gymnasium* was often celebrated for opening the broad world of culture for talented young people regardless of their ethnicity and religion. Along with the civil service and the army, the school was a major integrating force that kept the empire together by educating its subjects in the spirit of discipline and loyalty to the throne. Iwona Ewertowska-Klaja writes in her study of Polish novels about school years in Habsburg Galicia, "In the Galician Arcadia, the *gymnasium* with all its school-day requisites was not a Utopia but rather the harsh reality. It formed the focal point of conflict situations, which the young man had to resolve, and served as a model for the society, in which he had to function later."[23] One of the major sources of conflict was the increasing tension between the growing national aspirations of the minorities, in the first place Poles and Ukrainians, on the one hand, and the dominant cosmopolitan German-language culture of the empire. The situation of Jews was even more complicated, because no matter how careful they tried to navigate between the conflicting sides, they were bound to antagonize one of them without winning the other. It is not surprising, therefore, that the Galician school was often remembered as a place of alienation, confrontation, and conflicts. It generated a sense of spiritual loss, separation, and lack of contact. Ewertowska-Klaja sums up her astute observations based on three Polish novels: "The Galician school novels, in which the childhood experience represents a point of departure for complications in later life, essentially vary the scheme of a psychologically colored novel of education, but the cliché is used in the opposite way: the 'bad guys' win, the 'good' ones lose."[24] The school experience in Galicia leaves the protagonists of Polish novels with two lasting pieces of legacy: passivity and perplexity. Childhood nostalgia turns into a traumatic disorder.[25]

Ewertowska-Klaja's analysis of the novels by the Polish authors Jan Parandowski (1895–1978), Emil Zegadłowicz (1888–1941), and Andrzej Kuśniewicz (1904–1993), all of which were written later than Wiener's novel, in the 1930s and the 1970s, seems to be fully applicable to *Ele Faleks untergang*, but with one significant difference that sets the Polish novels apart from their Yiddish counterpart. Whereas the protagonists of the Polish novels remain alive and eventually find a place in post-Habsburg Polish society, the meaningless death of Ele Falek signifies the futility of Jewish integration into Polish or Austrian society. All the difficulties and conflicts of the Polish characters notwithstanding, they manage to establish positive relationships with their nation and family, whereas Ele Falek tries desperately but unsuccessfully to set himself free from both his Jewish legacy and his father's fate. Wiener deals with the issues of death and destiny at two levels: as a metaphysical issue and as a fact of life that is defined by social and psychological conditions. In the chapter on theology in his philosophical treatise *Von den Symbolen* (On the Symbols), Wiener formulates the main task of that discipline as theodicy, that is, justification of God's action in the world: "The great human sufferings, death and pain, the screamingly loud injustice are the greatest incentives for dialectical theology. There is a moment in

the history of religion after which religion concerns itself almost exclusively, in a dialectic scholastic fashion, with the justification of God."[26]
At the metaphysical level, Wiener treats in the novel the same question
from a secular existential perspective and comes up with a purely negative answer, finding no justifiable reasons for human suffering. He con-
demns the same old Habsburg world that some of his contemporaries
came to regard as nearly ideal. Like the biblical Job, Wiener rejects conventional explanations offered by the established religion of Judaism
and Christianity as inadequate and misleading.

The text is filled with references and allusions, which were addressed
to the members of Wiener's milieu, the half-modern, half-traditional
middle-class Krakow Jewish youth of the last pre–World War I decade.
This layer was hardly accessible for the Soviet readership back in 1929
and is even less accessible today. Stylistically and thematically, the
novel belongs in the tradition of Austrian-Galician noir literature, with
its dark irony, troubling sexuality, and social pessimism, invoking the
spirit of the most famous Galician writer of that kind, Leopold von
Sacher-Masoch.

Not surprisingly, the publication of the novel did not get much critical attention. *Ele Faleks untergang* had little to do, stylistically or thematically, with the Yiddish literary mainstream of the 1920s in Poland
or America, which focused on collective concerns rather than individual anxieties and valued an accessible and idiomatic style filled with
Jewish references; nor did it fit the new specific criteria of Soviet literature, which required the writer to represent the social reality according to the Marxist scheme of class struggle. The first review of the
novel appeared in the Warsaw Yiddish literary review *Bikher-velt* and
belonged to the prominent Bundist activist and literary critic Yankev
Pat. In Pat's view, the novel was out of touch with the contemporary
reality. It was a truthful, serious, compassionate, and well-crafted work
that would be in place in Vilna around 1907 but was not appropriate for
the Soviet Union in 1929. Pat perceived Wiener as a sad and distressed
man who was unable to sort out his feelings. He concluded his brief
review with a rhetorical question: "Why does Kharkov State Publishing
House need to dig up a Krakow corpse from a soldier's grave?"[27] Pat's
critical opinion was sympathetically mentioned by a Soviet reviewer,
who signed his brief article with initials A.A. Most likely, it was Avrom

Abchuk, an ambitious and talented young writer and critic who had fled from Poland to the Soviet Union in 1921 and was making a successful literary career in Kiev. His novel *Hershl Shamay* (1929) is often regarded as the best-written novel in Yiddish proletarian literature.[28] By the end of the 1920s, Abchuk was a graduate student (*aspirant*) at the Literary Section of the Institute for the Jewish Proletarian Culture, which perhaps explains the relatively balanced tone of his review of a novel that was written by one of his mentors.

The Soviet reviewer demonstrated his erudition by claiming that the influence of Dostoevsky and the Austrian writers Arthur Schnitzler and Stefan Zweig had prevented Wiener from writing a proper social novel. The main artistic fault of the work, according to A.A., was Wiener's identification with his main character and the resulting inability "to differentiate between his own artistic individuality and his artistic object." Instead of taking control over the material, Wiener let the material take control over his narrative, producing an unacceptable atmosphere of gloom and decline. A.A. liked the novel as a work of art but could not approve of it ideologically. He skillfully summed up his insight into the novel's symbolic meaning with Soviet ideological clichés: "The impression from this first work is, nevertheless, that we are dealing with a writer of high and refined artistic culture. Wiener has an original manner of writing and knows the secret of weighing his words and measuring his style. One can only wonder why, in our time of storms and struggle, he chose the theme of Job and wasted his creative energy on it."[29]

Conclusion

Despite the obvious differences in style and subject matter, the three texts by Der Nister, Godiner, and Wiener share common concerns of moral and existential nature. They all end with the death of their male protagonists as a result of an absurd trial which brazenly violates recognized legal norms. All three stories involve a sado-masochistic erotic relationship between the protagonist and the authorities, which adds ambiguity to the situation. Under Soviet conditions, the problem of the moral and legal justification of violence acquired a special poignancy. The officially sanctioned approach required the writer to demonstrate the supremacy of the "law of revolutionary necessity" over other, more traditional secular or religious legal concepts based on the presumption of innocence. This was the message of David Bergelson's 1929 novel *Midas hadin* as well as of the classical Russian Civil War thriller *Razgrom* (The Rout, 1927) by Aleksandr Fadeev.[30] Der Nister, Godiner, and Wiener, each in his own fashion, exposed the ambiguity of this attitude. They did not draw a clear line between the aggressor and the victim, focusing instead on the problematic, both from a psychological and a moral point of view, love-hate relationship between them. They showed sympathy for their victimized characters but did not rule out the possibility that their sufferings could have been partly self-inflicted, caused by their attraction, perhaps unconscious, to the figures of power and authority. This shift of emphasis, however disturbing it might seem for those who prefer a black-and-white picture, might open a new venue for the appreciation of the ambivalence of the position of an intellectual in a totalitarian society. These disturbing images and motives did not disappear completely from the Soviet literature of the 1930s, where they reemerged in the form of coded metaphors rather than leading themes.

NOTES

1. In more detail, the events of 1929 and their effect on Yiddish literature are described and analyzed by Gennady Estraikh, *In Harness: Yiddish Writers' Romance with Communism* (Syracuse: Syracuse University Press, 2005), 28–134; and Chone Shmeruk, "Yiddish Literature in the USSR," in Lionel Kochan (ed.), *The Jews in Soviet Russia since 1917* (Oxford: Oxford University Press, 1970), 249–52.

2. On Meir Wiener's life and career, see Mikhail Krutikov, *From Kabbalah to Class Struggle: Expressionism, Marxism, and Yiddish Literature in the Life and Work of Meir Wiener* (Stanford: Stanford University Press, 2011). On Bergelson's *Midas hadin*, see Mikhail Krutikov, "Narrating the Revolution: From 'Tsugvintn' to Midas-hadin," in Joseph Sherman and Gennady Estraikh (eds.), *David Bergelson: From Modernism to Socialist Realism* (Oxford, UK: Legenda, 2007), 167–182; and Mikhail Krutikov, "Rediscovered the Shtetl as a New Reality: David Bergelson and Itsik Kipnis," in Steven T. Katz (ed.), *The Shtetl: New Evaluations* (New York: NYU Press, 2007), 211–32.

3. Der Nister, "Unter a ployt (Reviu)," *Di Royte Velt* 7 (July 1929): 8–34; Der Nister, *Gedakht* (Kiev: Kultur-lige, 1929). The story was translated by Seymour Levitan as "Under a Fence: A Review," in Eliezer Greenberg and Irving Howe (eds.), *Ashes Out of Hope: Fiction by Soviet Yiddish Writers* (New York: Schocken, 1977), 193–218.

4. Der Nister, "Under a Fence," 217.

5. Delphine Bechtel argues that "one very probable model for Der Nister's hermit is Hoffmann's monk Serapion" from the cycle of novellas *Die Serapionsbrüder* (N.p.: Serapion Brothers, 1819). See her discussion of this connection in *Der Nister's Work, 1907–1929: A Study of a Yiddish Symbolist* (Bern: Peter Lang, 1990), 261–62.

6. David Roskies, *A Bridge of Longing: The Lost Art of Yiddish Storytelling* (Cambridge: Harvard University Press, 1995), 225–29.

7. Shmeruk, "Yiddish Literature in the USSR," 254.

8. Der Nister, "Under a Fence," 197.

9. Bechtel, *Der Nister's Work*, 264–65.

10. Isaac Nusinov, "Der Nister," in Der Nister, *Gedakht*, xviii.

11. In more detail, Litvakov's position is discussed by Gennady Estraikh in *In Harness*, 130–31.

12. "Partey-baratung baym kiever kreyz-partkom," *Prolit* 5 (1929): 87.

13. Shmuel Godiner, *Figurn oyfn rand* (Kiev: Kultur-lige, 1929), 80.

14. Ibid., 90.

15. Estraikh, *In Harness*, 124.

16. *Di Royte Velt* 10 (1926): 46.

17. Wiener's letter to Vogel, 8 February 1926, Avraham Sutzkever Collection, Manuscript Department, JNUL, 1565.

18. Meir Wiener, *Ele Faleks untergang* (Kharkov: Melukhe farlag fun Ukraine, 1929). Subsequent references are to this edition and are cited parenthetically in the text.

19. Meir Viner, "Yugnt-fraynt," *Sovetish Heymland* 10 (October 1969): 118.

20. Meir Viner, "Der zeyde Binyomin," *Sovetish Heymland* 9 (September 1969): 115.

21. Stefan Kaszyński, introduction to Stefan Kaszyński (ed.), *Galizien—Eine Literarische Heimat* (Poznan: UAM, 1987), 7–8.

22. Zoran Konstantinović, "Das Stadtbild Lembergs in der Österreichischen Literatur," in ibid., 16.

23. Iwona Ewertowska-Klaja, "Überlegungen zu drei galizischen Schulromanen polnischer Autoren," in ibid., 207–8.

24. Ibid., 210.

25. Ibid., 217.

26. Meir Wiener, *Von den Symbolen* (Berlin: Benjamin Harz, 1924), 155.

27. Yankev Pat, "Ele Faleks untergang," *Bikher-velt* 8 (1929): 30–32.

28. Gennady Estraikh, "Soviet Yiddish Vernacular of the 1920s: Avrom Abchuk's *Hershl Shamaj* as a Socio-linguistic Source," *Slovo* 7.1 (1994): 1–12.

29. A.A., "Meir Viner: Ele Faleks untergang," *Di Royte Velt* 9 (1929): 185–86.

30. On the notion of justice in Bergelson's novel, see Krutikov, "Narrating the Revolution," 167–82.

Index

Adler, Cyrus, 11, 23, 24
Agnon, Shmuel Yosef, 185, 228
agricultural colonization: in Argentina
110; in Palestine 34, 110; in the USSR 38,
39, 41, 43–45, 107–109. *See also* Birobidzhan; Crimea
Agro-Joint, 93, 102
al-Hilū, Raduan, 134, 136
al-Mughrabī, Mahmūd, 131, 133, 134
Aleph Zadik Aleph, 22
Alexandria, 130
aliyah, 4, 56, 67
Almazov, Sol, 109, 117
American Committee for the Settlement
of Jews in Birobidjan (Ambijan), 119
American Jewish Committee, 12, 18, 20,
22, 23, 27, 32, 33, 57
American Jewish Joint Distribution Committee (JDC), 3, 4, 12, 37, 54, 59, 63, 74,
76, 93–104; in Brazil 159, 161; in the
USSR 38, 40, 44, 45. *See also* Agro-Joint
Amsterdam, 65
Anglo-Jewish Association, 27
antireligious campaigns, 44, 45, 49
anti-Semitism, 40, 55, 75, 87, 146, 157, 162,
189, 228
anti-Zionism, 28, 44, 120, 158, 161, 163
Arab riots in Palestine, 6, 20, 46, 47, 66,
132–34
Arabization of communist parties, 127,
129, 131, 133–37

'Arif, Amin, 135
Argentina, 22, 54, 67, 108, 110, 156, 157, 191
Armenian Marxists, 129
Armenian refugees, 58, 59
Asch, Sholem, 5, 46, 149, 150
Association for Jewish Colonization the
Soviet Union (ICOR), 107–20
Association for the Settlement of Jewish
Toilers on Land (OZET), 38, 108
Auschwitz, 68
Australia, 4, 19, 108
Austro-Hungarian (Habsburg) Empire,
30, 54, 58, 59, 222, 228–30

Babel, Isaac, 171–73, 176–82
Bank of United States, 73, 74, 84
Basel, 222
Belfast, 23
Belgium, 68, 96
Bergelson, David, 40, 201, 202, 205–207,
215, 218, 232
Berger-Barzilay, Joseph, 129, 130, 132
Berkman, Alexander, 61
Berlin, 4, 5, 21, 23, 40, 59, 64–66, 96, 102,
185, 199, 222, 223
Bernstein, Herman, 100
Bessarabia, 96, 101
Bialik, H. N., 185, 188
Bialistotsky, B. J., 145
Bialystok, 76–79, 81–83, 85
Bialystoker Relief Committee, 76, 78, 81, 82

Contributors

GLENDA ABRAMSON is Emeritus Professor of Hebrew and Jewish Studies at the University of Oxford.

AVNER BEN-ZAKEN is a Chair of the Humanities at Ono Academic College, Israel.

TOBIAS BRINKMANN is Malvin and Lea Bank Associate Professor of Jewish Studies and History at Penn State University.

HASIA R. DINER is Paul S. and Sylvia Steinberg Professor of American Jewish History at New York University.

DAVID ENGEL is Maurice R. and Corinne P. Greenberg Professor of Holocaust Studies at New York University.

GENNADY ESTRAIKH is Associate Professor of Yiddish Studies at New York University.

ERIC L. GOLDSTEIN is Associate Professor of History and Jewish Studies at Emory University.

REBECCA KOBRIN is Russell and Bettina Knapp Assistant Professor of American Jewish History at Columbia University.

MIKHAIL KRUTIKOV is Associate Professor of Slavic and Judaic Studies at the University of Michigan.

JEFFREY LESSER is Samuel Candler Dobbs Professor of Latin American History at Emory University.

GABRIELLA SAFRAN is Eva Chernov Lokey Professor in Jewish Studies at Stanford University.

JOSEPH SHERMAN (1944–2009) was the Woolf Corob Fellow in Yiddish Studies at the Faculty of Oriental Studies at the University of *Oxford.*

HENRY SREBRNIK is Professor in the Department of Political Studies, *University* of Prince Edward Island, Canada.

RAKEFET ZALASHIK is Guest Professor for Science and Jewish Studies at the Zentrum "Geschichte des Wissens" of ETH & Universität Zürich.